THEOLOGY INTERPRETED

A Guide to Christian Doctrine

Volume II
Christ, The Spirit and The Church

1993

To
Prof. Earle Waugh
with thanks and appreciation

Joe

THEOLOGY INTERPRETED

A Guide to Christian Doctrine

Volume II
Christ, The Spirit and The Church

Christian Doctrine of Christ
Redemption, The Holy Spirit, Salvation
Church and The Last Things

Joseph Pungur

UNIVERSITY
PRESS OF
AMERICA

Lanham • New York • London

Copyright © 1993 by
University Press of America®, Inc.
4720 Boston Way
Lanham, Maryland 20706

3 Henrietta Street
London WC2E 8LU England

Library of Congress Cataloging-in-Publication Data
(Revised for vol. 2)

Pungur, Joseph.
Theology interpreted.
Includes bibliographical references and indexes.
Contents: v. 1. God, the world, and mankind — v. 2. Christ, the
Spirit, and the church.
1. Theology, Doctrinal.   I. Title.
BT75.2.P83   1987   230'.044   87–8250

ISBN 0–8191–6354–6 (v. 1 : alk. paper)
ISBN 0–8191–6355–4 (pbk. : v. 1 : alk. paper)
ISBN 0–8191–8891–3 (v. 2 : alk. paper)
ISBN 0–8191–8892–1 (v. 2 : pbk. : alk. paper)

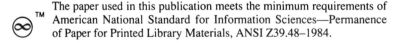

The paper used in this publication meets the minimum requirements of
American National Standard for Information Sciences—Permanence
of Paper for Printed Library Materials, ANSI Z39.48–1984.

To my former and present students

here and abroad

CONTENTS

Foreword
Preface

PART TWO

THE DOCTRINE OF CHRIST AND REDEMPTION

INTRODUCTION

SECTION 2. THE WORK OF CHRIST

SECTION 3. THE INTERPRETATION OF THE WORK OF CHRIST

PART THREE

THE DOCTRINE OF THE HOLY SPIRIT, SALVATION, CHURCH AND THE LAST THINGS

INTRODUCTION

The Importance of Pneumatology

SECTION 1. THE PERSON OF THE HOLY SPIRIT

SECTION 2. THE WORK OF THE HOLY SPIRIT

SECTION 3. THE DOCTRINE OF THE CHURCH

SECTION 4. THE DOCTRINE OF THE LAST THINGS

FOREWORD

Readers of Vol. 1 appreciated the perspective presented in Theology Interpreted (University Press of America, 1987); Dr. Pungur sketched the developement of the Christian tradition in a brief yet thorough manner. This volume continues his evaluation of the critical doctrines which have exercised the minds and hearts of believers from the beginning. Theologically, Christology is of such importance that scholars are constantly redefining the essence of this fundamental issue. Pungur insists that the meaning of Christ cannot be understood apart from the history of the debate, and indeed, one should continually look to the Scriptures as the foundation for the main interpretive principles.

In our day, concerns about pneumatology have been enriched by the dramatic movements of the Church in the Eastern Block countries. There, the Spirit has revitalized and renewed the church in ways few could have thought possible only a handful of years ago. Pungur strives to show that the doctrine of the Spirit should be understood throughout its history as having this powerful vivifying effect. Hence, the amazing recovery of the Church after so many years of persecution is a living proof of God's continuing influence in the world.

The problems we face are obviously not solely of a material nature; true, thousands, even millions continue to perish from lack of food or from the scourge of vicious governments. Yet the direction of the Church, from Pungur's perspective, is that God has control of affairs, and has His ultimate plan in place. Matters of eschatology are generally discounted in the contemporary scene. The wisdom of this survey is that the end times are just as God has detailed them, and that the faithful believer can read the signs of the times in a level-headed, reasonable manner despite the exaggerations of the marginal groups so evident all around. There is something reassuring about this perspective. It stands as a fortress in a milieu that offers little assurance.

I hope you find Theology Interpreted: Vol. II an informative and insightful overview of the Churches' important doctrines. It certainly presents one very reasonable, easily comprehended vision of the Church from the engaged mind of a committed Christian. In that sense, this writing, too, is part of the intellectual ferment which marks the contemporary church. That ferment, I am sure Rev. Pungur would insist, will not end with his contribution, but will continue in each of us as part of God's grace.

Dr. Earle H. Waugh
Professor, Religious Studies
University of Alberta

PREFACE

Some years ago when the first volume of my book on Christian Theology was published it was promised that a second volume would follow it. The first volume presented the Doctrine of God, Revelation and Providence, Man and Sin; this volume deals with the rest of Christian Doctrine. Its subtitle indicated three major themes: Christology, Pneumatology and Ecclesiology. These include the doctrine of Christ and Redemption, the doctrine of Holy Spirit and Salvation, the doctrine of Church and the doctrine of the Last Things. The material is arranged in two parts.

This study of Christian Doctrine, like the previous study, was designed and written primarily for those who want to understand better the tenets of Protestant tradition. It can also be used as a springboard to the deeper study of Christian Theology. Last but not least, because many Christians lack a comprehensive awareness of doctrine, they feel themselves insecure when confronted by those who develop some kind of philosophy, this volume together with the first one, is intended to provide a comprehensive and systematic explanation of the basic teachings of protestant Christianity to those who want to understand their faith better and strive for a Christian world-view.

In this volume, the pattern of the first has been followed. Questions are raised, problems indicated, accusations against Christian doctrines are pointed out.

I am obliged for their help to Rev. David Buttler, Dr. Robert Anderson, Dr. Earle H. Waugh, Dr. Iain F. Clayre, for offering comments, suggestions and stylistic editing of the manuscript and to Sandra Smitten for typesetting the manuscript. A special thanks is due to the University Press of America for publishing this book.

Dr. Joseph Pungur
University of Alberta
Edmonton, Alberta
CANADA

PART TWO

THE DOCTRINE OF CHRIST AND REDEMPTION
INTRODUCTION

Chapter 1

The Importance of Christology, What is Christology?
Christology as the Centre of Christian Theology
Its Consequences

1. What is Christology?

At the very outset of this study of Christology we are obliged to deal with the question: What is Christology?

Christology is a Greek word, coined from two words *Chrystos* meaning "Christ", and *Logos* meaning "word" or "speech". "Christ" is a term meaning "anointed" and is functionally equivalent to the Hebrew "Messiah" meaning "Redeemer", that is, one who is sent by Jahweh who authorizes Him by "anointing" him. Hence the meaning of Christology is "talk about Christ". In Christian doctrine Christology is the study of the person and work of Christ the Redeemer, and the redemption of humans.

2. Christology as the Centre of Christian Theology

Christology is not simply one part of Christian theology but its centre: the core and the foundation of Christian theology[1]. Without Christology we cannot talk about Christian theology at all. Christology is the main constituent of Christian theology because Christology gives it its distinctive feature, precisely because Christian theology is a theology of redemption. No other world religion has this unique feature. In all other religions man is the one who somehow tries to achieve his salvation, or his eternal life, or everlasting happiness. Only in the Christian religion does one find that the salvation of man is a free gift of God. God made possible salvation for the whole of mankind by the Redeemer, Saviour and Messiah, who is the Son of God: Jesus Christ *(Luke 2:11, 19:10; John 12:47; 1 Tim. 1:15; Titus 2:11; 1 John 4:14).*

At this point a question arises: on what basis could Christians claim that their religion is a religion of redemption? Its verification can be found in the special revelation of God in the Bible, which reaches its climax in the person and work of Jesus Christ. God's plan for the redemption of mankind gradually became clear. In the religion of Old Testament, the claim of God upon His elect people became apparent and obvious. Early Judaism conceptualized this claim in the Decalogue. But the Prophets were the ones who began to understand and prophetized a divine vision: that the religion of Law is not the final stage of God's revelation but that God intended to say something more to man. According to their vision, there will come a True Man, the Servant of God, the Son of God, the Prince of Peace. He will make peace between God and man by perfectly fulfilling the Law and he will suffer vicariously for mankind's sin. By doing this, he will break the power of Sin and abolish its deadly consequences and will lead people back to God and finally He will establish the Kingdom of God in its fullness. *(Micah 5:2-4; Mal. 3:1; Isa. 9:2, 6-7, 11:1-9, 53; Jer. 23:5-6; Zach. 9:9-11; Dan. 9:25)*

This Messiah and Redeemer came in the human-divine person of Jesus Christ, who through His teaching, work, suffering and death achieved and completed the great task of redemption of mankind and the establishment of the Kingdom of God. He not only announced this program; his followers recognized and experienced it all and many have recognized and experienced the same since that time, generation by generation. This is how Christianity as a development of Judaism has become the religion of redemption. In this light we can rightly say that Jesus Christ is the peak and centre of special revelation of God. What was ever revealed by God reaches its meaning in the person and work of Jesus Christ. Without this centre, the special revelation of God falls apart and loses its most obvious relevance; no one can put it into a full, comprehensive and really coherent whole. This has already been discussed in the first volume[2].

3. Its Consequences

That Jesus Christ is the peak and centre of the special Revelation of God has far reaching consequences.

First of all, K. Barth rightly says that theologians would be silent without Jesus Christ. But, because of the revelation in Jesus Christ, theologians may speak about God, because God Himself, through Jesus Christ, has broken the silence[3]. E. Brunner calls God's revelation in Jesus

Christ the "source of light" of Christian theology. Only in Christ can we find theology's *ratio cognescendi,* ie, the reason for understanding, because He is the foundation of all Christian truth[4]. In emphasizing this "importance of Jesus Christ" as the basis of Christian theology, they are absolutely right. Without the revelation of Jesus Christ, man's talk about God, his theology, would be weak, uncertain and relying mainly on guesswork. Without Jesus Christ, not much certain and true about God could be spoken and virtually nothing could be said about the true relationship between God and man. Christian theology certainly could not exist without Jesus Christ. Theologians, divorced from the revelation of Jesus Christ, could not talk about God[5].

Secondly, the person and work of Jesus Christ is critical to the Christian faith. The Apostolic Creed dedicates its second and the longest section to the person and work of Jesus Christ, the Son of God, and expresses the Christian faith in Him. This is because Christ is the real basis of Christian faith. What we believe about God the Father is grounded in the revelation which Jesus Christ brought to us. What we believe about the forgiveness of sin and the mercy of God, the resurrection of body, the Kingdom of God and eternal life - all are founded in the person and work of Jesus Christ who became the Master, Saviour and Lord. Beside these objective benefits, there is the subjective importance of his person for the life of his followers, namely, that Christ is the leader, the protector, the friend and example in the life of Christian believers who take seriously His calling to "Follow me". These believers desired that the new being which appeared in Jesus Christ should be realized and manifested in their lives also. For those who want to take seriously the program of *imitatio Christi* - the imitation of Christ, the idea deriving from Paul and Thomas Kempis, Jesus Christ becomes the centre of their life. They relate everything to him, they try to act according to his will and they care that His "New Being" should grow in themselves while the "Old Being" should weaken and gradually wither away *(Gal.2:20; Eph. 4:22-24).* As E. Brunner said, Christology can transform into *"Christo vita"* if the talk about Christ turns into a life according to Christ. Without the transformation of Christology into "Christ-like life", Christology inevitably deteriorates into hollow religious philosophy.

Thirdly, Christ is not only the centre of Christian Theology - and as a consequence the centre of Christian Faith; Christ is the centre of human history too[6]. One might say this ambitious statement originates from a Christian pride or exclusiveness, that Christian enthusiasm exaggerates the importance of Jesus Christ and imagines Him to be the centre of history. Christian conviction always must be based upon the revelation of God; it

3

does so in this case also. It was God who made His Son Jesus Christ the centrepiece of human history by giving Him to this world *(John 3:16)*, and by raising him from the dead *(Acts 2:25; Rom. 8:11)*. Hence Jesus Christ is the beginning of the new creation *(2 Cor. 5:17; Gal. 6:15)*. The Son of God not only participated in the work of Creation *(Col.l:l6)*, but in Him, by Him and through Him a new creation had begun *(Eph.2:10, 3:9; James l:l8)* and with Him a new beginning of human history *(2 Peter 3:13)*. As a consequence of sin, human history went astray because the course of human history lost God as its ultimate end. Instead of its approaching towards God and the Kingdom of God, that is, towards a state of divine order, human history took the opposite, fatal and tragic direction: it is running away from God. This means that the goal of history is being lost and also that history has lost its very meaning. This is the reason why human history is so tragic, full of suffering, destruction and death. God, motivated by His love, wanted to stop this course of history: He gave to the world His only begotten Son *(John 3:16)* and in Him God wanted to turn radically the course of history towards Himself. This had been done by the saving event in Jesus Christ. To put it in a theological formula: God added to history the history of salvation *(Heilgeschichte)* - by sending His Son Jesus Christ - the Saviour. The Son, by completing the work of redemption, gave human history a new turn, a new perspective and a new direction. In doing so He established Himself as the centre of human history.

How did the direction-change of history actually take place? The process is this. In the life of those who believe in Christ and repent and accept Him as their Saviour, Christ stops their course of running away from God and redirects it towards God. The people of God willingly join God in His history-shaping activity. They offer themselves to God as His co-workers and they do everything possible so that the negative course of History will be changed in everyone by calling everybody to repentance and asking them to be reconciled with God and directing their life towards God *(2 Cor. 5:20)*. As they work for that end their subjective conviction will become objective reality. They know in faith that Jesus Christ is the centre of history, they work so that every man may accept Him and they wait for the time when the objective reality will be manifested to all at the second coming of Christ in His glory at the end of human history. *(Acts 1:11; Col. 3:4; 1 Cor. 15:23, Rev. 1:7)*.

4

NOTES

1. See Part I, Section I, Chapter 4, Point 6.
2. See Part I, Section 1, Chapter 6, Point 5.
3. K. Barth: Church Dogmatics, Vol III.1 Edinburgh (T&T Clark, 1956) p.45 f.
4. E. Brunner: Dogmatics, Vol II (London, Lutterworth Press) p.239 f.
5. See Part I, Section 1, Chapter 1, Point 3.
6. E. Brunner: Dogmatics, Vol II, p.237.

Chapter 2

Jesus of History and the Christ of Faith

The "Jesus of History" Movement
The Roots of the Movement, Its Main Representatives
The "Christ of Faith" Movement

1. The "Jesus of History" Movement

In dealing with Christology, we are obliged to mention a trend which flourished in the 19th century, called "the Jesus of History" movement. This raised the question of the historicity of the human person of Jesus Christ. It was concerned with the historical truth about the person of Jesus of Nazareth, that is, his real life-story beyond and apart from the Church dogmas which grew up around his person. Throughout Church history, Jesus Christ was presented as a dogma of the Church. The "Jesus of History" movement began to scrutinize the historical basis of the Church's dogma about Christ. This movement therefore was interested primarily in the historical facts about Jesus.

2. The Roots of the Movement

As to the roots of this movement, we can find at least three. The first root can be found in the movement of the French Enlightenment of the 18th century, which has connections with the Renaissance and the rationalistic philosophy of Descartes, Spinoza and Liebniz along with the empirical philosophy of Bacon, Berkeley and Hume. The ideas of Enlightenment spread over Europe and fell on fertile soil among the European intelligentsia. One result of this was that the majority of European intellectuals around the beginning of the 19th century became sceptical of church dogmas. This phenomenon triggered research into the historical facts about Jesus the founder of the Christian religion.

The second root of the "Jesus of History" movement goes back to new discoveries in archaeology. These discoveries began in Italy with the locating of Herculeanum and Pompeii in the mid 18th century. Both of these towns were destroyed by the eruption of the volcano Vesuvius in 79

AD. Archeology as a science had been founded by J.J. Winkelmann (1717-1768). The Napoleonic war in Egypt (1798-1801) gave a new impetus to the development of archaeology and the development of research on ancient Egyptian culture - the Pyramids, Temples and Tombs of the Kings. Later H. Schliemann (1822-1890) discovered ancient Troy and the Cretean culture. In the meantime, J. Champollion decoded the inscription on the Rosetta Stone allowing scholars to read the Egyptian Hieroglyphes. P.E. Botha found ancient Nineveh and deciphered the cuneiform writings of clay tablets. All these discoveries had raised interest in the past culture of mankind and as a consequence in the historicity of the Bible and particularly in the historicity of Jesus of Nazareth.

The third root of the "Jesus of History" movement was in the Bible criticism. Bible criticism as a branch of Biblical Science came about as the result of the above mentioned movements. It came into existence in the late 18th century and has developed an important but sometimes controversial science, as was later seen in the work of R. Bultmann and his school in our century.

3. Its Main Representatives

Out of the science of Bible criticism grew the "Jesus Research" movement. Its aim was to reconstruct the real life of Jesus of Nazareth, the founder of the Christian religion, an attempt that has resulted in scores of books on the "life of Jesus" (Das Leben Jesu). Let us briefly review this movement.

The beginning of Jesus research goes back to H.R. Reimarus, the German Oriental linguist (1694-1768), who wrote a long criticism of the Christian religion which he did not publish. After his death some seven sections of his manuscript were published by G. Lessing, the German poet and philosopher (l729-1781); this was called the "Wolfenbuttel Fragments".

More than sixty books were published on this subject. There is no space here to deal with this matter in depth. It is sufficient to point out the main groups and to mention the most important names. There was a group of theologians such as J.J. Hess; F.V. Reinhard; E. A. Opitz; J.A. Jakobi; and J.G. Herder, who followed Reimarus' path and tried to portray a rationalistic understanding of Jesus' life. This trend reached its peak in the work of H.E.G. Paulus. The last attempt of this type of interpretation can be found in K.A. Hesse's work and that of F.E.D. Schleiermacher. The aim of this rationalistic interpretation was to eliminate all supernatural and miraculous elements of Jesus' life by replacing them with rationalistic interpretation. For example, the divine conception of Jesus Christ was denied and an intensive search for a possible father started. The nature miracles were explained as illusion. For example, Jesus' walking on water was explained by the supposition that there the water actually was shallow and he was leaping from stone to stone hidden just under the surface of the water which gave the impression of walking on the surface of the sea. It was thought that the miracles of healing were performed by Jesus' spiritual power or by secret medicines or by unusual methods of healing. It was supposed that Jesus' death was not real; he probably fell into a coma from which he was resuscitated. His ascension was a simple departing; he got lost in the clouds surrounding the peak of the mountain-actually walked away on the other side of the mountain - acknowledging the failure of his mission and no one knows when and where he died.

Another group of theologians, whose main representative is Dr. F. Strauss (1808-1874), produced liberal "Lives" of Jesus, which satisfied requirements of Protestant liberal theology. Of the two "Lives" written by Strauss the first (1835) falls under this category while the second (1864) is in many points different from the first and gets near to the "Eschatological" type of Life of Jesus. In the first Life of Jesus, Strauss used the Hegelian method and Jesus' historic person was understood as a manifestation of the higher idea of God-Manhood. Strauss categorically rejected the supernatural elements of the Gospel as having no historical foundation and qualified them as pure legends and myths which were added to Jesus' life story after his death. He gave rationalistic or psychological interpretations to Jesus' miracle healings and visions. No wonder that Strauss, too, did not accept the literal resurrection of Jesus. Having radically criticized the Gospel, Strauss did not attempt to reconstruct the "life" of Jesus. However, he reached a philosophical conclusion, namely, that in the life of Jesus the "infinite manifested itself in the finite and the finite spirit remembering its infinitude"[1].

Beside the nationalistic and liberal Lives of Jesus, there were other genres of "lives". B. Bauer (1809-1882) wrote a sceptical Life of Jesus in which he arrived at the view that Jesus was not an historical person at all. Other authors wrote fictitious, imaginative "Lives of Jesus". Among them

8

a French Roman Catholic, E. Renan's, Life of Jesus is the most remarkable because it is an artistic, aesthetic and lyrical book about Jesus. This literary masterpiece achieved three aims at one stroke; presented the criticism of the contemporary German theologians, presented Jesus' person in an attractive way and presented Jesus' life as he could have lived it[2].

One more circle of theologians has to be mentioned: those who insisted that the person, work and life of Jesus could be understood only from the eschatological point of view. Among the theologians belonging here were T. Colani; G. Volkmar; W. Weiffenbach; and W. Baldensperger. The most famous was Albert Schweitzer (1875-1965), the French-German from Alsace, theologian, missionary-doctor and organist. He took over the idea of Johannes Weiss (1863-1916) about the importance of eschatology in Jesus' life (Die Predikt vom Reiche Gottes, 1892). On this basis, Schweitzer tried to reconstruct the historical Jesus. He criticized liberal theologians' dependence on the moral teaching of Jesus and their ignorance of his teaching concerning the eschatological Kingdom of God which Schweitzer held was the main axis of his teaching and of his life. At first, said Schweitzer, Jesus expected the immediate coming of the Kingdom when he would be revealed as the messianic "Son of Man." To prepare for the messianic era he sent off his disciples. When the arrival of the Kingdom of God was seemingly delayed, Jesus wanted to force its coming by his messianic suffering. Schweitzer also wanted to eliminate the supernatural elements from Jesus' life as all of his predecessors had done. His conclusion was that life, not history, shows who Jesus really was[3].

In the book, "The Quest of Historical Jesus" (1901) Schweitzer reviewed the last century Jesus research. This book is usually regarded as the end of the quest of historical Jesus. However, the issue came up again around the middle of this century in the Bultmannian school, mainly in the work of J. M. Robinson who launched a new quest for the historical Jesus[4].

What did this "Life of Jesus" movement achieve? The result was a surprisingly meagre one; namely, the attempt to reconstruct the historical Jesus has fallen short of the real Jesus of Nazareth. Does this mean that Jesus of Nazareth, the founder of Christian religion, never lived? That he is a fictitious person or an imaginary figure only? History proves that at the

9

birth of an important movement there is always its founder. Without Napoleon there could have been no "Second Empire" in France, without Hitler there would have been no "Third Reich" in Germany, without Marx could there have been no Marxist movement. Without the historical person of Jesus of Nazareth there would have been no Christianity. The failure of the "Life of Jesus" movement was rooted in its inadequate method. But it could happen in the future that, by inventing and applying a new method to the Jesus research, positive results might yet be yielded.

4. The "Christ of Faith" Movement

After the fiasco of the "Jesus of History" movement, attempts were made to understand Jesus from the point of view of Faith. This sparked a long debate between the representatives of the "Jesus of History" group and the exponents of the "Christ of Faith" school. Three theologians should be considered.

The German theologian, Martin Kähler (1835-1912), was dissatisfied with the achievement of the "Jesus of History" movement because it went too far and in many cases led to scepticism. In his lectures and in his book entitled "The so-called Historical Jesus and the Historic, Biblical Christ" he pointed out that the quest for the historical Jesus had led to a deadlock. He made a subtle distinction betwen "Historical" and "Historic" Jesus (German: Historisch, Geschichtlich). The historical Jesus is to be discovered by the historians. The historic Christ is who exercised effect upon history. Kähler's opinion was that the historical Jesus is almost hidden from us - as the meagre result of the "Jesus of History" movement proved. He suggested a brilliant solution, namely that the Christ who is preached is the historical Christ. It is not the "Jesus of History" that is important but the "Christ of Faith". However, he did not want to deny the importance of the historical foundation of Christianity; rather he only wanted to change the emphasis. He went further in arguing that only a historical person could exercise an historic effect. The historic effect of Christ is verified by two thousand years of existence of the Church; behind this effect there must be present the historical figure of Jesus of Nazareth. For Christ has an effect upon the world, this confirms the existence of Jesus of history[5]. Kähler skillfully applied the ancient method of Aristotle and Thomas Aquinas which, concluding from the effect to the cause, was used by them to prove the existence of God.

Kähler's standpoint was accepted and fully developed by the so called "Neo-Reformation" theologians such as K. Barth, E. Brunner and R. Bultmann and their followers. With their mediation the "Christ of Faith" movement created a remarkable impact on Contemporary Protestant Theology. Beside all its positive contribution, however, this movement had the tendency of neglecting the historical roots and foundation of the Christian religion. As a consequence of it, a danger appeared, namely, the shift of Christian theology from its unique position of being historically founded into the swampy category of Religious Philosophies.

Christian theologians have to take both trends seriously. On the one hand, they are dealing with the Christ of faith and on the other hand they must look at the results of the "Jesus of History" movement which supplies the data of the historical fact of Jesus Christ.

NOTES

1. D. F. Strauss: The Life of Jesus Critically Examined (SCM 1973) p.780.
2. J. E. Renan: The Life of Jesus (The World Publishing Co. USA, 1941).
3. A. Schweitzer: The Mystery of the Kingdom of God. (1901), 1956, London.
4. J. M. Robinson: A New Quest of the Historical Jesus (SCM, 1959).
5. M. Kähler: The So-called Historical Jesus and the Historic, Biblical Christ. p.63 f. Translation edited by C. E. Braaten (Fortress Press, 1964. Philadelphia).

Chapter 3

The Question of Method

Christology "From Above", Christology "From Below"
An Intermediate Standpoint

In contemporary theology the question of a proper Christological method has become a significant issue. There are at least three groups of dogmatic theologians who represent three different opinions on this question. Each of these groups take a different starting point in its Christology. Let us review them in turn[1].

1. Christology "From Above"

The first group of theologians pursue a method commonly known as Christology "from above." A capsule description of this Christological method is that these theologians emphasize the paramount importance of the Son of God who became flesh *(John 1:14)*. For them the important thing is the divine Logos who descended from "above", from the realms of God, and became flesh in the person of Jesus of Nazareth.

This concept of Christology is not new; it was already common in the ancient Church. Theologians who represented this standpoint include Ignatius of Antioch; Athanasius; and Cyril. Its Scriptural basis can be found in *John 1:14; Phil. 2.5 f; Rom. 8:3; and Gal. 4:4.*

The basis of this concept was in Platonic philosophy, which regarded reality as the materialization of ideas. For a man with a hellenistic background it was quite acceptable that in Jesus of Nazareth the Logos became flesh. But it was hard to accept that Jesus of Nazareth became the Son of God.

In modern theology K. Barth and his followers developed this line of Christology. He speaks about the Son of God who goes into a world which is foreign to him and through humiliation the Son of God becomes a man by uniting himself with the Man Jesus[2].

2. Christology "From Below"

The second group of theologians follow another line in Christology. They began Christology from "below", that is they emphasize the human nature of Jesus Christ and move upwards toward His divine nature. This perception was already present in the ancient Church. It was also followed by M. Luther. Some of the 19th century theologians like F. Schleiermacher and A. Ritschl also took this line. There are contemporary theologians, mainly among the Liberals, who occupy this standpoint in Christology. Among whom we may mention F. Gogarten; G. Ebeling; R. Bultmann and W. Pannenberg.

In the Christology of the German theologian, W. Pannenberg, we can find some characteristic arguments for this method. First, he criticizes the other perspective. He cannot accept it because of its dependence on the presupposition of the doctrine of Trinity, in that it is stated that the Son, the second person of Trinity, became human. This method thus accepts as an axiom the divinity of Son, whereas the proof of the divinity of Son is the very task of Christology. Further, he says, the "from above" method has difficulties in recognizing the real significance of the historical Jesus of Nazareth. This method would be feasible only if one would be in the position of God to follow the Son's descent into the world. Therefore, Pannenberg suggests one must begin with the man Jesus, ie. from "below" to understand the divinity of Christ. To start with the man Jesus means that one starts with the historical reality of Jesus. He maintains that knowledge about Jesus' life is clear enough to build a reasoned Faith[3].

3. An Intermediate Standpoint

There is another circle of theologians who occupy a middle position between the above-mentioned two, quite extreme, standpoints. They unite the two extremist views and work out a more acceptable method.

The German theologian, Jurgen Moltmann, can be mentioned in this context. He says that the difference between the method of "below" and that of "above" is only apparent. Jesus Christ was the Son of God from the beginning, but it became known only gradually to his followers. Christ's deity - His sonship - became obvious only at the end of his life - on the Cross and in the Resurrection. But in fact, Jesus Christ was the Son of God before his life-history took place. The difference in method is basically the difference between *ratio essendi* and *ratio cognoscendi*, that is, that Jesus Christ was really the Son of God but this only gradually becomes

13

obvious to human understanding. In this light the sharp contrast between the two methods disappears[4].

According to Paul Tillich, Christology cannot be put only in the terms of "from above" or "from below" because it is unique. Therefore he uses both methods. He starts "from above" but he takes the perspective of "from below", or that of the man Jesus. Further, he disagrees with the Johannine incarnation concept by arguing that God cannot become flesh - in which case God ceases to be God. He accepts the "Adoptionist" solution as one in which the term incarnation can be understood: The man Jesus had been adopted by God as Son of God. He insists that Jesus as the Christ is both a historical fact and a subject of faith[5].

Our standpoint in the method of Christology is near to that of J. Moltmann. On one hand we agree with the testimony of the scriptures, that Christ is the Son of God in whom "the "Word became flesh"(John 1:14). On the other hand, however, we have to recognize our situation: that we have access to christology from the human level only, which means that we ought to start "from below".

All this seems to be a purely academic matter. However, it has practical importance in the ministerial service. The preacher may talk about Jesus Christ from the point of view of God, that is, "from above". In this case it is doubtful that his audience will understand and accept the message. But if he preaches about Jesus Christ "from below" looking at Him from the human perspective, he may expect that his audience will understand and may accept the message. Only then can he show the thoughts, gifts and blessings of God that are to be found in Jesus Christ. Approaching Jesus Christ from "below" and understanding him from "above" is the most proper method of Christology.

NOTES

1.   See Part I, Introduction, Chapter 4.
2.   K. Barth: Church Dogmatics, Vol IV.1
3.   W. Pannenberg: Jesus - God and Man,(SCM 1968) p.34 f.
4.   J. Moltmann: Theology of Hope, Ch III.1 (SCM 1964) p 139 f.
5.   P. Tillich: Systematic Theology, Vol II (Chicago University Press) p. 94.

Section One

The Person of Christ

Chapter 1

The Fullness of Time

Preparation for the Coming of Christ in the Old Testament
The Historical Conditions, The Spiritual Conditions

The arrival of Christ the Messiah, the Redeemer and Saviour, was not unprepared. God had prepared His Son's way in a manyfold manner by creating the necessary conditions in the life of the Elect People, in history and in culture. The Christ did not come earlier or later but at the optimum moment in the life of humanity. This moment is what the Bible describes as the "Fullness of Time" - the *Pleroma Tou Kronou (Gal. 4:4)*. Let us look at its details.

1. Preparation for the Coming of Christ in the Old Testament

God did not abandon man in his fallen state. He wanted to rescue man from sin and its tragic consequences. Therefore, according to God's fore-ordained plan, He put into practice His rescue operation. Its first phase was the election of Israel as his covenant people. By giving the Divine Law to the elect people, God wished that a part of mankind learn to withstand the corruption of Sin by committing itself in full obedience to the will of God. To the elect people God gradually unfolded His plan of Salvation which would be achieved by sending a unique person who would bring about the salvation of Israel and of humanity. The name and character of this person became known more and more through the prophecies. Lastly, he was called the "Messiah", which means "Annointed" or *Christos* in Greek. This means a special person in nature, character and aims - who is annointed for the execution of his special task, appointed, authorized and sent by God.

God promised the Messiah after the fall of man. According to *Genesis 3:15* God gave a promise to Adam and Eve that the "seed" of the woman "will bruise" the "head" of the "serpent". This means that one of the descendants of the woman will break the power of the evil. The first promise is called the *Proto-euangelion* - the first Good News. The elect man Abraham also received a promise from God in *Genesis 22:18*: "By your descendants shall all nations of the earth bless themselves". This is an obvious reference to the Messiah. Balaam the prophet in a prophetic vision saw "a star which shall come forth out of Jacob" *(Num. 24:17)*. In the prophecies of the Prophets many details of the person, character and work of the Messiah were brought to light. Micah talks about the Ruler who comes from Bethlehem *(5:2-5)*. Malachi speaks about the Messenger of God *(3:1)*. Haggai expects the arrival of the Treasurer of all nations *(2:7)* Zachariah speaks of the "Servant" *(3:8)* and the "King" *(14:9)* who is coming. Jeremiah prophesies about the "righteous branch" who shall reign *(23:5)*. Ezekiel predicts the arrival of the "Shepherd" *(34:23-31)*, of a "New Heart" and a "New Spirit" that are given by God *(36:26-27)*, and he looks forward to the Resurrection of Israel *(37:1-14)*. Job dreams about his "Redeemer" *(19:25)*. Daniel foretells the coming of the "Prince of Princes", the "Anointed Prince" *(8:25, 9:25)*. But first of all Isaiah offers abundant and clear prophecy about the Messiah. He calls him the "Son of a young woman" and "Immanuel" - God with us *(7:14)* who will be "Light" for his people *(9:2)*. "To us a child is born, to us a son is given, "and He will govern", and "His name will be called Wonderful, Counsellor, Mighty God, Everlasting Father, Prince of Peace" *(9:6-7)*. Deutero Isaiah prophesies about the Suffering Servant who will be slaughtered like a Lamb and "He was wounded for our transgressions, He was bruised for our iniquities: upon Him was the chastisement that made us whole, and with His stripes we are healed ..... and the Lord has laid on Him the iniquity of us all." (Ch. 53).

God revealed to his people the person, character and the work of the coming Messiah in due time[1].

2. The Historical Conditions

God not only promised the coming of Christ: He also created the necessary historical conditions for the arrival of Christ. It is not incidental that Christ was born when the Roman Empire was at its zenith. This empire was the first modern state in many respects. Its army, organized in legions, was an highly effective one. It would preserve the Western part of the empire for a thousand years and for two thousand its Eastern part. The Imperial Roma had a network of stone roads. The communication system was excellent with a service of couriers. The organization of the empire was highly efficient. The Empire, which ruled the whole

16

Mediterranian basin, was made up of provinces and beyond its borders the rulers of the barbaric nations were the vassals of Rome. The empire had a developed legal system based on the *Lex Romana* - the Roman Law, and a flourishing political life. Political parties had programs and elections were held. The populace experienced the blessings of democracy and the vices of tyranny. The *Pax Romana*, the Roman Peace, was forced upon the known world and it was guarded by the legions - which also secured the privileges and rights of the Roman citizens against the poor, the oppressed and the slaves. Until the introduction of the cult of the Emperors, the Roman state was quite lenient to the religious and cultural life of subjugated people. Judaism was, for example, a *religio licita* - licensed religion [2].

Palestine was under Roman rule at that time. The mighty kingdom of David and Solomon had disappeared long ago. In 931 BC the Jewish state split into two: Israel on the North and Judah on the South. Israel was soon overrun by Assyria in 722 BC. Sargon II took the Israelites into captivity, Judah meeting with similar fate in 586 BC. After the Babylonians occupied Jerusalem, Nebuchadnezzar took its people into captivity in Babylon. After the fall of the Babylonian empire the Persian king, Cyrus, gave permission to the captive people to return to their homeland and many of the Jews came home. They returned in two groups: in 538 BC with Nehemiah and Ezra and in 458 BC with Esdra. The Jews restored the Temple and the walls of Jerusalem and rededicated themselves to their ancient faith (515 BC). In 333 BC the Jews fell under the rule of Alexander the Great and subsequently they were ruled by the Hellenistic monarchs. As a reaction to the forced Hellenization of Antiochus Epiphanes IV, the Jews rebelled against him and, under the leadership of Judas Maccabee, they won independence in 165 BC. It lasted for only one century. In 63 BC, the Roman general Pompey occupied the country. Later the Romans appointed the half-Jew Herod the Great as king, and it was around the end of his life that Jesus was born in Bethlehem (c 5 BC). After the death of Herod the vassal kingdom was divided among his sons: Archelaus, Herod Antipas and Herod Philip. The Romans soon dismissed Archelaus and procurators administered his former territories: Judea, Samaria and Edom. Pontius Pilate was one of these procurators *(Luke 23:1)*. Later Herod Agrippa I, the grandson of Herod the Great, ruled the whole country as king. Both the Herodian dynasty and the governors exploited and oppressed the Jews and they were hated by the people. In this political context we may well understand why and how the longing for the arrival of the long-expected Messiah, who would liberate his people, was at its climax.

3. The Spiritual Conditions

In the Roman empire there was a mixed cultural and religious life, the result of great variety of ethnic groups with particular cultural and religious heritage. Extensive trade, inner migration of the populace, slavery and even tourism contributed enormously to the mingling of cultures and religions. Beside Roman culture and religion there were Greek culture, religion and philosophies together with Oriental culture, religion and costumes. This was the age of "Hellenism" and "Syncretism" - a colorful amalgam of various languages, ways of life, and religions, with an eminent role given to the Greek language, style and manners.

Where so many cultures, philosophies and religions were present none of them could become truly dominant and a feeling of relativism, uncertainty and disppointment took hold in the mind and the soul of the people. Confusion of thoughts, the feeling of lostness and meaninglessness intensified and as its consequence the longing for a better, consolidated and spiritually secure world grew rapidly. No wonder that in the Empire there was a general longing for a *"Soter"* - a Redeemer. This longing was skilfully utilized by the Roman emperors for political purpose. They were eager to present themselves as the *Soter* of mankind, declaring themselves divine persons who appeared in this world - sent by the heavens - to fulfil the aspiration and wishes of mankind by giving them peace, order and prosperity. The coins of this age bear the name "Soter" above the relief of the Emperor.

If the longing for the Soter was general in the Empire, it was particularly accentuated among the Jews in Palestine and in the Diaspora. This once mighty and independent people was now living under the Roman yoke and in miserable conditions surrounded by unfriendly gentile nations. The Jewish dream of the restitution of David's glorious kingdom always remained one of their most sacred expectations. The promise of God to His elect and covenant people would turn into reality by the arrival of the Messiah. He would free the covenant people of Jahweh and restore their power and might again. Because of this ever living hope about the sudden coming of the Messiah, self-proclaimed Messiahs appeared from time-to-time. They led the Jews into suicidical rebellions against the Romans, finally resulting in the destruction of Jerusalem in AD 70 and the abolition of the Jewish state in AD 135.

God had prepared for the coming of His Son in history, in culture and in the spiritual life of the Jewish people and of humankind. These are the reasons why Jesus Christ did not come earlier or later, in another age or in another place. He was born in an occupied country, amidst an oppressed people, in a stable among animals. God stretched his saving hand as deeply as the position where men had fallen. Christ came in the right age, in the right time and in the right place. This is what the "fullness of time" means[3].

For the Christians it is important to know that the coming of the Messiah was not an unprepared, abrupt event; God carefully planned and prepared it by creating the best conditions for it. The same providence of God is still at work: God carefully prepares for the arrival of Christ in the life of each individual person and in human communities. God prepares every person for "the fullness of time", ie. for their acceptance of Christ.

NOTES

1. E. Brunner: Dogmatics, Vol II, p. 233.
2. Op.cit, P. 235.
3. P. Tillich: Systematic Theology, Vol III, pp. 369.f.

19

Chapter 2

The Incarnation

Models of the Messiah, The Logos Doctrine
The Doctrine of Virgin Birth

The word Incarnation is derived from the Latin word *Incarnatio* which means to enter into flesh or body. As Christian theological doctrine it means that the Son of God, the second person of Trinity became a true man in the person of Jesus of Nazareth; who is therefore the promised messiah, the Christ, the saviour of humanity. In dealing with this important Christian doctrine we try to answer three questions. Firstly, "Which kind of messiah arrived?" Secondly, "What is the meaning of the divine side of incarnation" or to put it in other words: "What is the meaning of the *Logos* doctrine?" Thirdly, "What does the human side of incarnation mean," including the "Doctrine of virgin birth?"

1. Models of the Messiah

We have already noticed that the person, character and the work of the messiah gradually became clearer in the Old Testament revelation [1]. However, in the intertestamental period in the last couple of centuries before Christ, two models of the messiah emerged and existed side by side in Jewish expectation.

The first model was that of messiah as a son of man. This concept was based chiefly on the writings of Ezra, Daniel and Enoch. According to this expectation the promised messiah would be a chosen human person, a prince, or a king. But sometimes he was imagined in a more humble form: such as a shepherd, or a servant. His main task was to liberate the elect people from their oppressors in a holy war where even the heavenly army of angels would fight if necessary. After having defeated all enemies the Messiah would restore the Kingdom of David; and finally he would establish the Kingdom of God on the earth.

The second model type of messiah is that of the Son of God type of messiah. According to this concept the messiah would be an angelic being, not an earthly one, and his name would be Messenger, Redeemer and Mighty God. This messiah would break the power of sin, Satan and evil, and would grant forgiveness and bring this world to a sudden and abrupt end. After this he would establish the heavenly Kingdom of God. This concept was based primarily on the writings of the great prophets - eminently that of Isaiah.

The Messianic Kingdom, the Kingdom of God or Kingdom of Heaven (Hebrew: *Malkothammaim*, Greek: *Basileia tou Ouranon*) also had two concepts or models of messiah. The first is, that the Kingdom of God would be a secular kingdom, established by the "Son of Man" who wages war against the enemies of the elect people and would be victorious over them. In this case the messiah is basically a political figure. This idea of messiah was accepted by the Zealots - the ardent Jewish patriots. Hence, we can understand the various rebellions of the Jews against foreign oppressors from the Maccabees to Bar Kochba. This messiah concept can be regarded as the deepest root of modern Zionism. The second concept is that the Kingdom of God will be not earthy but a heavenly, a spiritual one, which will be established by the Son of God. Those who accepted this idea were the pious rather than political people such as the Essenes, the members of the Qumran sect and the followers of John the Baptist. They expected a messiah who would fight against sin, call for repentance and for ascetic life-style, require inner change and an involvement in a spiritual community with God. This type of messiah would not establish an earthly kingdom, rather he would abolish this sinful world and would lead his elect, pious and righteous people into the Kingdom of Heaven. This spiritual concept of Messiah reached its fullness in Christian theology[2].

God's answer to these expectations was Jesus Christ, in whose person and work both concepts of messiahship were present. He is both the Son of God and the Son of Man.

2. The *Logos* Doctrine

When we turn towards the mystery of the incarnation we look firstly at its divine side. We can understand something of it because God revealed it. In the incarnation of the Son of God in the form of Jesus of Nazareth "The *Logos* became flesh" *(John 1:14).* To understand the divine side of the incarnation, therefore, we have to look into the Logos doctrine.

The word *Logos* is Greek and means word, thought, reason - *ie.* the word by which inward thought is being expressed. In Greek philosophy it is a technical term which denotes the general law which is the basis of the universe. Heraclitos (544-483 BC) understood *Logos* as the universal reason which is eternal, general and necessary. Everything occurs according to *Logos*. The Stoic Philosophers (4th-1st centuries BC) also considered Logos as the law of both the spiritual and the physical world.

The Jewish philosopher and theologian, Philo (20 BC - 40 AD), in Alexandria, Egypt, worked out the *Logos* doctrine which became influential for John's Gospel and the writer of the Epistle to the Hebrews. Philo said that *Logos* is actually the mediator between God and the world, creating, animating and directing it. The *Logos* is the creative power of God, immanent in the world.

Early theologians took over the *Logos* doctrine and modified it applying it to Jesus Christ by saying that Christ is the *Logos*, the eternal Son of God, the second Person of the Trinity, who participated in the work of Creation and who is the immanent reason of the world. Christ as *Logos* is the vessel of God's inner thoughts in whom God has disclosed His eternal purpose of the creation, His eternal idea of Redemption and His eternal plan of Salvation. Christ is the eternal Word of God in whom all God's promises had been materialized. Christ as *Logos* is the mediator between God the creator and fallen man and the universe. He is the redeemer of all creation including mankind[3].

In the process of the incarnation this *Logos* became flesh. The timeless, eternal and divine *Logos* became a man and entered into human history. With him and by Him a second creation, a new genesis commenced which reaches its fullness at the end of this world.

3. The Doctrine of the Virgin Birth

Beside the divine side of the incarnation there is a human side. According to the second Article of the Apostolic Creed, Jesus Christ was "Conceived by the Holy Spirit, born of the Virgin Mary." This statement of faith is based on the Revelation of God *(Matt. 1:18, Luke 1:35)*. The problem involved in it is the following: How was it possible that the Son of God became a human person? The doctrine of the Virgin Birth excludes the fact of previous sexual intercourse; no male sperm fertilized Virgin Mary's egg. This sharply contradicts human experience, we have to accept that the Holy Spirit performed a miracle. The conception of Jesus Christ was the act of the same Holy Spirit who created the world and its life, including man without material means. At Jesus Christ's conception the same Holy Spirit was creating in a spiritual way.

22

Theologians in every age have tried to understand this miracle. John of Damascus said that Mary's ear was the bodily organ of the miraculous conception of Jesus Christ; she believed in the word of God which was announced to her by the Angel (Luke 1:26-38). Augustine stated that Christ was conceived by faith. K. Barth said that "Jesus was born as none of us was born, not because of male generation, but of female conception." He also stressed the importance of the divine initiative in the Incarnation. The virgin birth of Jesus Christ was the beginning of the humiliation of the Son of God[4]. J. MacQuarrie says that the question is whether the doctrine of virgin birth helps us to understand the person of Christ. His standpoint is that both birth and death are mysteries, so this doctrine simply indicates that the origin of Christ is in God[5]. He sees three truths in the doctrine of Incarnation: the initiative in the God to man relationship lies with God and it shows God's deep involvement in and with His Creation, and this initiative and involvement have their centre in Jesus Christ[6].

Why is the doctrine of the virgin birth important? The answer is that It is important from the point of view of Soteriology. If Jesus Christ was not the Son of God incarnated then he was just another among sinful men. Consequently, the vicarious death of Jesus Christ would lose its validity; he died because of his own sin and not because of our sins. In this case his death could not achieve atonement at all. With the doctrine of the virgin birth the early Church wanted to stress that Jesus of Nazareth, the man who embodied in Himself the eternal Son of God, constituted a unique, sinless and true man; the "Second Adam" whose vicarious death had the redemptive value. The problem of the virgin birth of Christ could only be understood in the light of His death. However, it is not the case that the doctrine of virgin birth was invented later, after the death of Christ in order that the redemptive meaning of His death should be validated. The case is that the disciples and followers of Jesus Christ understood properly the importance of His virgin birth after His death and resurrection.

The doctrine of the virgin birth gave impetus for the development of "Mariology" in the Roman Catholic Church. In its extreme expressions this growth led to theories such as the bodily assumption of the Virgin Mary to practices such as the worship of Virgin Mary, and even a trend to announce her as Co-Redeemer. Protestant theology rejects these views and practices because of the lack of Biblical foundation for them. This, however, does not mean that Protestant theology gives to her no significant place in the gallery of the great figures of the Bible.

23

The doctrine of the virgin birth is not without ethical consequences. The fact that Christ was conceived by the Holy Spirit means that the act of conception was sanctified. Therefore Christians cannot misuse the gift of sex which is related to it. They have to live in a highly responsible way, in the presence of God. Consequently, Christians reject the irresponsible sexual liberalism of our age.

NOTES

1. See Part I, Section 1, Chapter 6, Point 5.
2. E. Benz: Evolution and Christian Hope (London, V. Gollanz) p. 3 f.
3. K. Barth: Church Dogmatics, Vol IV.1 p. 51 f. and IV.3 p. 97 f, 239 f.
4. K. Barth: Church Dogmatics, Vol I.2 p. 127 f.
5. J. MacQuarrie: Principles of Christian Theology, p. 280 f.
6. J. MacQuarrie: The Humility of God (SCM, 1978) p. 26 f.

Chapter 3

The Humanity of Christ

Christ the true Man, The Problems of Christ's Humanity: The Knowledge of Christ, The Sinlessness of Christ His Messianic Consciousness

From the doctrine of incarnation, that is, the Son of God the second Person of the Holy Trinity took up a human body and dwelt in the person of Jesus of Nazareth who therefore is Jesus Christ, follows the Christian doctrine of the twofold nature of Jesus Christ. This means - as the Synod of Calcedon (451 AD) conceptualized - that Jesus Christ is *vere deus et vere homo*, that is he is true God and true man. He had both divine and human natures in His person which qualified Him to be the true Messiah of humanity. The twofold nature of Christ is a basic tenet of Christian faith. Let us study firstly His human nature, secondly His divine nature, and thirdly, the problems of the two natures.

In this chapter we deal with the human nature of Christ. However, we do not intend to give a comprehensive study of Jesus Christ's earthly life nor do we attempt to write a sort of "Life of Jesus". This is simply not the task of doctrine. But we have to point out some important facts of Jesus' life and in so doing we try to argue that He was really, fully and truly human. The goal is to indicate the truth of the early Christian experience: that Jesus Christ is thoroughly human is true.

1. Christ the True Man

We can easily gather facts, first of all from the Gospels and also from the Epistles, which provide proofs of the human nature of Jesus Christ. there are at least two irrefutable truths about the real manhood of Jesus Christ. The first is that He was born of woman just as we are *(Matt. 1:28 f; Luke 2:7; Gal. 4:4)*. The second is that He died *(Mark 15:37; Matt.27:50; Luke 23:46; John 19:30)* and was buried *(Mark 15:45-46; Matt. 27:59-60; Luke 23:52-53; John 19:42)*. From beginning to end His was fully a human life, the life of the Son of Man. The child Jesus was brought up in the family of Joseph the carpenter in Nazareth. He learned the law, the writings of the Prophets and the tradition as Jewish children were expected to, and He trained in carpentry in order to earn His living. He was barely twelve years old when He surprised the priests and teachers by his profound knowledge in the Scriptures and by his theological skill *(Luke 2:39-52)*. He became a devout person, reading the scriptures, meditating, praying and singing the psalms. He became an itinerant teacher because He wanted to help all who needed assistance, counsel, or healing. He attracted sinners, outcasts, and sick people. He was both admired by his followers and hated by his adversaries. In the end He was arrested, put to trial and sentenced to death on the cross. Jesus Christ's earthly life shows that He was a man like ourselves. He shared in our common human life and destiny[1].

That Jesus of Nazareth was a real human person is generally accepted not only by Christians but by even those who do not follow Him. However, a few atheist thinkers insist that He was never a real living person. To them we would answer: history proves that at the origin of any important movement there must be a real person: its founder, originator and creator. There is no Marxism without Marx, no Naziism without Hitler and no Stalinism without Stalin. There is no Christianity without the real person and work of Jesus Christ. A non-existent or imaginary figure could not have launched the movement Christianity. One has to accept the fact of the real, true and authentic human existence of Jesus Christ.

2. The Problems of Christ's Humanity

We have emphasized the true human nature of Jesus Christ. However, we have to point out that this human nature is not without problems if we want to understand it more fully. Classical theology usually mentions two problems in relation to Jesus Christ's human nature. The first is the problem of his knowledge and the second is his sinlessness[2].

2.1. The Knowledge of Christ

When we look into the humanity of Christ the question arises: "Was His human knowledge limited or was it limitless because it was divine?" The root of this problem lies in the double nature of Jesus Christ who was not only truly human but truly divine as well. In that case, how far did His divine nature influence his human nature? Or more precisely, how did the human Jesus have the omniscience of the Son of God? In the light of *Philippians 2:7* we may say that the son "emptied himself, having taken the form of a servant". When He took the form of a man, He left behind His divine power. Therefore we may say that Jesus Christ's human knowledge was limited with exception of his knowledge about God, knowledge that

26

helped Him to be the true man. In this respect we can say that He was the "Second Adam" *(1 Cor. 15:45, 47).* His humanity means that He shared the limitation of fallen man including its limited knowledge. He acquired human knowledge as a child like any other child; as *Luke 2:5* says; "Jesus increased in wisdom and stature". Towards the end of His life He was asked about the time of the end of the world. He plainly said: "But of that day or that hour no one knows... not the Son, but only the Father" *(Mark 13:32).* His limited knowledge also proves His true humanity; He was like one of us and not a "Superman". Amidst the limits of human conditions He was fully obedient to the will of God.

2.2. The Sinlessness of Christ

In relation to the true humanity of Christ the question of His sinlessness has to be faced. If Christ was a true human like us, does it mean that He was also a sinful man? The answer is a definite "No". Christ did not commit sin, consequently He was not a sinful man. He came in the likeness of sinful flesh *(Rom. 8:3)* but He was without sin. Jesus himself asks: "which of you convicts me of sin? *(John 8:46).* However, many attempts were made by His adversaries in this respect so that Jesus' person could be tarnished. He was called a "Friend of sinners" *(Matt. 11:19),* and was accused of not keeping the Sabbath *(John 9:16).* In His staged trial the main accusation against Him was that He claimed to be the "Son of God" *(Matt. 26:63-66)* which was regarded as a capital sin. Jesus Christ was tempted but He never sinned *(Matt. 4:1-11; Heb. 4:15).*

Christ came into the world, into the abyss of man's sin, without the abyss of sin in Himself, to lift up mankind from His fallen state. He Himself was not fallen. Only this sinless character of Christ qualified Him for the office of Messiah. But the lack of sin would not in itself make the Messiah. Something positive must be present in Him. This is the complete obedience to the will of God. Jesus Christ was obedient to God unto death on a cross *(Phil. 2:8).*

Why is the doctrine of sinlessness of Christ an important one? It is important from the point of view of Soteriology similarly to the doctrine of Virgin Birth. According to W. Pannenberg the reason behind it lies in the concept of the "High Priest" *(Heb. 4:14, 15).* In the Old Testament the High Priest had to have ritual purity when he offered sacrifice for sins on the day of atonement; otherwise the sacrifice was thought to be worthless. So Jesus Christ, who offered his self-sacrifice on the cross as the true "Great High Priest" had to be sinless, otherwise His sacrifice for the redemption

27

of humanity could not be accepted by God. The dogma of the virgin birth also served this purpose, that is, to prove the sinlessness of Jesus Christ from the very beginning of His human life. From the same point of view the account of temptation of Christ was important *(Matt. 4:1-11)*. He was tempted but He defied the temptation[3].

3. The Messianic Consciousness of Jesus

Jesus of Nazareth was born, grew up and lived in a political, spiritual and religious atmosphere in which the longing for the promised Messiah was in its climax. The oppression and exploitation of the Jewish people by the Romans and their collaborators, the presence of the Zealots, the Essenes, the Qumran sect, and the followers of John the Baptist all fuelled this longing for and belief in the immanent arrival of the Messiah. This expectation produced pious people like Simeon and Anna who were living in the Temple of Jerusalem waiting for the Messiah *(Luke 2:25-38)*. Jesus not only knew about the idea of Messiah, but He gradually became convinced that He was the promised Messiah and decided to dedicate His life to its implementation.

As Jesus became aware that He was the promised Messiah, the messianic consciousness strengthened in Him until He was absolutely convinced about His messianic mission. In this process He distinguished Himself from the Prophets, regarding Himself as the One in whom the promised Kingdom of God has already arrived *(Luke 4:16-21, 11:20)*. The decisive question was which of the two types of messiahship he should follow: the popular political-secular type or the spiritual one? He opted for the spiritual type of messiahship. Evidently, Jesus made efforts to transform the popular expectation of a political Messiah of his people into a spiritual type but He failed in this effort. Humanly speaking, this failure largely contributed to His rejection as Messiah by the majority of the Jews.

There is a strong trend in contemporary theology which puts emphasis on the human nature of Christ. This was started by D. Bonhoeffer and continues through the theology of P. Tillich, J. Moltman, W. Pannenberg, and J.A.T. Robinson.

Jesus Christ's humanity has great importance for Christians. In the human Jesus Christ man receives the mercy of God and salvation; all this is being communicated to us through the human Jesus Christ. His human nature is therefore the proof and seal of the redemptive love of God.

NOTES

1. E. Brunner: Dogmatics, Vol. II, pp. 322 f.
2. ibid p. 324.
3. W. Pannenberg: Jesus - God and Man, pp. 354 f.

Chapter 4

The Divinity of Christ

In God's Revelation, In Christ's Teaching and Deeds
In the Disciples' and Others' Testimony

Jesus Christ was not only truly human *Vere Homo* but truly God, *Vere Deus* at the same time. Christian theology teaches the eternal Godhead of the Son of God. The divinity of Christ is a unique Christian teaching which distinguishes the Christian concept of Christ from all other understanding of Christ and from all other religions. The divinity of Christ is a basic Christian dogma, and also the most characteristic distinguishing one. As we said before Christian theology is basically Christology[1]. The core of Christology is the teaching about the twofold nature of Christ: He is both human and divine. The divine character of Christ makes Him an extraordinary person: consequently it makes Christology a unique Christian doctrine. Having seen Christ's human nature, we have now to look at the divine nature of Christ, who is the Son of God, the second person of the Holy Trinity (See: Part I, Section 2, Ch. 2, and Part III, Section 1, Ch. 2).

1. In God's Revelation

The doctrine of divinity of Christ, first of all, is based upon the revelation of God. We may distinguish three stages in God's revelation which are relevant to this issue. First is the promise of God about the coming messiah who will be a divine person. We have dealt with this issue above [2]. This promise culminated in the announcement about His Son at the conception of Jesus: "Therefore the child to be born will be called holy, the Son of God" *(Luke 1:35)*. Second, there is the testimony of God at the baptism of Jesus Christ by John the Baptist at the river Jordan. This event is important not only from the point of view of the messianic consciousness of Jesus Christ but because God publicly confirmed the sonship of Jesus Christ by saying: "Thou art my beloved Son, with thee I am well pleased" *(Luke 3:22)*. Third, there are the resurrection and ascension of Jesus Christ, which are the highest proofs given by God that Jesus Christ who was resurrected and has ascended into Heaven is indeed the Son of God *(Acts 2:24, 3:26; Phil. 2:9)*[3].

2. In Christ's Teaching

Jesus Christ plainly and self-consciously proclaimed that He regarded himself not only the Son of Man but the Son of God as well. This is based upon His profound conviction that: "I and the Father are one" *(John 10:30).* Christ also emphasised that He has His divinity in His own person because "The Father... has granted to the Son also to have life in Himself: *(John 5:26).* Christ's real nature is, however, a mystery, because: "No one knows who the Son is except the Father" *(Luke 10:22).* The benefit of the Son's mystical unity with the Father is that: "He who has seen me has seen the Father" *(John 14:9).* When at his trial the high priest directly asked him: Are you the Christ, the Son of the Blessed"? Jesus gives the plain answer: "I am" *(Mark 14:61).* After the resurrection and before His ascension Jesus Christ, in the mission - commandment, sent out His disciples to baptize not only in the name of the Father and that of the Holy Spirit but in the name of the Son - in His own name *(Matt. 28:18-20)*[(4)].

3. In Christ's Deeds

Jesus Christ's claim that He is the "Son of God" is one thing, but to prove it is the other more crucial issue. Jesus' contemporaries were weary of false Messiahs who misled many people and brought upheavals, wars and misery. They did believe that the Messiah would come but they were very sensitive about the credentials of the genuine Messiah. Therefore they wanted "signs" ("Greek: *Semeion*) which proved His Messiahship. It is no wonder that Jesus Christ's contemporaries always asked Him for signs *(Matt.16:1, Luke 11:16).* Jesus Christ refused to answer this provocative demand by providing some special signs. However, His whole messianic activity can be understood as a continuous and profound sign-giving about His true messiahship including His Sonship. There are at least three elements in Jesus Christ's activity which unanimously prove His sonship and divinity.

The miracles of Jesus Christ can be understood as "signs" of His divinity. In His miraculous deeds, whether healing *(Matt. 8:2-3)* or raising the dead *(eg. Luke 8:49-56)* or showing His power over the forces of nature *(eg. Mark 4:37-39),* an extraordinary transcendental power was present which proved to be stronger and superior to any destructive power, either embedded in human nature such as sickness or death or in the blind forces of nature. In the miraculous deeds of Jesus Christ the creative power of God the creator was present. These deeds - apart from the fact that they gave relief to men involved in the miracle - proved two things. First, that in Him God is at work and second, that Jesus Christ's claim for divinity is well founded.

Not only Christ's miracles but His authority to give forgiveness of Sin also proves His divinity. No one can forgive sin except God - against whom every sin is aimed. But the Son of God, who is one with the Father, also has the authority and power to forgive. Christ says: "The Son of Man has the authority on earth to forgive sins" *(Mark 2:10)*. The forgiveness of sin is always linked to the healing of man *(e.g. Matt. 9:2-7)*. Both activities of Christ aim at the restoration of Man to his original state. Therefore Christ rightly announced that with Him the Kingdom of God is already here (Luke 11:20). Only Christ the divine Son of God can bring this new state into existence.

Beyond Christ's miracles and the forgiveness of sins, Christ's death, resurrection and ascension prove His Sonship and divinity. His death on the cross was offered by Him as sacrifice for the expiation of the sins of humanity *(Matt. 20:28, 1 John 2:2)*. Only Christ, who is not only man but God, could achieve this *(Rom. 8:32; 2 Cor. 5:19)*. Christ's resurrection shows that the Father accepted the son's sacrifice, which in turn demonstrates the divinity of the Son. This is obvious from the Apostles' witnessing: "...Designated Son of God in power... by his resurrection from the dead" *(Rom 1:4)*. The Ascension of Jesus Christ is the crown proof of His deity: "No one has ascended into heaven but he who descended from heaven, the Son of man" *(John 3:13)*.

4. In the Disciples' and Others' Testimony

The deity of Jesus Christ became evident to some of the people who were around him. The Disciples and Apostles bear witness to the deity of Christ. But the earliest testimony comes from John the Baptist. He says: "I have seen and I have borne witness that this is the Son of God" *(John 1:34)*. Peter at Caesarea Philippi exclaims: "You are the Christ, the Son of the living God" *(Matt. 16:16)*. Thomas bears witness at his encounter with the resurrected Lord: "My Lord and my God" *(John 20:28)*. The writer of the Gospel of Mark starts with this introduction: "The beginning of the gospel of Jesus Christ, the Son of God." *(Mark 1:1)*. John confesses: "For God so loved the world that He gave his only Son *(John 3:16)*. Paul was convinced about the Sonship of Jesus Christ, stating: "And the life I now live in the flesh I live by faith in the Son of God" *(Gal.2:20; I Cor. I:9; Col. I:13; Eph. 4:13)*.

Jesus Christ's friends and followers also provide us with testimony of His deity. Nathaniel says: "Rabbi, you are the Son of God" *(John 1:49)*. The boat people whom He saved on the stormy sea worshipped Him, saying, "Truly you are the Son of God" *(Matt. 14:33)*. Having witnessed the death of Jesus Christ the Roman centurion exclaimed: "Truly this was the Son of God" *(Matt. 27:54)*. Even Jesus Christ's adversaries bear witness concerning His deity. The Tempter approached Him saying: "If you are the Son of God "... *(Matt. 4:3)*. The unclean spirits cried: "You are the Son of God" *(Mark 3:11)*. The crowd at His cross mocked Him by saying: "If you are the Son of God, come down from the cross" *(Matt. 27:40)*.

From all this it is obvious that the New Testament communicates to us without any doubt that Jesus of Nazareth is regarded as the promised Messiah, the Christ, the Son of God who has divine nature. We are told so by Jesus himself, by the Disciples and Apostles, by His followers and by the early Christians and even by His adversaries. In the early Church, accepting Jesus as Christ was the difference between Christians and other people. Confessing Jesus Christ as Son of God, that is, confessing His deity, was the main criterion of being a Christian.

Nothing has changed in Christianity in this respect. Today, as it was yesterday and will be tomorrow, one faces the same condition if he or she wants to become a Christian: the acceptance of Jesus Christ by faith as the Son of God. The Christian minister always has to remember this in his parish work and in his preaching ministry.

NOTES

1.   See Part II, Introduction, Chapter 1.
2.   See Part II, Section 1, Chapter I, Point 1.
3.   E. Brunner: The Mediator, (London, The Lutterworth Press, 1934) pp. 232 f..
4.   L. Berkhof: Systematic Theology (The Banner of Truth Trust) pp. 316 f.

Chapter 5

The Problem of the Two Natures of Christ

The Docetic Heresy, The Ebionite heresy
Nestorians and Monophysites
Monothelites; Unorthodox Views in Modern Theology

In the previous two chapters we have seen how Jesus Christ was both truly human and truly God. Now the question inevitably arises as to how is it possible that two natures - *physes* - that of the human and the divine, could dwell in the same person at the same time without one nature adversely affecting the other. The Early Church had already faced this serious problem and much of the so called "Christological Debate" (1st-4th centuries) revolved around this question. As has been mentioned before (Vol. 1, Part I, Section 2, Ch. 3. "God Misunderstood") the Christological Debate was concerned with three major issues. First, what is the right relationship between the three persons of the Trinity? Second, what is the correct relationship between the two natures of Christ, and how this twofold nature of Christ can be interpreted. Third, whether Holy Spirit proceeds both from the Father and the Son or only from the Father? We intend to review the most important heresies concerning Christ's double nature and the Church's solution in the Chalcedonian definition. We shall also point out how far heretical views are present in modern theology.

1. The Docetic Heresy

The name comes from the Greek word *Dokein* which means "to seem, to look like". In Christian theology this means a certain understanding of Christ: namely, that He only looked like a man while He was not really a man, but God. This was an attempt to understand the mystery of the twofold nature - by overemphasizing His divine nature at the expense of His human nature. In the age of Hellenism this solution to the Christological problem was understandable. Because this age was influenced by the philosophy of Plato, who developed a world view in which he distinguished between the world of "Ideas" - which was considered the real world-and the world of "Phenomena", this world - which was regarded only as the "shade" of the perfect world of Ideas. It is no wonder that people with a hellenistic upbringing naturally accepted that Jesus Christ's divine nature - the ideal one - was more important than His human nature in which God appeared in this world[1].

The Docetic heresy first appeared in "Gnosticim". Basilides (ca.130) taught that no real union took place between Christ and Jesus. The human person was only a transitory form for Christ. The link between them was dissolved before the crucifixion. Jesus was a real man and He was just a starting point of the *eon* - age - of Christ. Christ ascended to heaven before the crucifixion and He laughed at the devil. Valentinus (ca.135-165) insisted that the body of Christ was not a human body, that Christ simply came through Mary. Saturninus (ca.150) denied that Christ ever had a human body; he insisted Christ was not even born and He only simply appeared to suffer.

The main representative of the Docetic heresy was Apollinaris of Laodicea (ca. 330), a Syrian bishop and a brilliant theologian. He thought that the *"Logos"* had taken upon himself the nature of man with *Sarx* - flesh - and *Psyche* - self - but he had not taken up the *Nous* - mind - of a human being. Instead of *"Nous"* the *"Logos"* was the reasoning Spirit in him. So Apollinaris denied the full incarnation of God in Christ; he allowed only an incomplete one. But if the incarnation is not complete, the redemption He brought is consequently incomplete.

To secure the full unity of the person of Christ, the early theologians introduced the "Doctrine of *Enhypostasia*". According to this doctrine, on the one hand, Jesus was fully human with *sarx, psyche* and *nous*. But on the other hand Jesus had not his own *hypostasis* - the special characteristic nature of a person - but that of God, so that Christ's existence was the existence of God[2].

2. The Ebionite Heresy

The name "Ebionite" comes from the Hebrew word *Ebjonim* - the poor. The Jewish Christians were called by this name first in Jerusalem, later on the eastern side of the river Jordan. Paul mentioned them in *Romans 15:26* as "The poor among the saints in Jerusalem" for whom he organized an aid campaign. They survived about three centuries. These Christians, because of their Jewish origins, strictly observed the Mosaic Law. They could not accept the Pauline interpretation of the Gospel that one can be Christian without previously being a follower of Judaism. Understandably, the Ebionites had a strong belief in a monotheistic God: the God of the Old Testament. Consequently, for them even the thought of Jesus Christ as God beside the God of the Patriarchs was a blasphemy. Moreover God never could turn Himself into a creature because God would thereby cease to be God. Then how could they accept Jesus Christ as a divine person? Their solution lies in their Christological standpoint: they understood Christ basically as a human who was elevated by God to a divine status. It is no wonder that they never accepted the pre-existence of Christ or His supernatural conception. They believed that Jesus Christ was a unique creature of God, who at His baptism was accepted as Son of God and under the guidance of the Holy Spirit He was obedient to the will of God. Jesus Christ was not God in and of Himself but through development He became God. He was not God in substance but at a certain moment He received a special kinship with God[3].

3. Nestorians and Monophysites

A new controversy broke out in the 5th century which was connected with Nestorius, the Patriarch of Constantinople (died c 451). This controversy can be regarded as a clash between the two theological schools of Antioch and Alexandria. Neither of these schools denied the twofold nature of Christ, or His divinity or His humanity. However there was a difference between them in emphasis. The Alexandrian theologians in Egypt emphasized the unity of the two natures and the one personality of Christ as basically divine in character. They emphasized the *mia physis* - "one nature" of Christ - hence the followers of this doctrine were later called Monophysites. The Antiochan school in Syria somehow overstressed the human nature of Christ. They did not deny His divine nature but they never described the two natures as one. Instead of speaking of union *(henosis)* they preferred to talk about the combination *(synopheia)* of the two natures.

The controversy between the two schools broke out when Cyril, Bishop of Alexandria, learned that one of Nestorius' associates delivered a sermon, allegedly written by Nestorius, in which Mary was described as *Christotokos* - the bearer or mother of Christ - but not *Theotokos* - the mother of God as was commonly held at that time. The argument behind Mary's new title was "that God should be born of a human being is impossible". Cyril accused Nestorius of denying the deity of Christ. After two Councils of Ephesus (AD 443, 449) the Council of Chalcedon (451) finally dealt with this controversy and took an orthodox standpoint by condemning Nestorius. Eutyches (ca. 378-454), the most ardent adversary of Nestorius, was also condemned. Eutyches taught that Christ's human body was different from other human bodies in nature.

The Council of Chalcedon (451) reaffirmed the Niceno-Constantinopolitan Creed (381) and stressed that the two natures in Christ were without confusion (against Apollinaris), without division (against Nestorius) and without change (against Eutyches). The Son was defined as perfect in Godhead and also perfect in manhood, truly God and truly man, consubstantial with the Father...and with us. However, not all Eastern Christian Churches accepted the resolutions of Chalcedon. Those who opposed it were henceforth called Monophysites. Today the Coptic, Syrian, Armenian and Ethiopian Churches follow this line in Christology.

4. Monothelites

The monophysite debate triggered off the Monothelite controversy. The question arose whether Christ had "One will" (Monothelite) or "Two wills", that is, one divine and one human will. After a long controversy, the 6th General Council in Constantinople (680-1) declared that: "Christ has two wills...not contrary one to another, but...His human will is subjected to His divine and omnipotent will". This Council condemned the Monothelites.

5. Unorthodox Views in Modern Theology

One might think that there is not much sense in mentioning old heresies and extreme views as we have done above. These unorthodox views however do not belong to the past only, they can be found sometimes in milder form in modern theology.

It has already been mentioned that the Monophysite teaching is prevalent in some Eastern Churches to this day. Apart from this, Docetic and Ebionite elements can be found in the writings of some modern theologians. Docetic elements are in the theology of such theologians as Schleiermacher and Ritschl. F. Schleiermacher (1768-1834) based his theology on the "God-consciousness" of man. This was fully possessed by Christ who therefore is the example for man. The docetic danger is that Schleiermacher begins with an idea which he then applies to Christ. The concept is more important than Christ. Christ is important so far as the concept works perfectly in Him. A. Ritschl (1822-1889) in his theology regarded Christ as the symbol of the values of the ideal man. Christ is God only because of the value-judgement of the Church. The Docetic danger is that he degrades Christ to a symbol[4].

Some elements of the Ebionite teaching can be found in the writings of those modern theologians who take the Christological starting point "from below": They stress the humanity of Christ who gradually became divine. W. Pannenberg and his followers can be regarded as theologians who are near this kind of teaching[5].

Christian theologians and ministers must be the guardians of the orthodox view of tradition in Christology. The preacher has to avoid extreme teachings in Christological issues and also has to prevent the spread of old or modern heretical views of the person of Christ.

NOTES

1. W. Walker: A History of the Christian Church (T&T Clark) p.53-190.
2. D. Bonhoeffer: Christology (SCM 1978) p.76 f.
3. ibid, p.78.
4. ibid, p.82 f.
5. W. Pannenberg: Jesus - God and Man, p.354 f.

Chapter 6

Other Interpretations of the Person of Jesus

The Religious Genius, The Example, The Great Teacher, The Healer The Humanitarian, The Hero

The extraordinary person of Jesus Christ has always been an object of human speculation. Apart from the Christian interpretation there are many other, mainly secular, theories concerning His person. Sometimes these originated in a particular age or in an extreme of the Church; sometimes they began outside the Church, but affected the teaching of the Church about Jesus Christ. It is therefore valuable to make a short survey of some of the characteristic interpretations of the person of Jesus.

1. The Religious Genius

Many of the non-Christian religious philosophers regarded Jesus as a religious genius who had a unique talent, intuition and sensitivity for religious questions. He worked out His religious thoughts in a more or less comprehensive religious philosophical system and by doing so laid the foundation of a major world religion: Christianity. By all this He is qualified to occupy a place in the pantheon of religious geniuses along with Buddha, Confucius, Zoroaster and Muhammad. This view of Jesus takes account only of the fact that Jesus successfully founded the Christian religion with its characteristic religious ideas whose religious community still occupies a major position among world religions[1].

2. The Example

With His moral ideas and simple life-style and His gentle and helpful attitude in dealing with people, Jesus is frequently regarded by both non-religious and religious people as the best example for humans to follow. From this perspective Jesus is considered as the ideal man or the True man, who embodied in Himself the best and most perfect characteristics of mankind. The impulses, inspirations and ideas that Jesus offered enabled humankind to become the best that could be. Therefore it is worth following His example because of man's own interest. This concept can be found outside the Christian circle. For example, Mahatma Gandhi was influenced by Jesus' ideas and this exercised a remarkable impact

39

upon his political philosophy. But this concept of Jesus was also present in the protestant liberal theology of the last century. Both Schleiermacher and Ritschl and their followers regarded Jesus Christ as an example[2].

3. The Great Teacher

This idea emphasises that Jesus was a genuine teacher, perhaps the greatest ever, who was able to communicate the most difficult religious and ethical ideas in the most simple and effective way so that even a child could understand them. He did it in such a way that His ideas became a living and decisive factor in the life of His audience. His greatness as a teacher can be seen in the fact that He successfully shaped the inner and the outer behaviour of humans by transforming them. This perception exalts Jesus because of His teaching techniques and method and their lasting effects upon human life[3].

4. The Healer

Jesus performed many miraculous healings, delivering people both from physical and mental sicknesses; He even raised the dead. In so doing, Jesus proved himself the greatest medical doctor who ever lived. Consequently He is praised for his healing skills. Here the priority is given to His healing ability, and He is regarded as the great healer of mankind. Apart from this, Jesus was an excellent psychologist who read the innermost secrets of men's hidden motivations. It is believed that the healing forces of Jesus came from his person and teaching. This concept of Jesus is very popular in the contemporary charismatic movement which practises healing by faith.

5. The Humanitarian

Jesus is sometimes regarded as the great humanitarian. The representatives of this concept of Jesus point to the fact that He loved people and always sought their benefit. He was the perfect altruist. His life was spent in constant service of His fellow men. He fed the hungry, healed the sick and cared for the suffering, gave advice to those who felt lost, gave forgiveness to those who needed it. Lastly, He sacrificed himself for the benefit of mankind. He proved to be the greatest humanist and altruist who ever lived. Therefore His footsteps have to be followed by all who want to do something for their fellow men.

6. The Hero

There are people who appreciate Jesus because of the way He pursued the truth through misunderstanding and suffering. He was even ready to die for His conviction. By His life and death He became the symbol for those who have life-affirming convictions. Jesus' example teaches man integrity, perserverance and fortitude. He showed an individual should never deny His convictions but be ready even to die for the truth. Jesus' example shows that the true life is the life of the tragic hero.

Another view of Jesus' life is the one which regards Him as a revolutionary. This perception emphasizes Jesus' rebellion against the establishment, both political and religious. He disregarded the conventions, customs and laws and He tried to clear the ground for His new and radical ideas. He did not succeed but he set a heroic example for revolutionaries of later ages.

Last, but not least, in our age the person of Jesus frequently is understood as one who is a liberator or a freedom-fighter, mostly in the theology of liberation. Here Jesus appears as one whose main aim was to liberate men from bondage. He was on the side of the oppressed, exploited and outcast. Jesus gave them inner freedom as the precondition for total freedom and taught them to live in freedom[4].

The common weakness of these interpretations is that they emphasize one feature of the person of Jesus at the expense of others. All these attempts fail to emphasize that Jesus Christ was primarily the redeemer, and that redemption was the centre of his ministry. All other features of his person can be understood rightly only from this central point. The Christian theologian has to watch carefully which interpretation of the person of Jesus Christ prevails in the Church. If he detects abberrations he is bound to make the necessary correction. Belief in Jesus Christ is important but equally important is that this belief should be in the real, true and full Jesus Christ.

NOTES

1.   E. Brunner: Dogmatics, Vol II, p.331.
2.   ibid. p.330.
3.   ibid.
4.   G. Gutierrez: A Theology of Liberation, (SCM 1974) p.175 f.

SECTION 2

The Work of Christ

Chapter 1

The Prophetic Office of Christ

Jesus Christ the Prophet, His Teaching
The Miracles of Jesus Christ

Having seen the person of Christ in the previous chapters we now turn to study the work of Christ. The work of Christ, stated briefly, is the redemption of humanity. This section of dogmatics is traditionally called Soteriology - the doctrine of salvation - and it constitutes the very centre of Christian theology. Because Christian theology is grounded on the fact that its founder Jesus Christ's messianic work - His teaching, activity and death - was dedicated to the sole purpose of the redemption of humanity, and by it He desired to lead humanity back to God. Through His redemptive work, Jesus Christ proved to be the true Messiah, the true Christ, and because of it His followers accept Him as Christ.

For practical purposes we shall follow the traditional pattern of "offices" of Christ to study Jesus Christ's work in the following chapters. These are grouped into three units. We shall consider His "Prophetic Office", His "Priestly Office" and lastly His "Royal Office"[1].

1. Jesus Christ the Prophet

Jesus Christ was frequently regarded by His contemporaries as a prophet *(Matt. 16:14, 21:11, 46; Luke 24:19; John 4:19)*. However, some asked whether He was more than a prophet because He had authority *(Mark 1:22)*. Jesus never claimed that He was a prophet because He was well aware that the time of the prophets had passed away. He regarded Himself "more than a prophet" *(Matt. 12:41)*. His claim was that He was the fulfillment of the prophecies *(Matt. 12:17)*. He was the one about whom the prophets had prophecied, therefore He was the end of prophets and prophecies. *(Heb. 1:1)*. With Him the Kingdom of God had arrived and it could be seen "In the midst of you" *(Luke 17:21)*. He never commenced His teaching like the prophets: "Thus saith the Lord". But: "I say to you"

(John 14:12, 16:20, 23). This is because the prophets always pointed to the promised One who is beyond them, but in Him this promised Messiah is fulfilled. In His person, the Word of God is being materialized *(John 1:14)*. Thus the Word is in His Person and through Him God himself is acting in the world *(John 10:30, 9:4, 17:8, 14, 5:21)*[2].

2. His Teaching

Jesus Christ was popularly known as a rabbi or teacher, whose main task was to teach people about God *(John 1:38, Luke 13:22)*. The core of His teaching was the good news about the arrival of the Kingdom of God in his person who is the Messiah, Saviour and the Son of God *(Matt. 10:7, 12:28)*. With Him a new age has commenced which is characterised by the restoration of the sovereignty of God over mankind and with it the return of man to his original state. With Him the New Creation has started. In its process Evil and Sin will be eliminated, sickness, pain and death will be abolished and man will live again in the nearness of God. All these become possible because Christ offers Himself for redemptive suffering and death for the forgiveness of sin. By His sacrifice He makes a new Covenent between God and man. By calling man to conversion, He establishes a new relationship between man and God which is based on faith, love and obedience *(John 12:44, 45, 14:1, 13:35, 15:10; Matt. 26:26-28)*.

After this general outlining of Jesus Christ's teaching, let us look at its details. His teaching can be grouped into three categories: the relationship between God and man; that of man to man; and that of man to himself. Let us examine them in turn.

In Jesus Christ's teaching God's attitude to man is one of love. God is the loving Father who wants to give humans the fullness of life. There are many signs of God's love which surrounds all men, but its unique proof is that "God so loved the world that he gave his Son, that whoever believes in him should not perish but have eternal life: *(John 3:16)*. God's love is manifested in manifold ways. It appears as providence to all men: Not only the good but even evil men. Beyond mankind the whole created Universe is under the providential care of God *(Matt. 6:25-34; Luke 6:35)*. God's love becomes apparent in a special way as the fatherly concern of God appears in compassion towards His creatures *(Matt. 10:29)* and it materializes in forgiveness to sinful man who is willing to repent *(Mark 2:10; Luke 15:7)*. God's mercy becomes obvious in the New Covenant which He offers to men *(Matt. 26:28)*. By it God wants to draw men into

His presence *(Matt. 5:45)*. Secondly, the mercy of God aims at the salvation of all men *(1 Tim. 2:4)*. Those who accept His forgiveness and the New covenant already participate in salvation *(John 1:12)*. Thirdly, the mercy of God becomes full in the New Creation which has already begun in those who have faith in Him. These are the ones who have gone through the New Birth *(John 3:3)* which is the work of the Holy Spirit *(John 3:8)*. Those who belong to Him will live with Him in the Kingdom of God *(Matt. 25:31-45)*[3]. But those who reject God's mercy and do not accept God's saving plan and refuse to repent will be judged severely on the day of the Last Judgement when Christ returns in glory.

As to the teaching of Jesus Christ concerning man's relationship with God, it is also based on love according to the Great Commandment: "You shall love the Lord your God..." *(Mark 12:30)*. Man's response to the love of God can be no less than love. God's love for man precedes man's love to God and kindles it *(John 3:16; 1 John 4:9,19)*. Man's love to God has to materialize first of all in Faith in God *(Mark 11:22)* and in Jesus Christ *(John 6:29, 14:1)*. This faith which is generated by love, must be shown through two things. First, Faith has to lead to true worship of God *(John 4:24; Matt. 4:10)*. Second, Faith in God must lead to utmost obedience to the will of God *(Matt. 6:10, 24)*. This obedience must show itself in man's acceptance of the mercy of God, in repentance *(Matt. 4:17, 9:13)* and in doing the will of God *(Luke 11:28)*. Only in this way can man expect to enter the Kingdom of God *(Matt 7:21)*.

Man's relationship to man also has to be based upon the principle of love according to the teaching of Jesus Christ. He spelled it out in the Great Commandment; "You shall love your neighbour as yourself" *(Mark 12:31)*, which Jesus himself followed in his dealing with men. His activity was motivated by love to men. Hence we can understand the real reason for His teaching and healing work, and this is also the ultimate motivation for His death which He offered vicariously as a ransom for the salvation of sinful humanity. His basic attitude to men was compassion which originated from his love *(Matt. 9:36)*. Even when He was rough to His adversaries it was because He wanted to protect the poor, the helpless and ignorant from their "blind" leaders who exploited and misled them *(Matt. 15:14)*. Jesus taught His followers the correct behaviour to others *(Matt. 5-7)*, and set an example to his followers in their attitude to other men. This attitude must be based on love and must show itself as compassion. This will materialize itself in forgiveness *(Matt 5:7, 6:12, 15, 18:21-22)*, in service to others *(Luke 22:26-27; Matt. 25:40; John 13:14)* and in brotherhood *(John 13:34; Matt. 23:8, 12:50)* which is based on the belief that God is Father of all, and all the children of God *(Matt 6:9, 5:45)*.

44

Concerning the personal conduct of His followers Jesus also gave consistent teaching. His principles can be found mainly in the Sermon on the Mount *(Matt. 5-7)*. Jesus' teaching derives from the love of God to man; thus man's inner life must be radically changed. Man, motivated by his love to God, must live a sanctified life. He must turn from sin, committing himself to obeying the will of God. Jesus held with utmost seriousness the ethical standard of the Old Testament where God said: "Be holy, for I am holy" *(Lev. 11:44)*. This saying was radically interpreted by Jesus *(Matt. 5-7)*. He preached the highest ethical standard for men which was ever preached. He did it because He knew that He and the Holy Spirit would enable His followers to implement it *(John 14:15-16)*. Motivated by love, men have to live a dedicated life both to God; in worshipping, praising and obeying Him, and to others; offering help, service and even sacrifice. Such life conduct is meant to alleviate the consequences of sin upon the life of men *(Luke 10:25-37)*. Man has to live a life which yields good fruits *(Luke 13:23)*; and which promotes the growth of the Kingdom of God *(Matt. 10:5 f, 28:19)*. Only a life with such positive content pleases God and earns reward *(Matt. 6:19-20, 25:14-30, 31-34)*.

3. The Miracles of Jesus Christ

We have already dealt with the miracles in general (Vol. I, Part I, Sect. 3, Ch. 5:3). Here we have to study the miracles of Jesus Christ in particular. The miraculous deeds that Jesus Christ performed during His ministry can be viewed in relationship to His Prophetic Office. In the Old Testament the "Men of God" or the Prophets - sometimes perform miracles *(Ex. 7-14; 1 Kings 17:14-16, 17-24, 18:30-38; 2 Kings 2:6-8, 4:42-44, 5:9-27, 13:21)*. The miracles of Old Testament served at least three purposes. Miracles were considered as the revelation of God's almightiness, and sign that the prophet was sent by God. The miracles, also were the channels of communicating either the mercy or judgement of God. In Jesus Christ's miracles we can also find these three elements. By performing miracles Jesus Christ proved that He is not less than the prophets of the Old Testament. But the number and magnitude of His miracles point beyond that of the prophets; they are the proofs of His messianship. The absence of destructive miracles against men particularly proves His messianship. But, by withering the fruitless fig tree Jesus demonstrated His judging authority and power *(Matt. 21:18-22)*. The miracles of Jesus also proved the almightiness of God and demonstrated that the Messiah-Saviour came to destroy evil. With Him, God's good work of restoration in the world and in man had begun. By performing miracles Jesus announced not by words but by deeds that the Kingdom of God had indeed arrived.

45

The miracles of Jesus Christ can be grouped into three types. First, there are the natural miracles, such as turning water into wine *(John 2:1-11)*, calming the stormy sea *(Mark 4:37-39)*, multiplying the bread *(Matt. 14:15-21)*, withering the fig-tree *(Matt. 21:18-22)* or the miraculous catch of fish *(Luke 5:1-11)*.

Second, there are His miraculous healings, including exorcism and the raising of the dead. We need only mention a few of these such as the healing of the ten lepers *(Luke 17:11-19)*, the healing of blind Bartimaeus *(Mark 10:46-52)*, the healing of the paralytic *(Matt. 9:2-7)*, exorcising the legion of demons *(Luke 8:26-39)*, raising the daughter of Jairus from the dead *(Mark 5:22-24, 35-43)* and the raising of Lazarus *(John 11:1-44)*.

Third, there are miracles which are connected with Jesus Christ's person. These include His sudden disappearance *(Luke 4:30)*, His walking on the sea *(Mark 6:48-51)*, His transfiguration *(Matt. 17:1-8)*, but most important of all: His resurrection *(Matt. 28:5-10)* and His appearances afterwards *(Luke 24:13-43; John 20:11-21:25)*. By all these Jesus Christ proved that He was indeed the Son of God and therefore the true Messiah.

We have to point out that by His teaching and miraculous deeds Jesus Christ had at least three messages that He wanted to communicate to mankind. First, that He had really been sent by God and in Him the wisdom and power of God were at work for the benefit of men; that he and God were one, and consequently, that He was the promised messiah. Second, that the Kingdom of God had really arrived and with it the beginning of the New Creation. Third, that the work of the Messiah was to destroy the work and power of evil and sin by teaching people about His new relationship with God, and by His messianic work making this new relationship possible; not only between man and God, but between human and human and human to himself. By performing miracles Jesus Christ wanted to show that God's power could destroy the works of Satan, evil and sin, and heal the tragic consequences to humans' life, restoring human to his original position previous to his fall. So Jesus Christ's teaching and miracles can be properly understood in relation to His messianic saving work, which culminated in His death on the cross[4].

The teaching of Jesus Christ has paramount importance both for Christian ministry and for the Christian life. Minister means the servant of the Word of God, including the good news of Jesus Christ about man's new relationship to God, to his fellow man and to himself. To be a Christian minister also means to be a teacher teaching people the way of God according to the teaching of Jesus Christ. This is an important task because "faith" in the salvation of God "comes from hearing" *(Rom. 10:17).* The Christian minister must also be aware that the "new life" could not be born in men because of his teaching alone, but as the miracle of God the Holy Spirit.

NOTES

1. J. Calvin: Institutes II, XV.
2. E. Brunner: Dogmatics, Vol II, p.275 f.
3. ibid, p.280.
4. See Part I, Section 4, Chapter 5.

Chapter 2

The Priestly Office of Christ

Responses to Jesus' Activity: His Followers and Adversaries
Jesus' Trial and Death
Jesus Christ's Interpretation of His Own Death

The idea of the priestly office of Jesus Christ comes from *Hebrews 9:11-12* where Christ is called "High priest" and described as "taking His own blood thus securing an eternal redemption". This points to the peak of Christ's messianic service: the only valid sacrifice, his self-sacrifice on the cross for the redemption of the world, which achieved God's plan for salvation of humanity *(John 3:16; Matt. 20:28; Rom. 8:32; Heb. 10:14)*. However, Jesus Christ's priestly office cannot be taken in isolation; it must be seen in the context of His prophetic office. The priestly office is basically the continuation of His prophetic office. He who taught about the love, mercy and the forgiveness of God and about the possibility of a radically new relationship between God and man, man and man and man to it - now by His priestly office or work creates the basis for all this. What He taught and did during His messianic service have their basis, ground and verification in His priestly work, that is, in His voluntary self-sacrifice on the cross. This unique, unparalleled and unrepeatable self sacrifice was for breaking the monolithic power of sin; for abolishing the consequences of sin and for leading mankind back to God. What He taught and did were consistently related to His coming sacrifice, and His sacrifice gives proof that what He taught and did were true, valid and according to God's plan for salvation. Only in this context can we properly understand Jesus Christ's priestly office.

1. Responses to Jesus' Activity: His Followers

In the following paragraphs we shall see the causes which led to Jesus Christ's trial, passion and death and we shall look at Jesus Christ's interpretation of His own death.

Jesus Christ's messianic activity in the last three years of His life did not go unnoticed; it evoked response. There were two kinds of response: positive and negative. There was a group of people who received Jesus

48

Christ's activity with symphathy and responded positively. There was another group of people who received Jesus Christ's activity with suspicion and with enmity and responded negatively. Let us look at these in turn.

We can discern three groups of those who accepted Jesus Christ's activity favourably. First, there were His disciples. Jesus Christ was an itinerant teacher who was followed by disciples whom He selected and called. There were twelve disciples, after the twelve tribes of Israel and Judah: Simon-Peter and Andrew his brother; James and John the sons of Zebedee; Philip and Bartholomew; Thomas and Matthew; James the son of Alpheus and Thaddaeus; Simon the Cananaean; and Judas Iscariot who betrayed Jesus. *(Matt. 10:2, 3)*. Jesus taught and trained the twelve. The subjects He taught included the secrets of the Kingdom of God *(Matt. 15:15-16; Luke 9:10)*, the secret of His Messianship *(Matt. 16:13-28)* and the secret of the future things *(Matt. 25; John 14-17)*. They were sent for mission by Jesus Christ in his lifetime *(Matt. 10:5-42)* and before His Ascension (Matt. *28:18-20)*. The purposes of Jesus Christ for the Disciples were twofold; that they should witness all that he taught and did and that they should spread the "Good News" all over the world. The Disciples accompanied the Master and they lived in a community which can be regarded as the nucleus of the Church *(Mark 3:4, 6:30-31; Luke 22:14; Matt. 16:18)*. Secondly, there was a broader circle of people who responded favourably to Jesus Christ's messianic activity. They were the "seventy disciples" *(Luke 10:1-11)* and His friends and followers such as Martha, Mary and Lazarus, Mary Magdalene, Joannah and Suzannah *(John 11:1-44; Luke 10:38-42, 8:2-3)*. There were secret followers of Jesus Christ like Nicodemus, Mark, Simon the Pharisee and Joseph of Arimathea *(John 3:1; Mark 14:51-52; Luke 7:40; Matt. 27:57)*. Lastly there was quite a large group of sympathetic people who were interested in Jesus' teaching and deeds. Jesus Christ was frequently surrounded by a large crowd *(Luke 8:4)* and there were thousands who from time to time listened to His preaching *(Matt. 15:32-38, 14:15-21)* and many of them believed in Him *(John 8:30)*. So Jesus Christ's messianic activity was not without a favourable response. He gradually became popular and attracted many people *(John 12:42)*. Presumably, many of these people later became adherents of the Church, constituting the Jewish wing of the Church known as "Ebionites"[1].

2. His Adversaries

There was another group of people who responded with hostility to Jesus' messianic activity. They were from the upper echelons of society.

They were from the higher clergy, from the Scribes, who were the guardians of the Mosaic Law, and from the two main religious parties of Pharisees and Sadduces. The reasons why they became Jesus' adversaries were as follows: They closely observed Jesus' activity, teaching and character and soon noticed its revolutionary character. It showed a marked divergence from the orthodox teaching of Judaism. Jesus openly broke with the strict prescriptions of the religious Law by doing work on the Sabbath day, healing the sick and plucking the ears of grain as He walked through a field with his disciples *(Matt. 12:9-14, 12:1-8)*. Jesus also disregarded the orders of religious authority *(Matt. 15:1-9, 23: 2-7)*, and even attacked them directly or indirectly *(Matt. 15:12, l6:6, 23: 13-36; Luke 11:42)*. They observed with jealousy how many people were attracted by Jesus and they wanted to stop this undesirable development *(John 7:1, 44; Mark 14:1-2; Matt. 26:3-5)*. Moreover, Jesus openly taught that He was the promised Messiah, the Son of God in whom the holy God was dwelling *(Matt. 16:16-17; John 5:18, 10:30)*. All this was too much for His adversaries and they decided to stop His dangerous, heretical and blasphemous teaching and activity. He was, they assumed, possessed by an evil spirit *(Matt. 12:24; John 8:48, 52)*. They wanted to lay a trap for Him and get rid of Him by killing Him in one way or another *(Luke 11:53; Matt. 22:15; John 7:1)*.

3. Jesus' Trial and Death

We do not intend to give a detailed description of Jesus' trial and death because it is not our task. We only give a summary of the main flow of the events.

Jesus' adversaries made several unsuccessful attempts to kill Him *(John 7:1, 10:31; Luke 4:29)*. They succeeded, but not without Jesus' willingness to give way to the events which God had prepared *(John 10:18)*. This opportunity came with the festival of the Passover when Jesus, who was working in the countryside, decided to go up to Jerusalem for the festival as other Israelites used to do. Jesus' enemies grasped this opportunity to get Him into their hands, put Him on trial and silence him by any means *(Matt. 26:4; Luke 20:19-20)*. With the help of Judas Iscariot they arrested Jesus *(Matt. 26:47-56)* and took him before the Sanhedrin, the Jewish Council, where he was accused by bribed witnesses in an unsuccessful attempt at charging him with blasphemy. *(Mark 14:56-59)*. Lastly, Caiaphas, the High Priest, asked Him the fateful question: "Tell us if you are the Christ, the Son of God." Jesus said to him: "You have said so" *(Matt. 26:63-64)*. This answer sealed Jesus' fate, because according to the Jews' religious law, one who make himself the Son of God deserves the death penalty *(John 19:7)*. The formal approval of Pilate, the Roman governor, was necessary for Jesus' execution, which they obtained by accusing Jesus before Pilate on not a religious but a political matter, using Jesus' claim that He was "The king of the Jews" *(Matt. 27:11)*. Pilate finally gave the permission for Jesus Christ's execution *(Mark 15:15)*. After severe beatings and mockery He was crucified on Golgotha together with two robbers *(Matt. 27:27-38)* where He died having committed His soul in God's hands *(Luke 23:46)*. He was buried *(Matt. 27:57-61)* with guards ordered to watch the tomb after it was sealed *(Matt. 27:65-66)*. All this happened amidst the joy and jubilation of Jesus' adversaries and an excited crowd, and the deep sorrow and mourning of Jesus' relatives and followers. Jesus Christ was innocent in every respect in the accusations against Him. He became the victim of the treachery, hatred and religious bigotry of His adversaries.

4. Jesus Christ's Interpretation of His Own Death

What has been said above about the trial and death of Jesus Christ is only the outer sequence of these tragic events. It is only the surface of these happenings, their visible side. It is only one side of His story. But there is another side of it, a deeper one, under the surface and hidden from the sight of onlookers, an aspect which was apparent to Jesus himself and later to the disciples and His followers. This is the divine side. As Jesus Christ was human and also divine, so His trial, suffering and death, have a human and also a divine side. In the previous paragraph we have seen the human side of these final events of His earthly life; we now would consider the divine side and look at how Jesus Christ interpreted His own passion and death.

Jesus Christ was well aware that His death did not happen by chance. He was deeply convinced that it was foretold by the prophets, most clearly by Isaiah who said that the Messiah had to undergo sufferings and even death to obtain our salvation. In Chapter 53 Deutero-Isaiah prophesies that the Messiah will be "despised and rejected by men", "oppressed and afflicted" and "judgement" will fall upon Him *(53:3,7,8)*. Therefore He will be the "man of sorrows" and aquainted with "grief" *(53:3)*. He "has borne our griefs and carried our sorrows), "He was wounded for our transgressions, He was bruised for our iniquities" *(53:4-5)*, and God "laid upon Him the "iniquity of us all" *(53:6)*. However, He was considered "stricken, smitten by God" *(53:4)*, "Yet it was the will of the Lord to bruise him, He has put him to grief, He makes himself an offering to sin" *(53:l0)*.

So He is "like a lamb that is led to the slaughter: *(53:7)*. This is because "upon Him was the chastisement that makes us whole, and with His stripes we are healed" *(53:5)*. These are the characteristics of the Messiah and this is what Jesus Christ fulfilled by His sufferings and death[2].

Jesus Christ anticipated and foresaw all this, and He consciously prepared himself to take up the messianic suffering and death for the benefit - the salvation - of His followers. He said this openly to His disciples: "The Son of Man came...to give his life as a ransom for many" *(Matt. 20:28)*. And Jesus was convinced that His messianic death would be of great benefit to others: "Truly, truly, I say to you, unless a grain of wheat falls into the earth and dies, it remains alone, but if it dies it bears much fruit" *(John 12:24)*. Jesus prepared Himself for this sacrifice, but to accept it was not easy for the human Jesus: "Now is my soul troubled. And what shall I say? Father save me from this hour? No, for this purpose I have come to this hour" *(John 12:27)*. His inner struggle can be sensed at the scene in the Garden of Gethsemane, until finally Jesus humbly submitted Himself to the will and plan of God *(Matt. 26:36-46)*. He regarded His sacrifice not only as a ransom, but as one which enables the making of a New Covenant between God and man *(Matt. 26:28)*. Jesus was convinced that His sacrifice provides for the redemption of humankind, the restoration of God's sovereignty in the world and the Glory of God *(John 12:27-28)*.

Jesus Christ anticipated, understood and accepted His sufferings and death in the sense of the Old Testament prophecies, and He interpreted them and offered them as a vicarious sacrifice for the sins of humanity. This is the essence of the priestly office of Christ. The office of which is the very cornerstone of Christian theology upon which all other tenets are built and without it there would be no Christian theology. By fulfilling it He proved Himself the true Saviour[3].

Christian theologians and ministers have to be aware of this, because there is always a temptation to play down the importance of Christ's vicarious suffering and death. Everything which is valuable in Christian theology is founded on the redemptive suffering and death of Jesus Christ the saviour. It is therefore the primary task of theologians to look at man in the light of Jesus Christ's suffering and death, and to preach repentance, forgiveness of sins and new life which are the fruits of Jesus Christ's suffering and death.

NOTES

1.   See Part II, Section 1, Chapter 5.
2.   E. Brunner: Dogmatics, Vol. II, p.283 f.
3.   ibid, p.281.

Chapter 3

The Royal Office of Christ

**Christ's descent into Hell, The Resurrection of Christ
The Appearances of the Risen Lord
Arguments Against the Resurrection of Christ
The Ascension of Christ**

Traditional theology speaks of the royal office of Christ as His third office. The royal office of Christ stems from His lordship, which is apparent from His resurrection and ascension *(John 18:36; Matt. 28:18; Eph. 2:20-23)*. In this office the former two offices, the prophetic and the priestly, are completed. Therefore the three offices organically belong together and constitute a unit of the work of Christ. The prophetic office reaches its peak in His priestly office, and the priestly work receives its validity from the royal office of Christ. To put it in other words: The teaching of Christ about the forgiveness of sins, the Kingdom of God and the new creation have their basis in His priestly work; that is, all he taught was shown to be true by His self sacrifice on the cross. The royal office is the proof and the seal that God accepted Christ's redemptory work, that is, by Christ's resurrection and ascension God proved that Jesus was the Messiah and the redemption He effected is therefore validated. These three offices of Christ became apparent by degrees. First His prophetic office came into view. His priestly office only became reality on the cross. His royal office became apparent only after His resurrection and ascension. But before we turn to study Jesus Christ's resurrection, ascension and His lordship, let us turn our attention to His descent into Hell.

1. Christ's Descent into Hell

Between Jesus Christ's death and resurrection something very strange happened. The Apostolic Creed expresses it as Christ's "Descent into Hell". This statement is based on the Scripture *1 Peter 4:6*, which says "The gospel was preached even to the dead", and *3:19*: "He went and preached to the spirits in prison", and *Ephesians 4:9*: "He had also descended into the lower parts of the earth". This apparently refers to *Isaiah 42:7*, where Isaiah prophecies about the servant of God who is "To bring out the prisoners from the dungeons, from the prison those who sit in darkness". This statement of the Apostolic Creed, we have to admit, is quite strange for modern man because of the concept of hell, yet we cannot conclude that this is an irrelevant part of the Creed and of the Christian faith[1].

This article of faith is a mystery, like the virgin birth or the resurrection or the ascension of Christ. But this does not prevent us from asking what is the meaning of Christ's descent into hell to us? The logical answer to the question "Where was Jesus' soul between his death and resurrection?" would be: His soul was with God, into whose hands He committed it on the Cross *(Luke 23:46)*. This would be in accordance with the general religious belief of mankind that after death the human soul returns to God. But here we learn something else, something special about Jesus Christ. Two questions arise at this point: Where does this teaching come from, and why was it stressed in the apostolic writings? The Apostles presumably received this revelation from the Risen Lord himself, who was with the disciples for forty days "speaking of the Kingdom of God" *(Acts 1:3)*. This revelation helped them to solve the following question: "If only those who live after Jesus Christ can enter the Kingdom of God, are those who died before Him excluded from it?" Obviously, this would be an injustice. This problem appeared in the Corinthian Church where the believers practiced baptism for the dead *(1 Cor. 15:29)*. The solution of the problem is in the doctrine of Christ's descent into Hell. This means that even people from the past are not excluded from salvation because they were also given a chance to enter into the Kingdom of God through Christ's vicarious death for all sinners.

This doctrine teaches us at least three lessons. First, that the mercy of God which appeared in His Son is so great that it opposes sin and its consequences from the very beginning. It is able to reach back into the past and can make radical changes in it. The past is closed only for man, but not for God. Second, that the extent of the mercy of God in Jesus Christ's redemptive work is not limited in any way. It can permeate not only the present and the future, but it can enter into the past as well. Third, this doctrine points in the direction of the controversial doctrine of universal salvation[2].

In the 16th and 17th centuries there was a debate between Reformed and Lutheran theologians on the theme of Christ's descent into hell. The question was about where Christ's descent fitted into the Divine scheme of things. The Reformed dogmaticians insisted that this was a part of Christ's passion, while the Lutheran counterparts held that it was the beginning of His exaltation. Actually, it was both, because it was the point when and where Jesus Christ's deepest abyss of humiliation turned into the beginning of His exaltation.

2. The Resurrection of Christ

The resurrection of Jesus Christ is as important a part of Christology as His death. Christian faith believes that Jesus Christ not only died, but He "rose from the dead on the third day" as the Apostles' Creed states. Here we find the uniqueness of the Christian faith the very ground of all that Christians believe in. At the same time it is the reason why Christians are Christians, because they have as their saviour Jesus Christ who was raised from the dead. By His resurrection Jesus Christ proved to be the true messiah. All that He said and all that He did, including His vicarious death for the sinful, from His resurrection obtained their divine verification, approval and seal. This means that the Kingdom of God is not a groundless utopia but is a glorious reality. It is really here; a new age has dawned where the power of sin is broken, evil is defeated, and humans can be free again. The broken relationship between God and man is re-established as well as the relationship between man and man and of man with himself. These are possible now because God in His mercy gave man His only Son "Who was put to death for our trespasses and raised for our justification *(Rom. 4:25)*.

We have to stress this because the resurrection of Christ is one of the most problematic parts of Christian theology. There are Christian believers who cannot accept this; they cannot imagine how one can come back from the dead, and they regard this doctrine as outdated or fantastic because it contradicts natural law. There are theologians in modern times who dispute this doctrine. For example, R. Bultmann did not accept the resurrection of Jesus Christ as historical fact, regarding it as an eschatological event, which happened only in the faith of the Disciples[3]. P. Tillich takes it symbolically[4]. We hold the belief that Jesus Christ indeed from the dead and this faith is based upon the witness of the Scriptures, to which we now turn.

The resurrection of Jesus Christ did not occur unexpectedly. Not only His death was prophesized by the Old Testament prophets, and predicted by Christ himself, but His resurrection too. Deutero-Isaiah prophecies that the Servant of God, having gone through suffering, humiliation and even death, - "shall see the fruit of the travail of his soul"...and God "will divide him a portion with the Great" *(Isa. 53:11-12)*. Hosea talks about the Lord who "on the third day will raise us up" *(Hos. 6:2)*. The Psalmist knows that God does not let "Thy godly one see the Pit" *(Ps. 16:10)*. The prophet Jonah's story, who "was in the belly of the fish three days and three nights" *(Jonah 1:17)* is understood by Jesus Christ himself as a prophecy about His three days in the tomb; "So will the Son of man be three days and three nights in the heart of the earth" *(Matt. 12:40)*. Jesus Christ prophesied His resurrection, that after His suffering and death he would "on the third day be raised" *(Matt. 16:21, 17:23; Luke 24:7; John 10:17)*. The new Testament writers unanimously comment on Jesus Christ's death and resurrection as events which occured "in accordance with the Scriptures" *(1 Cor 15:4; Luke 24:25-27, 46)*.

One of the evidences of Jesus Christ's resurrection is His empty tomb. All the four Gospels emphasize that the tomb, carved in rock, which was sealed after the burial of Jesus Christ with guards ordered to watch it - was found empty on Easter morning by the women and disciples *(Mark 16:1-6; Matt. 28:1-7; Luke 24:1-12; John 20:1-10)*. E. Brunner calls the empty tomb the "world fact" of Jesus Christ's bodily resurrection, which everyone, believers and non-believers, could perceive. Not only Jesus Christ's adherents, the women and the disciples, but the indifferent guards are the witnesses of the resurrection. But the latter were forbidden by the priests to spread this news and because they were bribed they told the people that His disciples stole Him away *(Matt. 28:11-15)*. However, the empty tomb remains historical fact of Jesus Christ's bodily resurrection[5].

3. The Appearances of the Risen Lord

Further evidence of Jesus Christ's resurrection were the appearances of the Risen Lord, the "Christophanies". The Gospels give details of these appearances: how He appeared to the women near to the tomb, to the disciples, to Thomas, to the disciples of Emmaus and to others *(Matt. 28:9; Mark 16:9, 12-13; Luke 24:13-35; John 20:11-30, 21:1-24)*. The oldest list of Jesus Christ's appearances can be found in *1 Corinthian 15:1-8*, which was written in Ephesus between 56 and 57 AD. According to this account the Risen Lord appeared to Peter, then to the Twelve, then to five hundred brethren, then to James the brother of Jesus, then to all the Apostles and finally to Paul himself. The purpose of this list of appearances is to give proof of the reality of Jesus Christ's resurrection by referring to witnesses. Paul says that he "received" this list *(v.3)*, presumably from Peter, when Paul was in Jerusalem three years after his conversion *(Gal. 1:18)*. This visit took place only five years after the resurrection. During this visit Paul received not only this account but a kernel of the Christian Creed, originally an Aramaic formula *(3b-4 vs)*: "That Christ died for our sins in accordance with the Scriptures, that He was buried, that he was raised on the third day in accordance with the Scriptures." Both this and the list constituted the so-called *Paradosis* - the basic teaching of the Apostles and the first Christians which they wanted to transmit to posterity. This *Paradosis* was formulated for at least three reasons. First, to preserve the fact of Jesus Christ's death and resurrection with its theological meaning and the names of the witnesses. Second, it had a didactic purpose for those who joined the Christian community. By this formula it was easy to memorize what Christians believed about Jesus Christ. Third, it had an apologetic purpose as well; by listing the names of the witnesses, Christians could defend the fact of the resurrection of Jesus Christ. There can be no doubt that the Apostles and many of those who belonged to the circle of Jesus actually experienced the resurrected Jesus Christ[6].

As to the content of the appearances of the Risen Lord we find the following: First, Jesus Christ wanted to convince His followers that He was alive. He who died was living again. His resurrection is the ultimate proof that all He said is true: He is the Son of God who has power to lay his life down and to take it again. *(John 10:17-18)* and therefore He is the promised true Messiah. And with it goes the implications that the forgiveness of sins, the arrival of the Kingdom of God, the beginning of the New Creation are not empty talk but serious reality: all these are sealed by His resurrection. It is important to note that Jesus Christ appeared only to His followers after His resurrection; to those who accepted Him and not to His adversaries who rejected Him. Second, by His appearances the Risen Lord wanted to re-organize His followers who were shocked, disillusioned and scattered because of His death *(Matt. 26:31, 56; Luke 24:21)*. By His appearances the Risen Lord gave them evidence that He lived again and gave them new faith and new commitment. *(John 20:19-23)*. Third, the Risen Lord was with His followers for forty days. He used this time to give them additional teaching about the secrets of the Kingdom of God and about their future life as His witnesses *(Acts 1:3; Matt. 28:18-20)*.

In connection with the appearances of the Risen Lord the question arises: What is the nature of His risen body? It is true that Christ returned from the dead recognizably in the same body in which He died. This body was seen to bear the signs of His wounds *(John 20:26-29)* which impelled the disciples to identify Him. The bodily resurrection of Jesus Christ is supported by the fact that He spoke and ate and could be touched *(John 20:27, 21:12; Luke 24:36-43)*. But His resurrected body was somehow a new body, a spiritual body, a *soma pneumatikon* which was fully under the power of the Holy Spirit. Hence we can understand how the Risen Lord could appear to His disciples who were assembled behind shut doors *(John 20:19)* and how He could disappear from the eyes of the disciples of Emmaus *(Luke 24:31)*, appear suddenly to Peter at the Sea of Galilee

(John 21:1-2) or to Saul on the Damascus road *(Acts 9:3-9)*. His body was like ours until His death, but after the resurrection His body was not only restored but newly created, the model of the body we will have *(1 Cor. 15:20, 22-23, 49)*. Therefore we insist that the appearances of the risen Lord were not those of a phantom or a ghost, they were not visions but the appearances of the real, living Jesus Christ.

4. Arguments Against the Resurrection of Christ

Since the first Easter there have always been people in every age who have taken a sceptical attitude to the Resurrection and have denied or rejected the thought that Jesus Christ was truly raised from the dead. They have put forward arguments to justify their unbelief. Let us now mention these most common arguments.

The most ancient argument, which we have already mentioned above was invented on the very first Easter morning by the adversaries of Jesus Christ *(Matt. 28:11-15)*. When the soldiers reported the resurrection of Jesus, the priests bribed them to say that His disciples had taken Him away. This falsification of what really happened was spread about among the Jews and they take this stand to this day. Mainly during the last century, liberal theologians were busy in trying to find an acceptable rationalistic explanation for Jesus' death and resurrection. A popular theory says that Jesus Christ never died on the cross. He put Himself into a state of a deep coma by the help of auto-suggestion or auto-hypnosis, a state which was very similar to real death. By so doing he tricked his adversaries, who buried Him assuming that He was dead. In the cave-tomb He recovered from the coma or hypnosis and walked out as if He had been resurrected from the dead. This theory shows Jesus as a trickster or a showman or a faker who cheated his followers. We can find no historical record or data which would support this theory.

Another theory puts the emphasis on the unreliability of the witnesses. This theory denies Jesus' resurrection but allows that Jesus' alleged appearances were the product of the excited imagination of the witnesses, the women and the disciples. If so, then how do we explain the case of Thomas who put his finger into the wounds of Christ *(John 20:27)*? Imaginary persons have no real wounds. Yet another hypothesis says that Jesus did not really appear to the disciples; they only saw a subjective vision. But visions are usually not eating breakfast as did the Risen Lord *(John 21:12-13; Luke 24:41-43)*.

The opponents of Jesus Christ's resurrection like to argue for the impossibility of resurrection by referring to the laws of nature which did not allow resurrection of dead. It is true that the resurrection of Jesus Christ is an unparalleled, unique event which broke "the laws of nature." But one has to look at it as the place where God the law-giver is at work, who can violate the unviolable laws because He is Lord over every law of nature. God created them. By the resurrection of Jesus Christ God wanted to demonstrate that the old age with its laws had reached its end and a new age - the Kingdom of God is here with its new laws. The laws of the old age say: "Every life must reach its end in death". The law of the new age says: "Even from death can spring new life", and this is exactly what Jesus Christ's resurrection demonstrates. This is how we understand Paul, who sings a jubilant hymn over the defeat of death by the resurrection of Jesus Christ *(1 Cor. 15:55-57)*. If every birth is a mystery, how much greater a mystery is the resurrection of Jesus Christ - the birth from death to eternity!

5. The Ascension of Christ

The resurrection of Christ was not the last stage of His messianic work and existence. According to the apostolic witness He was elevated into heaven after having been forty days with His disciples and He now sits at the "right hand of God" from where He will come again in glory *(Acts 1:4-11; Heb. 8:1; 1 Pet. 3:22)*. The Apostles' Creed also states "he ascended into heaven and sits at the right hand of God, from whence He shall come to judge the living and the dead".

We have to see that the resurrection of Christ and His exaltation belong together, because His resurrection is the first stage of His exaltation which reaches its fulness in His ascent into Heaven from where the Son of God came. His present glory is partly hidden, seen only by His followers in faith. But this becomes apparent to everybody, the living and the dead, when He comes back in glory at the end of time to judge the whole of mankind and complete the work of salvation. Therefore the resurrection of Jesus Christ cannot be described as a simple return to this life but as a transition from earth to heaven, from His state of humiliation to the state of exaltation[7].

The ascension of Jesus Christ has at least three messages: that He is victor, that he is lord and mediator. Let us look at these in turn.

The exaltation of Christ shows that He is *Nikator* - conqueror or victor. He overcame the evil forces of sin, death, satan and this world *(1 John 3:5, 8; 2 Tim. 1:10; Eph. 1:20-22; 1 Peter 3:22; John 16:33).* His conquering work will be completed at the end of this age when all the remnant of the evil forces will be completely destroyed and a New Creation will reach its fulness *(Revel. 21-23, 22:5).* Then He will hand over everything to God so that God will rule over all *(1 Cor. 15:28).*

The exaltation of Jesus Christ shows that He is lord. He is lord, because He is victor. The early Christians adored Him as Kyrios - king and lord *(Rev. 17:14; John 20:28).* His lordship is somewhat hidden in this world. It is now apparent only in the Church which is the community of His followers. He rules the Church as the head of the Church *(Eph. 1:22).* Christians recognize Jesus Christ as their lord and ruler whom they obey. His lordship is exercised both by His word and by the sacraments through the communication of the Holy Spirit. Jesus Christ's lordship is to some extent to be seen in the life of the world by the present witnessing and service of His Church. But Jesus Christ's kingship over the world will be full only in the eschaton, the end of the age. *(Revel. 21:1-6).*

In His exalted state, Christ now sits "on the right hand of God", which means that He shares in the lordship of God. This lordship does not mean simply "ruling". His ruling always includes the element of "serving." Hence His name in His exulted state is Mediator *(1 Tim. 2:5).* His ascension cannot be considered as an escape from the earth, the place of His suffering and death. He did not hide himself from men in heaven. He went into heaven for the sake of mankind whom he wanted to serve - by interceding for us even "at the right hand of God" *(Rom. 8:34; Heb. 7:25; John 14:13; 1 John 2:1).* By being in heaven, Christ opened for us a way into heaven, which is the holy presence of God *(Heb. 4:14, 10:19-21).* Christ is in heaven means that we have one in the heavens who still works on our behalf that we also will be where He is. *(John 13:2-3, 17:24).* Being in heaven Jesus Christ gave us a goal for life which cannot be less than heaven - the full presence of God *(Heb. 10:22-25).* We are created for this purpose by God and His Son the Mediator makes it possible. Every other life-purpose which is less than this misleads and destroys mankind and therefore is not worthy of man, the creation of God *(Revel. 1:8).*

The meaning and destiny of human existence rests in Jesus Christ's vicarious death, victorious resurrection and glorious ascension. Consequently, the very essence of the Christian ministry is in preaching, teaching and drawing people into the faith of Jesus Christ, the Son of God, who suffered for our sins, was raised from the dead for our justification and rules as King of kings to give us access to the presence of God. Upon the faithful execution of all this depends the very meaning of the Christian ministry.

NOTES

1. See Part III, Section 4, Chapter 2, Point 5.
2. See Part III, Section 4, Chapter 2, Point 7.
3. R. Bultmann: Kerygma and Myth (Harper Torchbook, 1961) p.38 f.
4. P. Tillich: Systematic Theology, Vol II, p.159 f.
5. E. Brunner: Dogmatics, Vol II, p.367.
6. W. Pannenberg: Jesus-God and Man, p. 89 f and A. Richardson: An Introduction to the Theology of the New Testament, p.193 f.
7. E. Brunner: Dogmatics, Vol II, p.372.

SECTION 3

The Interpretation of the Work of Christ

Chapter 1

The Views of Jesus Christ's Sacrifice in the Early Church

Atonement, Vicarious Suffering, New Covenant
Justification, Liberation

We have already seen how Jesus Christ understood and interpreted His own messianic work. There remain three tasks for us. First, to show how the early Church reflected upon the self-sacrifice of Jesus Christ. Second, to see how the theologians of the past understood this, and third, to look at the Christology of the present days. These themes will be dealt with in subsequent chapters.

In this chapter we are going to look at Jesus' self-sacrifice from the point of view of the early Church. There were at least five interpretations.

1. Atonement

The early Christians understood Jesus Christ's messianic work basically as atonement. The word atonement is coined from three words: "At-one-ment" which literally means "to make two parties at one" or "to reconcile two parties". Christ's messianic work was regarded as one by which His self-sacrifice achieved atonement between God and Man. This interpretation, based on the theology of the epistle to the Hebrews, comes from the practice of ritual sacrifice of the Old Testament religion. It is imperative to note that the conception of ritual sacrifice was common in ancient religions. The basic idea is that sin hurts and angers God. Sacrifice must be performed which restores peace between God and man. In Old Testament religion, the High Priest sacrificed animals on the Day of Atonement. But it was understood that the blood of animals somehow was imperfect for achieving full atonement. Only man, the perfect man, could atone for man's sin. The writer of the epistle to the Hebrews regards Jesus Christ as the true High Priest who, being that true man, sacrifices Himself on the cross and achieves the perfect atonement that was merely forshadowed or signposted by the Old Testament rituals. "Christ has offered for all time a single sacrifice for sins" *(Heb. 10:12)*, and "For by a single offering he has perfected for all time those who are sanctified" *(Heb. 10:14)*. Therefore, "The blood of Christ...shall purify your conscience from dead works to serve the living God" *(Heb. 9:14)*. So a righteous God is able to say: "I will remember their sins and their misdeeds no more" *(Heb. 10:17)*. Consequently, after Jesus Christ's single and perfect sacrifice, there is no need of further atonement offerings for sin *(Heb. 10:18)*[1].

2. Vicarious Suffering

This understanding of Jesus Christ's sacrifice has its origin in the experience of living in society. The regulation of any community is the law, which is either imposed upon the community by a higher authority, such as a ruler, or is constituted by the members of the community, defining it, accepting it and submitting their individual wills to it. From the principle of law comes the necessity of obeying it and keeping it. If the individual breaks the law, he or she is liable to punishment. When one lives in sin one breaks the law of God. Breaking the law of God brings punishment. According to the judgement of God the punishment of sin is a capital one: death *(Gen. 2:17, 3:19; Ezek. 18:4; Rom. 6:23; Heb. 10:28)*. But Jesus Christ voluntarily offered himself to bear the death-punishment, instead of and on behalf of man. This is what happened on the Cross. Consequently, we are released by God and set free. This interpretation of Jesus Christ's vicarious death is based mainly on Deutero-Isaiah's prophecy about the "Suffering Servant" *(Isa. 53)*. "The Lord has laid on Him the iniquity of us all" *(6.v.)* and "He was stricken for the transgression of my people" *(8.v)* and "He was bruised for our iniquities: upon him was the chastisement that made us whole" *(5.v)*[2].

3. New Covenant

A particular aspect of Jesus Christ's sacrifice is made clear by the idea of the New Covenant. Jesus Christ himself interpreted his death in this manner *(see Part II. Section 2. Ch 2:4)* and the early Church learned this insight from Jesus Christ Himself. It can be understood from its Old Testament background. Israel was God's elect people with whom God made a Covenant *(Gen. 15:18, Ex.24:8)*. The immediate purpose of this covenant was to bless Israel. But in God's plan of salvation it had a greater purpose far beyond Israel: God wanted to reach, bless and share salvation with every nation of the earth through the covenant people. Israel failed to remain faithful to this covenant and could not fulfill the role given her by God in His plan of the salvation for mankind *(Rom. 11)*. In spite of the failure of the covenant people, God determined to execute His plan of salvation. To this end God sent The Messiah who is His Son. In the self-sacrifice of the Son on the cross, God established a new covenant with those who believe in Christ irrespective of which nations they come from. In the pascal sacrifice of Jesus Christ when the blood of the Lamb of God was being shed this New Covenant is created. By it a new communion between God and Man was created. At the Last Supper, Jesus Christ clearly told His disciples that by His death, in His broken body and shed blood, a new covenant is created which replaces the old covenant *(Mark 14:22-24; I Cor. 11:23-26)*. Jesus Christ, himself a Jew, ordained the repetition of this Last Supper so that His followers should remember they are the people of this new covenant. This ritual practice became a sacrament in the Church and was known variously as the Lord's Supper, Holy Communion, the Eucharist or Mass. Christians consider themselves the people of this new covenant *(2 Cor. 3:6)* [3].

4. Justification

The early Church, following the theology of Paul's epistles, also understood the work of Christ as justification. Justification is the solution of the contradiction between the law of God and the love of God. According to the theology of the Apostle Paul, man is under the power of the law of God. Not only is this true of the Jews, the elect people of God to whom the divine law was given in the form of the law of Moses, but equally true of all men because they have the law of God written on their hearts or consciences *(Rom. 2:15; Ex. 20:1-17)*. Men are bound to live in accordance with the divine law and do good works which please God. In this way, humans will not be separated from God by sin *(Gal. 3:12)*. But in fact we could not keep the divine law and live according to it *(Rom. 3:23)*. Man knows that he has to live according to the demands and even the letter of the divine Law and some may even want to do so *(Rom. 7:22-23)*, but we are none of us able to live such a life and this is the sin of man *(Rom. 3:20; 1 Cor. 15:56)*. This is because there is the "Law of the flesh", "Desire", the "Law of the old man" which in our experience prevails over the "Law of Spirit" *(Rom. 7:21-25)*. Consequently all men, both Jews and Gentiles, are under the wrath of God and judgement which result in Man's death *(Rom. 2:12, 6:23)*. In the face of this desperate and hopeless situation, God sent His Son to this world, the True Man who sacrificed himself voluntarily for the sins of mankind *(Rom. 8:3)*. So Christ is the end of the Law *(Rom. 10:4)*. Whoever accepts Jesus Christ's saving death "in faith" trusting in his sacrifice instead of their own attempts at keeping the law of God, is justified before God *(Rom. 5:1-2)*. His sins and punishment are taken away by Jesus Christ and His righteousness is given to the believer. So Christ is the end of the Law *(Rom. 10:4)* Man is justified by faith alone and can live a new life, under the leadership of the Holy Spirit *(Rom. 8:2; Eph. 4:24, 1:5; Gal. 3:26; Rom. 8:26-27)*.

5. Liberation

The early Christians frequently looked at Jesus Christ's messianic work as the true liberation of man. The idea of God as liberator comes from the Old Testament and has both a political and a spiritual element. The first goes back to the ancient history of Israel, when God through Moses liberated His elect people from bondage in Egypt, where they had become slaves *(Ex. 3:7-8, 13:3, 20:2)*. By this mighty act God revealed Himself as liberator. The second notion comes from the ancient religious belief that there is a cosmic struggle between God and Satan, in which man changed sides by committing sin and thus became the accomplice of Satan. Man realizes he has become a slave in the bondage of sin and his fate is sealed because he is bound by death. Because of His love and mercy, God intends to free mankind from the captivity of Satan, and to this end sends the Messiah who liberates all. The early Christians were convinced that Jesus was the Messiah who through his messianic work rescued Man from the power of Satan, and in doing so, liberated Man from the bondage of sin *(John 8:36; Matt. 1:21; Col. 1:18-14)*. Jesus Christ is also the liberator of man "from the coming wrath of God" *(1 Thess. 1:10)*, from temptations *(Heb. 2:18)*, and even from the burden of everyday troubles *(2 Peter 2:9; 2 Tim. 3:11)*. Christians have always acknowledged Jesus Christ as their true liberator who gives them freedom and, if they understand this properly, become committed to the struggle for the full liberation of mankind[4].

If we compare the early Church understanding of Jesus Christ's sacrifice with the record of Jesus' teaching on the subject we recognize that the two interpretations are basically the same. What Jesus Christ revealed to His disciples and followers about His sacrifice was fully understood by them. They believed in it and therefore they were Christians - the adherents, followers and believers in Jesus Christ.

Today this is one of the fundamental criteria for being Christian: to believe in Jesus Christ's sacrifice as the peak of his messianic work, which he completed for our benefit, and follow Him in a life of self-giving service.

65

Christian ministers are called to the task of proclaiming Jesus Christ's messianic work to all, persuading them to accept it and believe in it.

NOTES

1.   E. Brunner: Dogmatics, Vol II, p.238.f.
2.   ibid, p.284.
3.   ibid, p.285.
4.   L. Boff: Jesus Christ Liberator (SPCK, 1980) p. 283.f

Chapter 2

Classical Views of the Atonement

Origen's Ransom Theory, Abelard's Exemplarist Theory
Anselm's Satisfaction Theory

Christian theologians made several attempts to understand more deeply and fully the various elements of Jesus Christ's messianic work, particularly that of His messianic self-sacrifice. In the course of Christian history several theories were developed, of which three are considered classical views of the Atonement. These are found in the works of Origen, Abelard and Anselm and we shall look at them in turn.

1. Origen's "Ransom Theory"

Origen (186-255) was one of the important thologians of the early Church, who expounded Jesus Christ's sacrifice as a ransom. This theory was based on Jesus Christ's own words: "The Son of Man came...to give his life as a ransom for many" *(Matt. 20:28)*. The word ransom is taken from military vocabulary. Prisoners taken in war might be freed if sufficient ransom money was paid. The size of the ransom depended on the rank and importance of the prisoner. The theological usage of the word ransom is quite proper, because theology recognizes the cosmic warfare between Satan and God. Man started out on the side of God, but became the prisoner of Satan when he committed sin. God would like to rescue man from captivity, but Satan has a claim to compensation which a righteous God acknowledges. Consequently, a ransom has to be paid to Satan in exchange for man. The ransom that God has paid is His Son, who offered Himself as a ransom to free man when He died on the Cross. Since then man, the former prisoner of Satan, lives as the "property" of God. This ransom theory was generally accepted in the early Church and it was worked out and interpreted in its various aspects by the Latin Fathers. It survived until the time of Anselm[1].

2. Abelard's "Exemplarist Theory"

The French theologian, Peter Abelard (1079-1142) based his theory of atonement on the love of God. He thought of the love of God as the motivating force both in the execution and in the implementation of redemption. God, motivated by love, sent his Son to redeem the world by sacrifice *(John 3:16)*, and to give Himself up to death for sinners (Rom. 5:8). This divine love was demonstrated by Jesus who was ready to "lay down his life for his friends", described by Jesus Christ as the "greatest love a man can have" *(John 15:13)*. Therefore the cross of Christ was the greatest manifestation and the greatest proof of the love of God. When man understands all this adequately, touched by the magnitude of God's love for man, exemplified in the death of Christ, it becomes a persuading power which leads man to repentence and conversion. This understanding generates an answering love toward God, which enables man to follow Jesus Christ as his true example[2].

This theory of atonement has both the advantage and disadvantage of subjectivity. The exemplarist theory became influential both in the theology of Protestant liberalism and neo-liberalism.

3. Anselm's "Satisfaction Theory"

Anselm of Canterbury in England (1038-1109) was one of the most important theologians of the medieval period. He proposed the satisfaction theory of the atonement in his famous book: *"Cur Deus Homo?"* (Why did God become Man?), a book which can be regarded as a critical milestone in the development of Christology.

Anselm argued against Origen's notion that a ransom had to be paid by God to Satan in exchange for man, teaching rather that Jesus Christ's passion and death was a compensation to God for the violation of His glory by man's sin. At this point God could have done three things. The first option was for God to annihilate sinful mankind, but that way God's plan of Creation would suffer. The second option was for God to tolerate sin and let sinful mankind live regardless. In this case God's glory as the fount of righteousness would suffer permanent violation. Anselm regarded both cases as unthinkable. The creation could not be destroyed nor could God's glory suffer indefinitely. There was, however, a third option open to God: the redemption of mankind by Jesus Christ His Son. Jesus Christ by His redeeming death achieved two things. First, His death resulted in the expiation of the sins of mankind. Second, His death as a sacrifice restored God's glory. Therefore Jesus Christ's death was basically a satisfaction; it satisfied both God's wrath because of man's sin and God's anger because of His violated glory. Anselm's Satisfaction theory of the atonement was accepted both by the Roman Catholic theologians and later by the theologians of the Reformation[3].

The above mentioned theories represent three complementary perspectives on atonement which do not contradict each other. Theologians and ministers have to know the various theories of the Atonement for two purposes. First, to avoid mixing them up, which frequently happens. Second, to learn the skill of using the various concepts of the Atonement in their pastoral work in general and in their preaching and teaching work in particular.

NOTES

1.   E. Brunner: Dogmatics, Vol II, p. 309.
2.   ibid, p.288.
3.   ibid, p.289.f.

Chapter 3

Major Developments in Christology

The Christology of the Reformers, The Kenotic Christology Contemporary Protestant Christology.

The first four centuries of the Christian era were decisive in the development of Christology. In the long-lasting and ardent Christological debates of early Christianity, the main features of the Church's doctrine of Christ took shape. We have already dealt with this (See: Part II, Section 1, Ch. 5). Not only have the nature of Christ and His status within the Trinity been formulated but His messianic work has also been expounded in many ways as we indicated above (Part II, Section 3, Ch. 1). After some initial turbulence, Christian conceptions of Christ have developed rather quietly, and it would be valuable to look at the important stages in their development. In the previous chapter we have already reviewed the classical theories of the atonement. In this chapter we concentrate our attention on three issues: The Christological stand of the Reformers, the so-called "Kenotic Christology" and Protestant Christology in our age.

1. The Christology of the Reformers

The main theological theme of the Reformers centered on the question: Does man receive forgiveness, justification and salvation by works of righteousness or by faith alone? Reformation theologians firmly taught the justification of man by faith alone, and it is in this context that we have to look at the role of Christology among the principal Reformers. They all accepted the classical theories of Christ's reconciliation, but with differences in emphasis. Luther emphasized the importance of the vicarious penal suffering of Jesus Christ, stressing that Christ bore the punishment of our sin. When confronted with the issue of how this vicarious penal suffering may benefit everyone, Luther introduced the idea of "happy exchange" arguing that Christ takes away our sin and in exhange gives us his righteousness. (Part III, Section 2, Chapter 1) Calvin and his followers preferred to accept the Satisfaction theory of Anselm and emphasized that Jesus Christ, being both divine and human, is the author of our salvation. In describing Christ's work, Calvin speaks of the prophetic, priestly and royal offices. In describing Christ's work, reformers were interested primarily in the ways and means by which salvation was made available to man as a result of Jesus Christ's redeeming work. Their problem was basically a practical one: man's access to the riches of Christ through salvation. They were not interested in theoretical christological issues *per se*. However, a christological debate did take place in connection with the interpretation of Holy Communion, which focused on the issue of how Christ was present in the Lord's Supper.

The Reformers could not accept the Roman Catholic doctrine of Transubstantiation and rejected it as contrary to the Scriptures. According to this doctrine, during the Mass the bread and the wine become literally the substance of the body and blood of Christ. This was intended to secure the "real presence" of Christ in the Mass, a doctrine we will return to later (See below: Part III, Section 3, Ch. 4.5). Here we are interested only with those views of the Reformers which have christological implications, especially those of Luther and Calvin.

Martin Luther (1483-1546) accepted the "real presence" of Jesus Christ at the Lord's Supper. His problem was just how Christ was present, how He could be present bodily and simultaneously wherever the Lord's Supper is observed. To solve this problem Luther evoked the ancient doctrine of *Communicatio Idiomatum*, the sharing of attributes. Based on *Colossian 2:9*, this doctrine asserts that "the glorified body of Christ participates in the divine attribute of the ubiquity (omnipresence) of God and can be really present wherever the Lord's Supper is administered"[1].

John Calvin (1509-1567) also believed in the real presence of Christ at the Lord's Supper, but his understanding of Christ's presence was a spiritual rather than a material, bodily presence. He insisted that a spiritual is no less a real presence than a material one. He developed Luther's teaching on the *Communicatio idiomatum* further into what became known as *Extra Calvinisticum*. The doctrine of *Communicatio idiomatum* presented a theological problem: where did the fullness of Christ's deity reside when the Son of God was in the world as Jesus of Nazareth? Was His deity fully in His human nature or was it retained in heaven? Calvin paradoxically stated: "Christ...is everywhere present as God. That He is God dwelling in the temple of God (that is in the Church) and in some place in heaven"[2] or, to put it in another way, God in His wholeness resides in the Person of Jesus of Nazareth and at the same time God in His wholeness resides beyond the person of Jesus.

2. The "Kenotic Christology"

Orthodox Lutheran theologians worked out a doctrine called "Kenotic Christology" based on *Philippians 2:5-10*, where Paul talks about *Kenosis* - the self emptying of Christ. Christ "emptied" himself when he was in the state of the Son of God by taking on the "form of servant". Subsequently God has "highly exalted him". According to this doctrine Christ went through two states. First there was his *Status exinanitionis* when Christ the Son of God deprived himself of his divine privileges and became Jesus of Nazareth, a human being who suffered and died. His second state is the *Status exaltationis*, when God exalted Christ through resurrection, ascension and by seating him at His right hand.

This doctrine answers questions about what is the meaning of Christ's humiliation with the explanation: Christ did not use His divine attributes during His earthly life. The "Kenotics", however, were not the only theologians who came to grips with this question. While they believed that Christ disassociated himself from His divine properties by renouncing them, that is "emptied them of use", another group, the "Cryptics", held that *kenosis* occurred by Christ concealing His divine properties, that is hiding them.

In the last century a new chapter of this debate opened. The debate centered on two questions. In which process did the divine *Logos* become the subject of humiliation? There were theologians who insisted that the process was: *Logos* - man - humiliation, so the *Logos ensarxos* (*Logos* in flesh) was the subject of humiliation. Other theologians held the view that the proper order was: *Logos* - humiliation - man, that is the *Logos asarxos* (*Logos* without flesh) was the one who humbled himself by "taking flesh". The second question concerned the character of the renunciation. They found a solution by making a distinction between God's relative and immanent properties. Immanent properties are those which belong to God's absolute nature such as love, truth and holiness, which Jesus Christ possessed, while the relative properties of God such as omnipresence, omniscience and omnipotence were renounced by Christ in His earthly life.

3. Contemporary Protestant Christology

When we attempt to draw even a sketchy map of the major trends in contemporary Christology, we have to recognize that it cannot be separated from the Christology of past ages. Recent trends in Christology came into existence either by agreement with or by opposition to older Christologies, and in all cases significant developments can be observed.

The Swedish Lutheran theologian Gustav Aulen (1878-1977) .wrote an important study on Christology entitled *Christus Victor* (1931). In it Aulen reaches back to the early theologians and points to the value of the classic atonement theory of Origen. He argues for this theory against the theories of Anselm and Abelard and, starting with Origen's teaching, worked out his own *Christus victor*. He based it on such texts as *Col. 2:15; Rom. 8:37-39; 1 Cor. 8:5; and Eph. 6:12* where the Apostle Paul affirms that Jesus Christ defeated the "principalities and powers", "spirits of the universe", "the so-called gods in heaven or on earth", and "spiritual hosts of wickedness in the heavenly places". Jesus Christ's messianic work can be found in the fact that He fought a battle and won victory over "evil powers" like Satan, sin and death, through which mankind was subjected to slavery. Therefore Christians, the inheritors of the riches of Christ, have the right to enjoy the fruits of Christ's victory[3].

The Christology of Karl Barth (1886-1968) has already been mentioned as our example of the "Christology from above" method of teaching about the work of Christ (See: Part II, Introduction, Ch. 3:1). Barth, the most productive theologian of the 20th Century, dealt with Christology intensively in the vast volumes of his *Church Dogmatics*. Barth understood the importance of the work of Christ in the tension between God and the world. Because of the sin of man there is a tragic gap between God and man. Christ's work is to bridge this gap by His cross and open a connecting way between God and man. The cross of Christ is the sign of divine judgement on the world, and in it the eternal "Yes" of God to man becomes apparent. Barth also looks at Christ in a dialectical way. Christ is the man who was rejected by God on behalf of us for our sake, and Christ is the Man who is fully accepted by God. Because of Him God accepts us. Barth stresses Christ's work of redemption, beginning with the incarnation of the *Logos* who descended upon the earth. The humiliation of the *Logos*, however, is the exaltation of man, because Christ redeemed not Himself, but man. The completion of Christ's redeeming work can be seen in His ascension. The *Logos*, having completed His work, returns to the Father[4].

The Swiss protestant theologian Emil Brunner (1889-1965), an excellent representative of the Neo-Reformation Theology, put forward his Christology in the second volume of his *Dogmatics* and in his book *The Mediator*. In his *Dogmatics* he criticises the classical theories of atonement because they failed to answer why redemption was necessary. He tries to provide the answer by pointing to Paul's solution in the concept of "Law". Man is separated from God because of his sin. This separation took place because of the Law which was imposed upon man. However, man did not keep the Law and now by himself cannot overcome this separation because of the power of Law which curses man's every effort. Only God can remove Man from this tragic consequence of his sin. This is exactly what was achieved by the suffering and death of Jesus Christ on the cross. Brunner sees three important meanings of the cross. First, the cross is the revelation of the incomprehensible and unconditional love of God to men. Second, the cross is the sign that God takes sin seriously, a warning to us not to take forgiveness lightly. Third, the cross became the clear demonstration of the human situation. Here man can understand fully the cost of his sin: it costs the crucifixion of Jesus Christ. By faith in Jesus Christ the "objective happening" of the cross becomes a subjective reality when the sinner makes peace with God and the atonement results in justification of the sinner. In this way, man is restored to his original position in the purpose of creation. Man is born again and sanctified; man becomes what God intends him to be[5].

The German Lutheran theologian Dietrich Bonhoeffer (1906-1945), who suffered martyrdom under the Nazis, delivered a series of lectures on Christology which were collected and published in 1963, while Christological themes can be found in his other works, in the *Communion of Saints* and *Letters and Papers from Prison*. The key concept of Bonhoeffer's Christology is *Christus pro nobis* - Christ for us. He recognizes three forms of Christ. First is "Christ as Word" *(John 1:1,3)*. Here Christ is the *Logos* of God, meaning that the Word exists in the classical Greek concept as idea. Christ as *Logos* is the embodiment of God's eternal idea, and as the Truth He is available to anybody at any time. The Word is not timeless, but occurs in history. It addresses us and requires response, seeks a community which responsibly faces up to the truth conveyed by the Word. Second is "Christ as Sacrament". The Word is embodied in the sacrament; sacrament is consecrated and interpreted by the Word. The meaning of the sacrament is the forgiveness of sins. Therefore the sacrament is a clear revelation; only he who perceives the Word in the sacrament has the whole sacrament. The third is "Christ as Church". Christ is present as the Church and in the Church. The Word is in the Church because the Word is proclaimed there and because, as Sacrament, it is in the Church. Christ is the head of the Church and Himself is the Church[6].

The name of Rudolf Bultmann (1884-1976) and his demythologization have already been mentioned in connection with theological method (See Vol. I, Introduction, Ch. 4:3). His demythologizing of the New Testament has remained a controversial area of theological debate. When he considers Christology, he sees difficulties in the claim of the New Testament that Jesus Christ is a historical person and at the same time the pre-existent Son of God. According to his view, history and myth are mingled together here. He supposes that the mythological language of the New Testament is "simply an attempt to express the historical figure of Jesus and the events of his life". If so, "We can see the meaning in them only when we ask what God is trying to say...through them"[7].

Bultmann insists that the cross and the resurrection are the two basic focal points of christology. The cross of Christ is a historical fact, originating in the historical event of the crucifixion of Jesus of Nazareth. The mythological language is only a medium for conveying the significance of this historical event. The cross not only belongs to the past, it is an eschatological event beyond the confines of any one time. It is an ever-present reality for those who accept the preaching of the cross by faith as the event of redemption and who are willing to be crucified themselves with Christ *(Gal. 5:24, 6:14; Phil. 3:10)*[8]. In Bultmann's view the resurrection of Christ was not historical. The historical fact is only that the disciples came to believe in the resurrection. The resurrection is only an eschatological event, and by it Christ will abolish death and bring life and immortality to mankind *(2 Tim. 1:10)*.

The German-American Protestant theologian Paul Tillich (1886-1965) represents a highly philosophical tradition in contemporary theology. We have already mentioned his methodological approach earlier. (See Part II, Introduction, Ch. 3:3).

In his *Systematic Theology (Volume II)* Tillich disagrees with the Johannine idea of incarnation, that "God became flesh". He argues that God does not become something other than God or God would cease to be God. He is in favour of the "adoptionist" theory: Jesus of Nazareth was chosen and anointed by God and accepted by his followers as the Christ. Therefore, Jesus as Christ is both a historical fact and the subject of faith. Tillich considers Jesus' death and resurrection to be symbols which contain factual elements. The important element in Christ is that He is the "new being". In Christ the "existence" and "essence" of being are united, making Him the new being in contrast to others in whom these two are separated. In Him the tragic features of existence - estrangement, conflict, meaninglessness, and self-destruction - which are evidences of sin - all come to an end. He is the meaning and the end of history. In Christ a new era has commenced.

Tillich rejects the classical theories of atonement and substitutes his own theory, the substance of which is the correlation between God's objective saving act in Christ and its subjective acceptance by man. He formulates this in one sentence: Redemption means that "I accept that I am accepted by God", which is, at the same time the heart of the Christian Faith[9].

The German Protestant theologian Jürgen Moltmann (b. 1926) who is the founding father of the "Theology of Hope" school, put forward his Christology in his book *The Crucified God*. His method has also been mentioned above (See Part II, Introduction, Ch. 3:3). According to Moltmann Christology has two tasks: "The first...is the critical verification of the Christian faith in its origin in Jesus and his history. The second task is a critical verification of Christian faith in its consequences for the present and the future". He regards the Cross as the "nuclear fact" in Jesus' life, which was the consequence of His ministry. He adds that the full meaning of the Cross can be seen only in the light of the Resurrection. He talks about not only the "Historical trial of Jesus" but the "Eschatological trial of Jesus" as well, which is in accordance with his basic theological premise - Eschatology. Moltmann accepts the literal resurrection of Jesus Christ, which was not a kind of revivification, a mere return to this life in which He would need to face death again. It was a resurrection into a "qualitative new life which no longer knows death". Moltmann concentrates upon the various consequences of the Cross in our human life. The consequence of the Cross upon our concept of God is that on the Cross we can see God who suffers. Only he who loves can suffer. On the Cross "God himself loves and suffers the death of Christ in love". Moltmann also points out the consequences of the Cross upon anthropology, politics and society. On this ground he condemns societies which "crucify" people today by exploiting, oppressing and humiliating them. He warns that Christianity must choose between being politically significant or remain just "an irrelevant sect on the boundary of society". Moltmann's Christology and its ethical implications helped the birth of "Liberation Theologies"[11].

The German Protestant theologian Wolfhard Pannenberg (b. 1928) also represents an important trend in contemporary Christology. His basic christological teaching can be found in the book: *Jesus - God and Man*. We have already quoted him in relation to christological method (Part II, Introduction, Ch. 3:2), where he can be regarded as the principal representative of the "Christology from below to above" trend. Having clarified the method of Christology, Pannenberg argues for the historical reality of Jesus. In contrast to Bultmann, he is quite satisfied with the historical facts about Jesus. He insists that the knowledge of Jesus' life provides enough solid ground for the anchor of reasoning faith. He emphasizes that Jesus' resurrection was a bodily resurrection and that it can be validated by historical methods. After the scepticism of the liberal and Bultmannian theologies, Pannenberg's new stand on the question of Jesus' resurrection is encouraging and has far-reaching consequences. For example, it sustains the credibility of the Christian message and validates the claim of Jesus Christ about the arrival of the Kingdom of God. Jesus, because of His resurrection, is a unique person and now it is rightly expected that He will reign in the Kingdom of God. Pannenberg holds that with the resurrection of Jesus the end of the world has already begun. This strong eschatological emphasis makes his Christology akin to that of the Theology of Hope[12].

The Christology of Process Theology closes this review of contemporary Protestant Christology. This theology came into existence under the impact of the Process philosophy of Alfred N. Whitehead (1861-1947), an English-American religious thinker and mathematician. His followers, Ch. Hartshorne, H. Cousins, W.N. Pittinger, S.M. Ogden, J.B. Cobb Jr. and others, worked out a system of Process Theology which has become a significant trend in theology in the Anglo-Saxon world. They tried to work out a theology on a Christian basis centered on the process principle of Whitehead. According to this view everything in the universe is in the state of process or development. From the point of view of this process principle they want to reinterpret and reformulate the entire structure of traditional Christian theology.

The Process theologians apply the characteristic Process principle in their Christology. They emphasize the humanity of Jesus Christ, Jesus regarded not as an intruder from the divine realm but as a real man. However, in Him, there was an "activity of divine". Jesus is the coincidence of God's action or agency and man's responsive action or agency, not in spite of but under the very conditions of genuinely human life[13]. They insist that Jesus cannot be isolated from what happened before Him. He is the Person in whom the past, present and future converge to a focus. In Jesus Christ God is acting because God is the "initiating agent" in every event. In the event of Jesus Christ they recognize an event of extraordinarily decisive importance. This is because in the event of Jesus Christ God shows how He acts in the world and how the world responds. The cross and resurrection of Jesus Christ are the disclosure of the suffering and victorious love of God. The consequence of the Jesus event is the recognition that God is love and man is created to be the lover, who in relationship with the "Cosmic Lover" finds the fulfilment of his existence[14].

As one can see from this short review, contemporary Protestant Christology has great diversity, many theologians are working to reach a better, deeper and fuller understanding of Christ and His work. They try to open up new paths in Christology. These trends seem to be contradictory in some respects, but this is due mainly to the different approaches and methods. The future development of Christology is expected to be towards the so called "Orthodox type" of Christology with the characteristics of acceptance of the Biblical record, acceptance of the bodily resurrection of Christ and the drawing of strong ethical consequences from this fact. The fermentation of contemporary Christology is a promising sign for the renewal of the whole of Christian theology.

At least three things are required from Christian ministers in connection with Christology. First, they should be well educated in this important part of theology. Second, they should continuously study the various issues in Christology. Third, they should develop their own Christology. This is for two reasons. First, Christology is the heart of Christian theology. Second, the minister's stand in Christology imparts directly on his work as minister, teacher and theologian.

NOTES

1.   D. Bonhoeffer: Christology, p. 56.
2.   J. Calvin: Institutes, IV. XVII. 28
3.   G. Aulen: Christus Victor, (SPCK 1945) p. 4.f.
4.   K. Barth: Church Dogmatics, IV, p. 211 f.
5.   E. Brunner: Dogmatics, Vol. II, p 289 f.
6.   D. Bonhoeffer: Christology, p. 49 f.
7.   R. Bultlmann: Kerygma and Myth, p. 35.
8.   ibid. pp. 32.f.
9.   P. Tillich: Systematic Theology, Vol. II. p. 94 f.
10.   J. Moltmann: The Crucified God, (SCM 1974) p. 84,
11.   ibid. pp. 84 f.
12.   C. H. Pinnock: Theology of Pannenberg, In Ev. Review of Theology, October 21, 1977, p. 21 f.
13.   M. Pittinger: The Doctrine of Christ in a Process Theology,   Expository Times, October 1970, p. 7.
14.   N. Pittenger: Bernard E. Melan, Process Thought and Significance of Christ in "Process Theology" ed. by E.H. Cousin, (Newman Press, New York, 1981) p. 203 f.

PART THREE

THE DOCTRINE OF THE HOLY SPIRIT, SALVATION, THE CHURCH AND THE LAST THINGS

Introduction

The Importance of Pneumatology
What is Pneumatology? Pneumatology as the Crown of Theology
The Branches of Pneumatology

1. What is Pneumatology?

At the outset of this part of Christian Doctrine we have to answer the question: What is Pneumatology?

The word Pneumatology has a Greek origin. It is coined from two Greek words: *Pneuma* meaning "Spirit", here referring to the Holy Spirit, and from *Logos* which means "word" or "speech". Hence Pneumatology means speech, teaching or study about the Person and the work of the Holy Spirit.

As we have said before, Christianity has a trinitarian concept of God: One God who is Father, Son and Holy Spirit (See Part I, Section 2, Ch.2). Each divine Person has its particular work. Traditional Christian Theology considers the work of creation as the work of the Father, but a work in which the Son and the Holy Spirit also took part. Likewise, Christian theology regards the work of redemption as the work of the Son, but a work in which the Father and the Holy Spirit also participated. Similarly, Christian theology holds that the work of salvation is pre-eminently the work of the Holy Spirit, but to it the Father and the Son also contribute. This trinitarian understanding of the works of the Persons of the Trinity is one of the basic characteristics of Christian theology[1].

We have already dealt with the work of the Father in Part One (Volume I), and that of the Son in Part Two; we will now examine the Person and the work of the Holy Spirit in this Third and final Part of this book (Volume II).

2. Pneumatology as the Crown of Theology

Pneumatology is so integral to Christian doctrinal theology that in it the former two parts - the Doctrine of God and the Doctrine of Christ - find their utmost meaning and fulfilment. To put this in another form: the creation and the redemption have their ultimate meaning in salvation. There is not much meaning in a world which is corrupted by sin unless there is a hope for its final restoration - what theology calls "the new creation". And what is the importance and meaning of Jesus Christ's work of redemption unless it results in salvation of the world at the end of time?

Consequently, there is an inner, logical and organic inter-dependence between the work of each of the Persons of the Trinity in creation, redemption and salvation. These three are the essential elements of God's eternal plan and decrees. Without each other the isolated parts in themselves are meaningless, irrelevant and in the last analysis, superfluous. Consequently, Christian theology looks at these three works of the Persons of the Trinity in their context and regards them as a complex organism. A synoptic view gives coherence to these three works and underlines the systematic nature of Christian theology. Therefore we can say that salvation as the work of the Holy Spirit is the crown of theology in which the other parts reach their meaning, fullness and ultimate aim.

Sometimes pneumatology is called by theologians the "applied" part of theology, because everything that the former two strands of theology taught about creation and redemption become actualized. Stated differently: what the former two parts of theology promised in this aspect of theology becomes reality. Here can be seen the "function" of Christian theology, how the redemption of Jesus Christ can become the experience of salvation. Pneumatology shows how the Holy Spirit works so that man can be free of sin, and how the new being can appear. How is this transformation of the complete being of man performed? Which helps are offered by the Holy Spirit for the growing of the new being? What are the characters of this new being? What can believers expect both at the end of their lives and at the end of this world? Here, the theories, concepts and tenets of theology confront everyday practice and experience. As a consequence, this part of doctrinal theology is of paramount importance[2].

Traditional theologians held that there was an age in which the work of the Father was dominant, ie. in creation. There was also a period which particularly belonged to the Son - when the redemption has been achieved by Christ. Since then the age of the Church especially belongs to the Holy

Spirit, which age will last until the end of time. This is because in and through the Church - and even beyond the Church - the Holy Spirit is at work in this world, acting to bring about the new creation. Jesus Christ promised the coming of the Holy Spirit to the Church *(John 14:16-17, 26; Acts 1:8)* which actually occurred at the first Pentecost *(Acts 2:1-13)*, an event which signifies the commencement of the age of the work of the Holy Spirit. Without the work of the Holy Spirit we would have only a vague knowledge of God, and the redemption of Jesus Christ would remain an event enveloped by the fading past. But because of the work of the Holy Spirit, this past becomes an ever-present reality for the successive generations of humanity. Moreover, the promises of God about the future of individuals and of the world can be present realities in faith because of the work of the Holy Spirit. And of first importance, the work of the Holy Spirit makes possible the "new life" - through repentance, forgiveness of sin and the new birth, a reality in those who accept Jesus Christ's redemption through the work of the Holy Spirit. People now can live in the presence of God because God lives in them *(1 Cor. 3:16)*[3].

There were periods in the history of the Church when the importance of the person and the work of the Holy Spirit were neglected by the theologians, in such periods as the late Middle Ages, the period of Protestant Orthodoxy and the period of Liberalism. This inveritably led to the spritual weakness of theology and of Church life. Its signs were the presence of intellectualism, scepticism and moralism in the theology and Church life of those ages. Whenever the understanding of the person and the work of the Holy Spirit is at a low ebb in the Church, the Church becomes weak, fragile and progressively lifeless and lacking its life-shaping power.

There have been other periods in the history of the Church - different from the above mentioned ones - when the importance of pneumatology was fully understood. These periods usually follow the low-tide awareness of the Holy Spirit in the Church and come into existence as a reaction to it. This "high tide" of the Holy Spirit in the Church evidences itself as revivalism and, in extreme cases, as mysticism and "enthusiasm". Church history provides enough examples of them. Today, the Church and theology are on the rising tide of the Holy Spirit, as can be seen in the growing importance of pneumatology in contemporary theology and in the growth of the revivalist movements both inside and outside the Churches.

81

3. The Branches of Pneumatology

The general statement that pneumatology is a part of theology which deals with the Person and work of the Holy Spirit needs a closer look. Pneumatology in a narrower sense means the study of the Person of the Holy Spirit. Pneumatology in a broader sense means the work of the Holy Spirit, which work is manifold. Classical theology recognizes the following subdivisions of pneumatology: (1) "Soteriology" - the doctrine of salvation; this deals with the different phases of how salvation occurs in man's life, how it comes about and the stages through which it progresses. (2) "Ecclesiology" - the doctrine of the Church; the Holy Spirit creates new life not only in individuals but in a new community which is the Church. Ecclesiology studies the questions related to the Church, and also is divided into branches which examine the various aspects of the Church: its structure, life and activity. These are: "Sacramentology", "Missiology", the "Doctrine of Ministry", "Ecumenology", and lastly "Eschatology" - the doctrine of the Last Things in which the work of the Holy Spirit is completed[4].

Christian ministers have to take serious account of pneumatology, knowing that we are living in the period which belongs to the Holy Spirit. Our worship, faith, love, service and our new life are possible only by the help, guidance and inspiration of the Holy Spirit. However, Christian ministers and theologians must maintain a balanced stance to avoid falling into the two extremes of neglecting the doctrine or overemphasizing it. The first could result in a poor lifeless theology, the second in an enthusiastic life without theology.

NOTES

1. L. Berkhof: Systematic Theology, p.424.J. Calvin: Institutes, I.XIII.
2. J. MacQuarry: Principles of Christian Theology, p.373.f.
3. E. Brunner: Dogmatics, Vol. III, p.6.f.
4. See Part III, Section 3, Chapter 1, (Introduction)

Section 1

The Person of the Holy Spirit

Chapter 1

Biblical View of the Spirit
The Holy Spirit in the Old Testament
The Holy Spirit in the New Testament

The Apostolic Creed states in its third article: "I believe in the Holy Ghost". While the first article expresses the Christian belief in God the Father and the second article does the same with the Son, the third article unequivocably expresses the Christian belief in God the Holy Spirit. The third article - like the former two - is based upon the Scriptures. Let us see now how the Bible gives evidence about God the Holy Spirit.

1. Holy Spirit in the Old Testament

The Old Testament uses the Hebrew word *Ruach* for the Spirit, a word which means "breath", "wind", "soul" and "spirit". This word first of all is related to the "Spirit of God" but the Old Testament also uses it to describe the spirit of man, and good or evil spirits as well.

In the Old Testament the expression "Spirit of Jahweh" can be found many times *(Gen. 1:2; Ps. 104:30; Job 27:3; Isa. 61:1)*. The "Spirit of God" has at least three meanings in the Old Testament. It means the presence of God, hence it means the power of God *(Gen. 1:2; Isa. 42:5; Job 33:4)*. The Spirit of God is interchangeable with the "Word" of God and with the "Wisdom" of God *(Gen. 1:3; Jer. 51:15)*. The expression "The "Spirit of God" is used by the Holy writers when they want to describe the initiative and action of the invisible God in the visible world *(Judg. 3:10, 6:34; Gen. 41:38)*. The Spirit of God is at work at The Creation *(Ps. 33:6)* in Providence *(Job 10:12; Isa. 42:6)* and at the Redemption *(Ezek. 37:1-14; Joel 2:28)*.

It is important to note that in the Old Testament, in special cases and circumstances, particular people did receive the Spirit of God. The Prophets had received the Spirit of God and this made them Prophets

(Num. 11:25; 1 Sam. 10:10; Micah 3:8; Isa 61:1; Ezek. 37:1). The leaders of Israel had the Spirit of God: judges like Jephthah *(Judg. 11:29)* and Samson *(Judg. 14:6)*. The kings of Israel also received the Spirit of God, for example, David *(1 Sam. 16:13)* and Saul who lost it *(1 Sam. 10:10, 28:15)*. The gift of the Spirit of God was not the privilege of the elite only; common people could also receive it, as we note with Amasai *(1 Chron. 12:18)* or Jahaziel *(2 Chron. 20:14)*[1].

2. Holy Spirit in the New Testament

The Old Testament concept of Spirit was taken over by the writers of the New Testament, where it was rapidly developed because of the teaching of Jesus Christ about the Spirit, and their experience of the Holy Spirit both at and after the first Pentecost. The Greek word which describes the spirit in the New Testament is *pneuma*. Its meaning is similar to the Old Testament *ruach* and means "breath, wind, ghost, spirit", and it relates to men, angels, demons and to God. God's spirit is called *Pneuma hagion* - Holy Spirit.

It is recorded in the New Testament that Jesus Christ lived and worked under the power of the Holy Spirit *(Luke 4:1)*.Not only was His birth initiated by the Holy Spirit *(Matt. 1:18)* but the Holy Spirit was seen to descend on Jesus Christ at His baptism *(Mark 1:10)*. He commenced His messianic ministry by announcing that "The Spirit of the Lord is upon me" *(Luke 4:18)*, by means of which He taught as one who had authority *(Matt. 7:29)*. His teaching and miraculous deeds strengthened the conviction of the disciples that the Spirit of God was dwelling in Him *(Matt. 12:28)*.

Although the Spirit was not yet known in person to the disciples *(John 7:39)*, Jesus in His farewell speeches promised the sending of the Holy Spirit, *Paracletos* or Counsellor who will be with the disciples as a constant companion *(John 14:26)*. The Spirit will not only comfort the disciples but will help and guide them in their witnessing for Christ *(Luke 12:12)*. Through the presence of the Holy Spirit Jesus Christ will be with his disciples *(Matt. 28:20; John 14:18; Gal. 4:6)*. Jesus Christ not only promised the coming of the Holy Spirit but He himself began to fulfil the promise. After His resurrection Jesus Christ had already begun to give the Spirit to the disciples by breathing on them *(John 20:22)*.

The turning point was at the first Pentecost when Jesus Christ's promise of the Spirit was fulfilled. *(Acts 2:1-13)*. The disciples received the gift of the Holy Spirit in a very visible way which completely transformed them and enabled them to begin their missionary work. Under its influence the disciples became Apostles. Other members of the first Church also received the Holy Spirit. The Apostles understood the outpouring of the Spirit to be as the fulfilment of both the Old Testament prophecies and those of Jesus Christ *(Acts 2:14-42).* The Holy Spirit was regarded by the first Christians as the gift of mercy and the proof that the age of the Messiah had indeed arrived. Church-membership was not only tied to repentance and baptism but was conditional upon participation in the experience of the baptism by the Holy Spirit *(Acts 2:33; 1 Cor. 12:13)*, the Spirit of adoption who made believers members of God's household and participants in Christ's heritage *(Gal. 4:6; 1 John 3:1).* The Spirit dwelt in the believers *(Rom. 8:9; 1 Cor 3:16)* and the Spirit assured them inwardly that they were the Sons of God *(Rom. 8:12-17).* In addition, the Spirit gave inner freedom to the believers *(Rom. 8:2; Gal. 5:13-18; 2 Cor. 3:17)* granting them the power of God by which they could live according to the will of God *(2 Tim. 1:7; Acts 1:8; Rom. 15:13).* Those who received the Holy Spirit were expected to bring forth the fruits of the Spirit for the benefit of men and for the Glory of God *(Gal. 5:22; 1 Cor. 12)*[2].

The New Testament puts emphasis on the eschatological character of the Holy Spirit. This suggests that the coming of the Holy Spirit in its fullness had a precondition, namely the redemptive death of Jesus Christ. Hence we can understand why the Gospels speak of the Holy Spirit yet to come. When in Jesus Christ's death this condition had been fulfilled the outpouring of the Holy Spirit duly occurred. This event proves three things. First, that Jesus Christ was the true Messiah. Second, that God's promise of the outpouring of the Holy Spirit was trustworthy. Third, that the age of the Kingdom of God has indeed arrived and God dwells amongst His people[3].

NOTES

1.   A. Richardson: An Introduction to the Theology of the New Testament, p.103 f.
2.   ibid, p.109 f.
3.   ibid, p.205 f.

Chapter 2

Holy Spirit within the Trinity

The Person of the Holy Spirit, Father and Spirit, Son and Spirit

We have already discussed this theme from another perspective when we dealt with the concept of the Trinity (See: Part I, Section 2, Ch.2). However, a closer look at the person of the Holy Spirit and his relation to the Father and to the Son is necessary.

1. The Person of the Holy Spirit

Concerning the Personhood of the Holy Spirit, it is tempting to consider the Holy Spirit as merely a simple means of communication, both between the Father and the Son and between God and Man. The danger involved in this is that the Holy Spirit is not considered as an independent and fully divine Person in His own right, equal with the Father and with the Son. If the Holy Spirit is only a means of communication between the Father and the Son, then the Holy Spirit loses His personal character and is placed in a subordinate position. In this case, the Trinitarian doctrine of God would be reduced to a Binitarian concept which falls far short of the Christian concept of God.

This temptation arises from the fact that man naturally uses the analogy of his experience of "human spirit," which he then applies to the Holy Spirit. The crux of the problem is that man cannot imagine human soul or spirit independently from the human body. Following this, it is assumed that the Holy Spirit has no independent existence either, that it is only the "Spirit" of God or the "Spirit" of Jesus Christ. But this is not the case with God, who Himself is Spirit. To talk about the "Spirit of the Spirit" makes little sense. The Christian teaching, which is based upon the Scriptures is that the three Persons of the Holy Trinity, Father, Son and Holy Spirit are truly, equally and fully God. Each of them is Godhead, an independent divine Person and co-equally God. But at the same time there is a basic unity between the three divine Persons, between the Father, Son and Holy Spirit. The uniting power between them is the perfect divine love which makes three Persons into One God.

Therefore we are right in saying that the Holy Spirit is one with the Spirit of God and with the Spirit of Christ because of the basic unity between the divine Persons. But we are also right when we speak about the person and work of Holy Spirit because of His independent nature. This independence does not mean that the Holy Spirit does something contrary to the will of the Father or of the Son, The Holy Spirit works independently of the Father and the Son, but in His work, the Father and the Son also participate. Moreover, the Father and the Son are communicated to man by the Holy Spirit. God - by the work of the Holy Spirit - can dwell in man, because of the redemptive work of the Son communicated to man by the work of the Holy Spirit. To sum up: In the activities of the three Divine Persons, it is always the One God who acts. This is formulated in classical theology as: *Opera Trinitatis ad extra sunt indivisa* that is "The works of the Trinity are indivisible outwardly"; each Person acts in all divine activity. This is the doctrine of *perichoresis* - co-inherence of the three divine Persons of the Trinity[1].

2. Father and Spirit

In the ancient Church there was debate about the precise relation of the Holy Spirit to the Father, a difference in viewpoint that has become known as the *filoque* controversy. Theologians of the Eastern group maintained the Father to be the sole source and origin of the Holy Spirit, *fons et origo,* as indeed they considered Him to be the source of the entire Trinity: *Pater est fons totius Trinitatis.* Western theologians on the other hand, basing their understanding on Johannine texts, insisted that the Holy Spirit "proceeds from the Father and the Son." Recognizing a single procession or double procession still distinguishes eastern and western theologians[2].

As to the question of how far the work of the Holy Spirit can be regarded as independent from the work of the Father the answer lies in the relation of the Person of the Holy Spirit to the Person of the Father. As we said before, this relationship is characterized by the dialectic of total unity and total independence. This paradox reaches its solution in the perfect divine love which is so sensitive that it is able to secure both the total unity and the total independence of the divine Persons at one and the same time. So the work of the Holy Spirit is independent; so far as the Person of the Holy Spirit is independent and His work is the work of the Father, so far the Holy Spirit is one with the Father. This is illustrated in the work of salvation and new creation, where the Holy Spirit is paramount but both the Father and the Son are also directly involved.

Hence, we are able to understand why and how the Holy Spirit participates in the works of creation and providence which are primarily attributed to the Father, while the Father and Son are also present in the works of salvation and new creation, works which are primarily attributed to the Holy Spirit. There is only one comprehensive divine plan or decree for creation, redemption and salvation, the plan of God, and this is being executed by God the Trinity.

3. Son and Spirit

The relation between the Son and the Holy Spirit needs special attention, because the Son is both incarnate and eternal.

According to the testimony of the Gospels, the Son Incarnate is submitted both to the Father and to the Holy Spirit. Jesus Christ - the Son Incarnate - is begotten by the Holy Spirit *(Luke 1:35; Matt. 1:20)*. At His baptism the Holy Spirit descends upon Jesus and the Father's witness is heard to the Sonship of Christ *(Matt. 3:16-17)*. Christ is teaching and acting under the power of the Holy Spirit *(Matt. 12:28)*. This submission of the Son is in harmony with His state of humiliation, in which the Son is living in the form of man, demonstrating the true model of man living in accordance with the will of God. The Scriptures conclude that He totally accepted and perfectly followed this model *(John 5:30)*. An integral part of His humiliation is the submission of the Son Incarnate to the will of the Father and of the Holy Spirit. However the total agreement of the divine Son with the will both of the Father and the Holy Spirit is not alien to Him, because of the eternal harmony between the three Persons of the Holy Trinity.

The situation of the Son Incarnate is radically changed after His resurrection, according to the testimony of the Gospels. Here the Gospels do not make a distinction between the activity of the risen Lord and that of the Holy Spirit. Now the risen Lord, the Son re-incarnated is not submitted to the Holy Spirit any more. The Resurrected Lord appears as one who is equal in every way with the Holy Spirit, having now received back His glory, power and state of divinity. Having completed the work of redemption, the Son is being lifted up from the state of humiliation and re-invested with His divine state. This is why the risen Lord could communicate the Holy Spirit to the disciples *(John 20:22)*. This is why, in the coming of the Holy Spirit, He himself is coming to be with and in the Church *(John 16:14-15)*. The Spirit of Christ is the one who interprets the Scriptures, illustrating the basic unity between the Son and the Holy Spirit *(Luke 24:17-35; 2 Cor. 3:16-17)*. The Son is He who sends the Holy Spirit

(Luke 24:49; John 16:7). It is true that the Holy Spirit proceeds from the Father, but it is also true that the Holy Spirit is sent by the Son. In this way the *filioque* clause can be justified.

In this light we can say that there is both unity and independence between the work of the Holy Spirit and the work of the Son. There is a unity of works between them as far as there is unity between the divine Persons of the Holy Spirit and the Son. This unity is founded in the perfect divine love. But this love secures the perfect independence of the works of both Persons because it guarantees the independence of the Persons. However, the Son Incarnate is clearly submitted to the Holy Spirit as well as to the Father, the Son ante-incarnate and post-incarnate is co-equal with the Holy Spirit and with the Father[3].

We have already shown that the Apostolic Creed plainly and firmly expresses the belief in the Holy Spirit. So does the Constantinopolitan Creed when it says: "We believe...in the Holy Spirit, the Lord and life-giver, who proceeds from the Father (and the Son), who is worshipped and glorified together with the Father and the Son, who spoke through the prophets..." Despite the controversy about the proceeding of the Holy Spirit, the Church has always accepted the Holy Spirit as Godhead and the third Person of the Holy Trinity. Thus priests and ministers always baptize people "In the name of the Father, Son and the Holy Spirit", believers worship Him together with the Father and the Son and the Blessing is spoken in the name of the three persons of the Holy Trinity.

NOTES

1.   A. Richardson: An Introduction to the Theology of the New Testament p.123.
2.   See Part I, Section 2, Chapter 3, Point 6.
3.   A. Richardson: An Introduction to the Theology of the New Testament p.121.f.

Chapter 3

Human Spirit and Holy Spirit
The Problem of Human Spirit. The Human Conscience
Human Spirit Under the Power of the Holy Spirit

One more issue needs to be clarified related to the Holy Spirit, the relationship between the human spirit and the Holy Spirit. The problem can be stated thus: Is there any similarity between the human spirit and the Holy Spirit? The answer is "Yes and No". The answer is "Yes" in so far as both the human spirit and the Holy Spirit are spirit, which implies a higher quality of existence than corporal entity. But the answer is No, because there is a qualitative difference between the human spirit and the Holy Spirit. While the similarity between the two is a phenomenological one, the difference between them is an ontological one. Man's spirit is a created entity, fashioned for his particular being. The Holy Spirit is not created; He is eternal and belongs to the very nature of God. According to Christian theology the relationship between the human spirit and the Holy Spirit was disrupted by sin. It can be restored, and both the disrupted and the re-established relationships have existential importance for man. Let us therefore look at this issue in detail.

1. The Problem of Human Spirit

No one can deny that a human being possesses a "spirit" which is one of the most characteristic features of the human. But there are divergent understandings about what is human spirit, where it originates and whether it has an independent existence apart from the human body.

First of all we have to remember that Christian theology makes a distinction between "spirit" and "soul". What we call "spirit" is the Hebrew *ruach*, Greek *pneuma*-spirit, while we translate as "soul" the Hebrew *nephes*, Greek *psyche* although the terms were to some degree interchangeable in the original languages. Man's soul implies that because of the "breath of life" he is a living being, an animated dust. Man's spirituality comes from the fact that he who was created "in the Image of God" *(Gen. 1:27)* has "spirit" in his make-up, as God is spirit *(Zach. 12:1; Job 32:8).* (See: Part I, Section 4, Chapter 1:3).

In everyday usage, as we might expect, there is a less than theological distinction made between soul and spirit. To clarify it, we might say that soul is the inner spiritual structure of man which includes selfconsciousness, associated with our intellectual, emotional and volitional life, the ability to remember, the subconscious realm and the realm of "super-ego" which sometimes is called conscience. The spirit of man refers mainly to the capability for spiritual activities like planning, decision making, and forming value judgements. Spirit is where creative imagination concerning life and arts, intuitions, insights and ecstacy find their impetus. It is in this area that some type of faith is prevalent, where it plays an important role in determining the main direction of life. This is where man's longing for higher values and his search for truth, beauty and eternity originates. The highest peak of the human spirit is the point where contact can be re-established between man and God. This is the point where the Holy Spirit enters again in the human being. We will see later why and how this happens. Here, let it suffice to say that the human spirit has an important role in Christian theology and especially from the point of view of the Work of the Holy Spirit.

The next question which we have to face is: Where does the human spirit originate? This question is as old as mankind. Man has always been interested in finding the answer to this question because it provides the key to man's self-understanding. Religions and philosophies have attempted from their very beginnings to provide an answer; in our view there are basically three.

The materialist philosophies provide two answers. The older school emphatically denied the existence of human spirit, which was considered as the idealist interpretation of the human being whom they accused of lacking a sound scientific foundation. The modern materialistic interpretation of the human spirit accepts its existence on the one hand but on the other insists that the human spirit has no existence apart from the human body. It regards spirit as the product of the higher nerve-activity of the human brain. Consequently, the human spirit depends on the material basis of the human brain; it is born from it and dies with it. According to this philosophy, man is basically an animal with higher mental activities which are commonly thought of as human spirit.

Idealist philosophies and some of the natural religions look at the human spirit in a twofold way. First, they accept the idea that the human spirit represents the "Divine spark" in man's being which is derived from the divine spirit. Therefore the human spirit, originated from God's spirit, has pre-existence as well as post-existence. This idea comes from two sources: from Platonic philosophy - it is likely that Plato borrowed this idea from one of the ancient religions - and from the theologies of some of the ancient religions. Second, they argue that the presence of the Divine spirit in man in the form of human spirit can be proved by the fact that man possesses the "Voice of God" in himself in the form of conscience. Therefore man basically has divine character, but unfortunately he lives imprisoned in the body. His task is to demonstrate by his thinking, life-conduct and activity that he truly belongs to the divine realm, the realm of the Spirit.

The teaching of theology concerning the human spirit is clear with respect to its creation by God. After he is resurrected man will have a new spirit in a new body. But Christian theology has at least three questions concerning the human spirit. The first is connected with the state of the human spirit or soul before birth, a question we have already dealt with in connection with the pre-existence of the human soul (See: Part I, Section 4, Chapter I:6). Second, there is the so-called dichotomy - trichotomy debate between theologians (See: Part I, Section 4, Chapter 1:5), that is, whether the human being has body and soul only, or body, soul and spirit. Third is the state of the human soul or spirit after death. We will consider this issue later (See: Part III, Section 4, Chapter 2:2-6).

As to the dichotomy-trichotomy debate: our standpoint is fundamentally the trichotomist one. The body has both soul and spirit, if we understand soul in the Old Testament meaning. In that case, soul means that which makes the body living. The human spirit is a special gift of God to man which gives man his unique human character and it is an important factor of man as the "Image of God" (See: Part I, Section 4, Chapter 1:3). However, the spirit of man, together with his soul, is corrupted by sin. This means that man's spirit has lost its original ability to enter into contact with God. This lost contact between the human spirit and God's spirit can be reestablished through the redemptive work of Christ and the activity of the Holy Spirit, making us again the "Sons of God". These are the people whom the New Testament describe as *pneumatikos*, that is, those who are living under the power of the Holy Spirit, who communicate in a living way between their human spirit and the Spirit of God.

2. The Human Conscience

The issue of human conscience inevitably comes up in connection with the study of human spirit. We have to deal with such questions as the nature of conscience, its origin and its theological importance.

The word conscience has its root in the Latin *Conscientia* which is equivalent to the Greek *Syneidosis*. Conscience describes the self-judging and controlling ability of the human spirit and also its capability of self-searching of the human spirit. It is a driving force for doing good and a restrictive force in avoiding sin.

There are two types of conscience concerning human activity. First, there is the *Conscientia antecedens* or antecendent conscience, which evaluates potential acts in advance. The conclusion is that conscience either agrees with the plan and urges man to act, or it disagrees with it and tries to prevent its execution. In the first case we talk about a good conscience, in the second case a bad conscience. Second, there is the *Conscientia subsequent* or subsequent conscience which judges man's own deeds that have already been done. It either applauds the deeds, in which case we speak of a good conscience, or it may condemn them, giving us a bad conscience.

What is the theological significance of the conscience? Sometimes conscience is called the "voice of God" in man, an affirmation that can be maintained only in the sphere of the universal grace of God. Paul says that even the Gentiles are not without the knowlege of the divine law because it is "written on their hearts" *(Rom. 2:15)*. This means that even fallen man is not without some underlying knowledge of God and His will. This makes possible an organized and enduring human life. But the affirmation made above cannot be maintained without reservation in the realm of the special grace of God. The voice of God in human conscience cannot be equated with the presence of the Holy Spirit in the human conscience or in other areas of the human spirit. This is because of sin. Fallen man cannot avoid the consequence of sin, among which the most grievous is man's separatedness from God. In effect, God withdrew his Holy Spirit from sinful man. God wants to give the Holy Spirit to man again, but under the condition of repentence and faith in Christ the Saviour. The Scriptures declare that this actually happens in Christian experience; for example Paul can say: "My conscience bears witness in the Holy Spirit" *(Rom. 9:1)*.

3. Human Spirit under the Power of the Holy Spirit

We touched upon this issue above but it needs further elaboration. Let us return to our standpoint in the dichotomy-trichotomy debate. Man in his original status possessed body, soul and spirit, including divine spirit. Because of the fall he lost the divine spirit, but man may retrieve it. He may regain the Holy Spirit. This is one of the main messages of Christian theology[1].

Why can man have the Holy Spirit again? Because Jesus Christ's redemptive death made it possible. As the consequence of sin man lost the Holy Spirit; sin and Holy Spirit cannot accommodate with each other. There is an ontological antagonism between the two. Either sin extinguishes the Holy Spirit, or the Holy Spirit expels sin *(1 Thess. 5:19; Rom. 8:2)*. When man lost the Holy Spirit, he lost the presence, power and guidance of God. Hence the tragic features of human life. Where there is no God there is no life. At this point sickness, pain and death came into human life. Where there is no God there is no power, hence man's weakness, fragility and inability to do what is good. Where there is no God there is no guidance; man loses his direction, aim and vision, contributing to the feeling of estrangement, lostness and meaninglessness[2].

This situation, however, can be reversed as a consequence of Jesus Christ's self sacrifice on the cross. Christ's death was not only the expiation of man's sin, but by it the obstacle of sin between God and Man was removed once and for all. The consequence of this healing work is that the Holy Spirit can again enter into man's spirit to re-establish the broken contact between God and man. This is a far-reaching event; by the presence and work of the Holy Spirit in man's spirit, the life undergoes a radical change. Man is re-introduced to the fullnesss of life, he regains his aim, direction and meaning for this life and has hope for the eternal life[3].

How then can man's spirit "have" the Holy Spirit? Man cannot acquire the Holy Spirit automatically or by manipulation. Man can have the Holy Spirit only if he accepts and fulfills its divine conditions. These are repentence from sin, prayer for the Holy Spirit and self-dedication to the will of God. There are examples which demonstrate the entering of the Holy Spirit into the human spirit. The great figures of the Bible offer many: the Patriarch, Moses, the Prophets, the Apostles and the first Christians. During the long history of the Church there always were men and women in every generation who received the gift of the Holy Spirit.

The whole of Christian theology is built upon the assertion that under certain conditions the Holy Spirit will dwell in man and restore Man to his original position in creation and status in relation to God. Man living under the power of the Holy Spirit can live a free, peaceful and relevant life which only is worth the name of life.

Christian theologians, priests and ministers should keep always in their mind that the meaning, relevance and usefulness of Christian theology lie in the fact that the Holy Spirit wants to enter into man and to transform man radically. The servants of God are the instruments of God in the process of the Holy Spirit's entering into and gaining power over every human being.

NOTES

1. See Part I, Section 4, Chapter 1, Point 5.
2. See Part I, Section 4, Chapter 5, Point 3.
3. See Part II, Section 3, Chapter 2.

SECTION 2

The Work of the Holy Spirit

Chapter 1

Holy Spirit as the Giver of New Life

The Holy Spirit and the New Life, *Ordo Salutis*
Conversion, Justification, Sanctification

1. The Holy Spirit and New Life

We have already stated that the work of the Holy Spirit is to create new life (See: Part III, Introduction Point 1). The part of Christian doctrine dealing with this operation is called Soteriology, the doctrine of salvation. The task of Soteriology is to study how the redemption of Jesus Christ becomes the salvation of man. Soteriology is the application of the doctrine of Redemption. The work of Salvation involves each of the three persons of the Trinity. First, God the Father's decree of salvation; God wanted to save the world and decided to accomplish it. Second, the work of redemption by Jesus Christ; the Son of God by His self-sacrifice expiated sin, thus removing the barrier between God and man and opening up the way for the coming of the Holy Spirit. Finally, the Spirit works incessantly to make God's plan a reality in human lives.

The work of the Holy Spirit in creating new life is manifested in two areas. The Holy Spirit creates new life in individuals by acting invisibly and secretly in individual souls. Moreover, the Holy Spirit creates a new community - the Church - from those who receive this new life. The work of the Holy Spirit in the Church is also twofold: it attracts people and gathers into the Church those who are elect, giving them a new life. Moreover, the Holy Spirit enables believers to remain and grow in the new life. The creation of this new life both in individuals and in the community, is possible because, according to the Biblical witnesses and human testimony, the Holy Spirit posesses the dynamism, energy and the power of God. The Holy Spirit, who participated in the work of the creation of the world, in so doing proved Himself capable for the creation of the new life. Our task is to deal with the work of the Holy Spirit. In this section, we will deal with this work in individuals. In the next section we will look at the work of the Holy Spirit in and through the Church.

2. The *Ordo Salutis*

The work of the Holy Spirit in individuals takes place by means of an orderly process, known in classical theology as the *ordo salutis* - the order or way of salvation. The *ordo salutis* establishes three different stages in the process of salvation.

There are two participants in the work of salvation: God who is acting through His holy Spirit for the salvation of man, and man who is responding to God's action. It follows that we can distinguish two aspects to salvation: the divine and the human.

The divine side of salvation has the following stages: election, justification and sanctification. The human side of salvation exhibits the following characteristics: conversion, regeneration and sanctification. On the divine side of salvation the driving force is the grace of God. On the human side the important factor is faith. We will examine them further in the following chapter.

It has to be stressed that these aspects of salvation, the divine and the human, constitute a unity in which the initiating, acting and executing factor is the Holy Spirit. Man only responds to the work of the Holy Spirit. According to reformation theology, even man's positive response to God is initiated by the Holy Spirit.

In connection with the work of salvation by the Holy Spirit, two erroneous standpoints must be challenged. The first is *Pelagianism* which says that in man's salvation everything depends on the human will: the acceptance of the salvation offered is dependent on the human will, either one wants to accept it or not. The second error is represented by *Quietism* which says that there is absolutely no contribution to salvation and everything depends on the sovereign will of God alone. The first error leads to the overemphasising of human works in salvation, the second leads to scepticism or fatalism.

We shall present the stages of salvation in such a way that both the divine and the human sides are seen to be present. The issue of "Election" has already been studied (See Part I, Sect. 2. Ch. 6). We shall deal now with three important stages of the *Ordo Salutis*; conversion, justification and sanctification.

3. Conversion

Conversion is the first visible sign of the work of the Holy Spirit in the life of the individual. Conversion is not the work of man, although it takes place in man's soul when the Holy Spirit moves the whole person of man to undergo the process of conversion. In this process the dominant factors are firstly the mercy of God, which is absolute, and secondly the faith of man, which is initiated by the mercy of God and generated by the Holy Spirit.

Conversion is a key concept of the Bible. In the Old Testament, the centre of the prophetic message is to call for repentance and conversion. The Hebrew word *shub* which embodies this concept literally means to return, to go back the way one came. Conversion means, therefore, to turn away from one's own way and turn back to God. This movement must be the wholehearted act of the decided person *(Isa. 44:22, 55:7; Jer. 18:11, 4:1; Ezek. 18:21; Isa. 44:22).*

In the New Testament the Greek word *Metanoia* conveys the ideas of both conversion and repentence. John the Baptist called his hearers to repentance *(Matt. 3:1-12).* Jesus Christ began his messianic work with the message: "Repent, for the Kingdom of heaven is at hand" *(Matt. 4:17).* In the first sermon of the Church at the first Pentecost in Jerusalem, Peter stressed the necessity for repentance *(Acts 2:38).* Paul strongly emphasized that man must "be reconciled to God" *(2 Cor. 5:20).*

The Bible provides several examples of conversion. Naaman *(2 Kings 5:15)*; Manasseh *(2 Cron. 33:12-13)*; Zacheus *(Luke 19:8-9)*; the blind man *(John 9:38)*; the Samaritan woman *(John 4:29)*; the Ethiopian eunuch *(Acts 8:38)*; Saul who became the Apostle Paul *(Acts 9:1-19)* and Lydia *(Acts 16:14)* are examples of conversion. Not only individuals but groups can undergo conversion *(Jer. 4:1; Isa. 44:22; Mal. 3:7; Acts 2:37-41, 11:21).*

The New Testament recognizes temporary conversion *(Matt. 13:20, 21; Heb. 6:4-6; 1 John 2:19)* and true, lasting conversion *(2 Cor. 7:10; Luke 19:8-9)* and repeated conversion *(Luke 22:32; Rev. 2:5, 3:3)* [1].

From age to age the central message of the Church's preaching has always been the same: to call people to repentance. Today, this message is a common element in evangelism.

We can, moreover, distinguish different moments in the process of conversion. First comes the acknowledgement or conviction of sin. Conversion starts with the understanding of one's own sins. In this stage one understands that something is basically wrong with his life. It is not what it should be. It has missed the ultimate goal, his life runs in the wrong direction because man lives to satisfy his desires, lust and selfishness, experiencing meaninglessness, alienation and despair. An inner crisis develops. In this stage man tries to do everything to extricate himself from this unpleasant and untenable situation. He is often fighting against everything and everybody, but it is a losing battle *(Acts 9.5)*. The sinner under conviction becomes gradually isolated from everybody and finds himself in a fight against God. This fight can take various moods such as: deeper immersion in sin, turning to alcohol or other drugs, choosing a new living-place or a new job or a new spouse or new friends, or fleeing into the asylum of atheist philosophy. At this stage the appearance of psychological disorders and sicknesses are common. At this point man either becomes lost forever, and sin and its tragic consequences will be triumphant over him, or he will gradually realize the inner cause of his miseries and try to detect his own sinfulness by the help of the Scriptures.

The sinner's understanding of his own sins leads to the next stage, which is known in theology as contrition. This is the point where man stops fleeing from God and tries to turn towards Him. Man retires within himself, and in an illuminated and often ecstatic moment he suddenly understands his miserable situation from the point of view of God. He not only sees his sins but understands his tragic situation as the direct consequence of his own sins. Now man begins to be ashamed of himself and of what he has done and feels remorse and great regret. This breaks his heart and soul and he accuses himself of his sins, misdeeds and mischief. He feels himself lost and understands at last the power of the sins which led him to this abyss. He begins to hate his sins as being the cause of all his misery, a hatred which sometimes is extended to himself as well.

This leads to the next stage, the confession of sins. Man, having recognized his sins and become contrite, turns in his soul to God in earnest by confession of his sins to God. The confession of sins may take various forms: in a soliloquy of the soul, or in the presence of a Christian, either a minister or a friend. Or it can happen publicly, if such a special occasion is provided.

After the confession, the sinful man at first experiences a relieving catharsis, inner cleanness and the relaxation of inner tensions. This is the immediate consequence of throwing out sins by uttering them in words. At the confession of sins man not only dissociates himself from his sins but casts them out from his life. However, this catharsis in itself is not enough. The feeling of relief can be also reached by psychotherapic means, as occcurs in psychoanalysis; man must yet reach the stage of absolution or remission of sins. Having confessed sins to God, one receives the answer of God in the form of absolution for one's sins; in effect when one confesses, expresses willingness to become free from his sins, man offers his sins to God, and God detaches sin from the individual. In the absolution, God actually takes away sins; man and sin are separated. The kernel of absolution is the forgiveness of sin. God forgives the sins of those who repent because Jesus Christ's vicarious suffering and death make it possible. This leads to the next stage; which is the justification. As the consequence of absolution man is aware of inner peace, relaxation and an acceptance by God. When he accepts God the relationship between God and man returns to normal. From this time man can expect a favourable turn in his life.

Classical theology distinguishes three elements in conversion. The intellectual element is when man recognizes his sin. *(Rom. 1:32; Ps. 51:3)*. The emotional element is when man feels sorrow for his sins by which he has ruined his life and hurt God *(Ps. 51:4; Heb. 10:27)*. The volitional element is when man wants to change his sinful state by seeking God's help, pardon and cleansing *(Ps. 51:2, 7, 10)*. The concept of *Metanoia* includes in itself these three essential elements *(Acts 2:37)*[2].

Conversion may take place in man's life in a lightning moment as we can see it in the case of the conversion of Paul *(Acts 9)* and that of Augustine. But there are other cases when the conversion is a long-lasting process, like the conversion of Luther or of Calvin. Sometimes the conversion is a rather stormy event, in other cases it is quiet.

We have to stress the initiative and work of the Holy Spirit in the process of the conversion. It is true that conversion appears to be the achievement of man because it is happening in the life of the human with his whole person involved in it. But this never could happen unless the Holy Spirit gave the initiative, inspiration and insight and unless he bent the human intellect, emotion and will towards God. It is the Holy Spirit that gives power and faith to man to go through the process of conversion.

100

4. Justification

If conversion can be understood as the human side of salvation, the doctrine of justification certainly can be regarded as its divine side. How is it possible for humans to regain their original position in which God regards them as just and righteous again? The doctrine of justification provides reasons why and how salvation is possible.

Justification is God's answer and solution to the problem of human sin. As we said in connection with sin, God could have eliminated sin together with the Sinner (See: Part I, Section 4, Chapter 6:1). In this case God would suffer a setback in His magnificent work of creation. God is not prepared to accept this solution, nor could God accept the second option of tolerating sin and sinful man in his fallen state forever. In both cases God's glory would have suffered. God opted for the third solution: the salvation of mankind.

God decided about it in His eternal counsel, where the Son undertook the work of redemption by His suffering and death in human form for the expiation of sins. And the Holy Spirit made effective the Son's work of redemption in man's life and in the world at large by recreating both man and the world and restoring them to their original status. Evil and sin will be eliminated and man, the creation and the glory of God, will be restored[3]. In the process of justification the dominant factor is the mercy of God which makes possible man's justification and generates faith through the work of the Holy Spirit; by this faith man can accept his own justification from God. Understood in this manner, justification is another work of the Holy Spirit.

Man's justification in time has its preliminaries in eternity. Justification of fallen men had been decided at the "Counsel of Peace" in eternity before creation. It is, in reality, the core of the eternal decree of redemption[4]. Redemption starts with justification because man's redemption depends upon how he can be regarded as a true, just and perfect creature before God without sin, rebellion and estrangement. Only when justified can man be reinstated to his original status with all the gifts, benefits and wealth from which he fell.

The decree of redemption was, in effect, God's decision in principle achieved in history by the redemptive work of the Son and made real to mankind by the restoring work of the Holy Spirit. God's election of man reveals itself in the subjective vocation of man, effective for those who are elected by God and are called by God *(Eph. 1:4)*. The vocation of man is both an inner and an outer vocation. Once again, this is the work of the Holy Spirit. The outer vocation of man is the work of the Holy Spirit; he creates conditions by which man is directed to the acceptance of God's mercy. The declaration of the mercy of God and the opportunity afforded man to listen to it and obtain knowledge of it are also the work of the Holy Spirit through the activity of the Church. The inner vocation of man by the Holy Spirit becomes apparent when man feels an urgent need for the mercy of God to find a permanent solution for his sins and re-establish his severed contact with God. Man's negative attitude to God becomes positive. Awareness of the intolerability of sin and the untenable situation towards God, the desire of man to be rid of sin and normalise his relations with God, are also the work of the Holy Spirit. In all this we see the constructive work of the Holy Spirit in man's inner vocation is that the Holy Spirit generates that faith in man's soul by which man accepts his own vocation for Salvation and is justified before God.

Let us now look more closely at what is happening in the moment of justification. E. Brunner describes it very aptly as "identification"[5]. In justification, a mutual identification takes place between man and Christ: Christ identifies Himself with the sinful man and the sinful man identifies himself with Christ on the cross. Christ, the Son of God, the true man on the cross in his salvatory death, identified himself with sinful mankind and thus with every sinful man. This means that He took upon Himself all the sins of mankind and He bore the burden and the punishment of all sin. These punishments are pain, suffering and death. His death on the cross is the vicarious death of sinful man: the sinless son of God dies because of the sin of men, because of our sins. In this death Christ shows His utmost and perfect identification with us. This identification of Christ with us was inspired by His love for us which aimed to free us from the bondage of sin and from our cursed and deadly situation of condemnation. By doing so, Christ executed the plan of Salvation of mankind which was decided by God in the Counsel of Peace in eternity. But Christ's identification with the sinful man on the cross is only half the story of justification; the second half of the story has yet to happen. It is also necessary that the sinful man should identify himself with Christ on the cross. This can happen only when sinful man understands that the Man on the cross is suffering and dying as the consequence of man's own sins. In Christ's death man dies together with sins as the consequence of sins. At this moment of man's identification with the One who is on the cross an "exchange" takes place which is initiated by God. God looks at Christ his own Son, the Man on the cross who is suffering and dying, in whom our sins reach the utmost consequence of the capital punishment of death, and reckons His death as yours. In Christ you are on the cross to suffer and die as the consequence of sin. But God looks at you, who identified yourself with Christ and are also identified by Christ himself, and God sees in you Christ, the true, just and perfect Man. This is possible because Christ has taken man's sins and granted to man His own perfect manhood. Man is on the cross in Christ in his death, and Christ is in you with his life. You and Christ become "exchanged" persons. This is why Christ died on the cross and the believer becomes a just, true and perfect man in the eyes of God. This is why one can say to God *Abba* - my Father *(Rom. 8:15)*. This is what happens In the moment of justification. This "exchange" of persons is the work of the Holy Spirit.

Conversion and justification are called by the Bible *Palingenesia* - new birth *(John 3:3, Tit. 3:5)*. The person who goes through the process of conversion and justification is "born again". Classical theology calls this process regeneration, because such radical changes take place in the inner life of the person that he is regarded as a new being. This change can be seen not only in man's attitude to God, to other men, to himself and to the world, but even more in that something absolutely "new" now appears which hitherto was lacking. This "new" is the new being, born by the Holy Spirit as the "New Creation" in man, a new man who is destined to inherit the Kingdom of God *(John 3:5, 6; 1 Pet. 1:23)*.

It has to be stressed that justification of sinful man before God is brought about solely as a result of faith and not by works. This is what the Bible stresses, particularly the Epistles of Paul. Only by faith man can be *dikaios* - just, righteous before God *(Rom. 3:24-28, 4:5, 5:1; Gal. 2:16, 3:11)*. This was the issue which led to the Reformation movement in the 16th century. The Reformers unanimously stressed the "*Sola fide, sola gratia*" principle, that is, man is justified only by the grace of God and by faith alone. This doctrine has become one of the central tenets of the Protestant Churches. We have to adhere to this precious heritage because this is the cornerstone upon which the salvation of man, the new life of man and the practical usefulness of Christian theology are founded. This principle indirectly says that the creation of new life in man is just such a sovereign act of God as our first creation was. We could not contribute to either; we can only accept both.

The *Sola fide, sola gratia* principle has to be maintained in Christian theology because there is always the temptation for man to try to make a contribution to his justification, to his new life, by some good works of merit or ethical value. In medieval theology this temptation was intense, reaching the point where a person's good works were considered as an important condition for his justification. It will be valuable to examine the process of how medieval theology reached this extreme position. The theologians of that time made an unjustifiable distinction concerning Faith. They discerned between *Fides generalis seu Catholica* (universal or catholic faith) on the one hand and *Fides implicita* (implicit faith) on the other. The *Fides generalis* could be acquired by clerics like priests and theologians only, because they went through proper education and training. It was regarded as enough for the laity, the mostly illiterate and uneducated common people, that they had *Fides implicita*, which was just barely enough for their salvation. *Fides implicita* meant an undeveloped, minimum kind of faith by which a common believer accepted what the Church believed, a faith in God based on faith in the Church. But the content of the faith of the Church remained hidden from the ordinary individual. Such a situation inevitably necessitates a display of visible good works on the part of the believer. Consequently, even if the common believer is unable to appreciate and understand the content of the faith of the Church, at least by his good works he will guarantee his salvation. Ultimately, this doctrine led to the remarkable position in which a person could "buy" salvation from God by "paying" with good works. In extreme cases, letters of indulgence were made available and people paid money for them. In these cases the good work was in the very act of buying, because precious money was "sacrified" for the purchase. The sale of letters of indulgence by a monk, Johann Tetzel, to raise money for the building of St. Peter's in Rome, precipitated the protest of Martin Luther that actually became the flashpoint that triggered the Reformation.

Without in any way defending this theory of two kinds of faith, we have to acknowledge that initially the numbers of people confessing Christianity grew rapidly. Waves of Euro-Asian people from the East were entering Europe in a period of intense migrations. They settled down and they took up the Christian religion. The Church had difficulties in coping with this situation. The introduction of the concept of *fides implicita* was born in such a crisis situation. The problem is that an emergency strategy became standardized as the norm, which led to the serious distortion of a fundamental principle of Christian faith. Hence we can understand the importance the Reformation placed on its affirmation of the original meaning and importance of faith in man's justification and redemption.

There still remain three questions to be answered: how is justification possible? What is the theological and what is the anthropological significance of justification? The possibility of justification is rooted in God, precisely in the three persons of the Trinity. Its first root is in the Father's will to save man and creation from sin and its tragic consequences. The second root is in the willingness of the Son to offer

Himself as a sacrifice for the redemption of man and that of the world. The third root is in the Holy Spirit's undertaking of the work of salvation, the application of the work of redemption which brings about the new creation of man and of the world. This has already begun, and reaches its fullness in the *eschaton*, the end of the age.

What is the theological significance of justification? To answer this question we have to realize that justification is related to sin. Justification is the divine answer to sin, so justification has to be dealt with in relation to sin. The perfect God created a perfect world, but sin entered into this world through man's folly. God has achieved His purpose: sin has been dealt a death blow, man has been returned to God, the spoiled creation has begun to undergo a new Creation and, in the fullness of time, His glory will be fully restored[6].

The crucial point in the plan of salvation is the justification of man. Why? Because the healing process of man and that of the world have to start at the very point where sin entered into this world. This point is the human soul. Since this is where the spoiling process started, here must also begin the healing process. This is why the justification of man is fundamentally important from the theological point of view. In the depth of the soul of man, where the rebellion against God started and the "No" to God was born and uttered, here the returning process to God has to begin. Here man must find an answering "Yes" to God's "Yes" in Christ. In this double "Yes" the justification of man takes place. With the justification of man the regeneration of man and that of the world have started and with it God's plan of salvation has begun to be implemented.

From the Christian anthropological standpoint the justification of man has enormous significance as we have seen (See: Part I, Section 4, Chapter 5). A fundamental teaching of Christian anthropology is that man, having sinned against God, lives under the judgement and punishment of God. Excluded from God's presence, man lives a life burdened with sickness, pain and misery, which life is destined to perish in death. Moreover, man faces the eternal punishment of condemnation. But there is an equally important statement of Christian anthropology, that sinful man does not necessarily travel towards a tragic end because His God appears to Him as Redeemer and Saviour, desiring to liberate him from sin and from its grave consequences. The Son redeemed man and the Holy Spirit carries out the work of Salvation. Christian anthropology does not propound a black and pessimistic view of man but offers a bright and optimistic vision. These two main teachings of Christian anthropology can be and must be seen as a unity. The two parts belong together and cannot be separated. If separated, they can be dangerous and misleading. Only their close relation to each other gives Christian anthropology a true, valid and comprehensive knowledge of man. Christian anthropology dares to speak about the tragically lost state of man only under the conditions of man's redemption, justification and salvation.

All this means that the story of man's fall in *Genesis 3* is only half the story of man. The second half is in Jesus Christ's parable of the Prodigal Son *(Luke 15:11-32)*. These two passages of the Bible closely relate to each other theologically and anthropologically. Man, the prodigal son, not only turned his back on the Father's house to pursue his own dangerous plan which ended in misery but, like the prodigal in the parable, he has the possibility of returning to his Father's home. Man has the possibility of returning to God, the only way out of the *cul de sac* of the sinful life. Justification is the embracing by God of the returned prodigal son, and with it commences the reinstallation of the prodigal into his full rights of sonship. This will be the subject of the next discussion.

5. Sanctification

The justification of man is not an end in itself; it has to be followed by sanctification. A plant which springs out of a seed is not a sufficient end; it is expected to grow and bear fruit. Justification is only the crucial beginning of new life in man. This has to grow daily until it conquers what the Bible calls "the old being", gradually and step by step transforming it until it yields good fruits for the benefit of mankind and for the glory of God. *(Gal. 5:22)*. Sanctification is a process of decisions and events in the justified and born-again individual by which this "new being" is growing at the expense of the "old man" *(Eph. 4:22-24, Col. 3:10)*. Theologically speaking, man in this process gradually becomes *Pneumatikos* - living under the guidance of the Holy Spirit - and less *Sarkikos* - living under the appetites of the flesh *(Rom. 8:5-14)*.

Sanctification is also the work of the Holy Spirit. Man cannot sanctify himself unless he is under the influence, inspiration and power of the Holy Spirit. Not only the beginnings of the new life - conversion and justification - are the works of the Holy Spirit in man, but the growth of this new life is also the work of the Holy Spirit.

The need for the sancitifcation of man is rooted in God. God is Holy. Consequently, all who belong to God also must be holy. This is the demand of God, who revealed clearly to the people of the Old Covenant:

"You shall be holy, for I, the Lord your God, am holy" *(Lev. 19:2).* The imperfect, unclean and sinful man must inevitably perish in the presence of the Holy God. Only the individual who is cleansed, purified and sanctified by God can live in His presence. In the justification which was conceived by Christ's vicarious suffering and death one is cleansed by God from sin. God looks at man in Christ and accounts him justified. But man in himself is still a sinful man. This principle was expressed by the Reformers in the following statement about man who is *"Simul justus et peccator",* that is, man is "at the same time both justified and sinful." Now in the process of sanctification the sinful character of man has to be progressively transformed to the character of the new life. This new life is made man's own by faith. God gave it to man in advance. But this new life also presents a task for man. God says to man in justification: "You are righteous again". In sanctification, He says: "Now really be the new man I have made you".

Thus sanctification is not completed in the work of the Holy Spirit alone. There remains a task for man, which E. Brunner calls "The imperative of discipleship"[7]. After conversion and justification man is indeed a new man, which fact is accepted by faith. If one accepts that he is a new man, now let him be this new man. At this point comes the human, ethical side of sanctification. God does not intend to carry out man's sanctification without the willingness and cooperation of man, both of which are required for the process of sanctification to be completed. *(Rom. 12:1-2; 1 Thess. 4:7; 2 Cor. 7:1; Heb. 12:14).* To sum up: justification and the birth into the new life are the acts of the Holy Spirit alone, but in the process of sanctification God requires man's cooperation with the sanctifying work of the Holy Spirit. However, even this willingness and cooperation are, in the last analysis, the product of the Holy Spirit secretly working in man's life.

The task of man in the process of sanctification can be described as *imitatio Christi* - the imitation of Christ, which means to follow the example of Jesus Christ. Of course, this imitation of Christ does not mean to mime Him in outer appearance, or to try to be another Saviour. After Him there is no need for saviours any more. But the imitation of Christ means to live according to the principles, ideas and teaching of Jesus Christ in the ever-changing circumstances of our life. To expound the content of this new life is the task of Christian ethics.

It suffices to say here that the Christian life in the process of sanctification can be characterized as a life lived in faith, hope and love, values which constitute the Biblical virtues. As a consequence, Christian life also follows the path of the cardinal virtues which are: prudence, justice, temperance and fortitude. In the third chapter of this section, we will expound the virtues more closely because of their importance in the process of sanctification.

What is said above about the life and conduct which are expected from those who enter into the opening stage of sanctification by conversion and justification, can be described as good works or, in the Biblical image, good fruits. These characterize the life of those who are in process of sanctification. These fruits are the consequence of both the secret work of the Holy Spirit in the believer and the justified believer's determination to follow the way of the virtues. However, an important aspect must be indicated: the good works which appear in man's life in the process of sanctification are really born out of gratitude to God; they are not offered as appeasement for past failure. Man, understanding that he has received forgiveness and justification as the result of Jesus Christ's self-sacrifice, now pledges in gratitude to yield his life to God, to live it in accordance with the will of God *(Gal. 2:20)*. Good works, in the Biblical sense, can be born only out of gratitude.

One more characteristic of sanctification has to be considered. Conversion and justification often take place in a moment; sanctification can be a long process. To be precise, it is a life-long task, a process which is never finished in this life and will be completed only in the *eschaton*, in the Kingdom of God *(Phil. 1:6)*.

There are two temptations we have to recognize in connection with sanctification: moralism and quietism. Moralism arises in the believer when he assumes that, having been justified, now he alone must carry on his own sanctification without the help of the Holy Spirit. This leads to frustration, stagnation and falling back in the Christian life. Quietism, on the other hand, is the opposite of moralism. The temptation in quietism is that the beliver feels himself so powerless that he fails to exert himself in his own sanctification as a human task and leaves it entirely to God. He forgets that the Holy Spirit wants to use the whole person, especially his will, in the process of Sanctification.

At the end of this chapter let us remind ourselves that one of the main tasks of ministers is that they are ordered by God to help people in their struggle towards conversion, so they may obtain justification by faith in God. They are to help people in the difficult process of sanctification by counselling, advising and leading them, so that they enter engergetically into their own sanctification by yielding "good fruits" to God and man in their lives. How can ministers help others unless they themselves have been through the pains and joys of the new birth, unless they themselves are living by faith and, with the help of the Holy Spirit, determinedly pursuing their own sanctification?

NOTES

1. L. Berkhof: Systematic Theology, p.483 f.
2. Ibid. p. 486.
3. See Part I, Section 4, Chapter 6, Point 1.
4. See Part I, Section 2, Chapter 6, Point 1.
5. E. Brunner: Dogmatics, Vol. III, pp 196.f.
6. See Part I. Section 4, Chapter 6, Point 1.
7. E. Brunner: Op. cit, p. 290.f.

Chapter 2

Grace and Faith

What is Grace? What is Faith? Faith and Grace as Unity

In the previous chapter we have seen how man can be justified before God on the basis of grace and faith. It is obvious that grace and faith are at the very foundation of Christian theology. The grace of God and man's faith in this gracious God make Christian theology and the Christian religion possible. God revealed Himself in Jesus Christ as a gracious God. We have the firm belief that human life in general is possible only because God is gracious, and in particular that man's justification and eternal life are possible only because God is gracious[1]. Because of the great importance of grace and faith we must probe them further.

1. What is Grace?

The word "grace" comes from the Latin *gratia* and is an important concept of the Biblical revelation. From God's perspective grace means that God, having been motivated by His love, shows understanding to man and deals with him tenderly, mercifully and lovingly for the benefit and fuller life of man.

In the Old Testament the Hebrew word for grace is *hesedh* which means the loving kindness and the mercy of God. The Old Testament speaks about Jahweh who is gracious to man and merciful *(Ex. 33:19; Neh. 9:17; Ps. 77:9; Joel 2:13)*. Because God is gracious, He is full of compassion, instead of being angry; He delights to grant pardon and He is abundant in mercy. In the Old Testament God's mercifulness also means that He is loyal and faithful to His covenant people[2].

In the new Testament the Greek words *eleos* and *charis* mean the mercy and compassion of God. Jesus Christ taught that God is merciful: "Be ye merciful even as your Heavenly Father is merciful" *(Luke 6:36)*. Jesus Christ was himself merciful to men, as can be seen from the Synoptic Gospels where it is recorded twelve times that Jesus Christ was motivated by compassion or mercy to help and heal needy people. The Apostle Paul also developed the concept of mercy in his theology. He did so because he wanted to maintain the meaning of grace according to

Jesus Christ's teaching against those who taught otherwise, mainly the rabbis. He underlined the gift-like character of mercy *(Eph. 2:8)* and its importance in the justification of man *(Rom. 3:24)*. Therefore the primal issue of Paul's theology is the relationship between grace on the one side and law or works on the other. Paul points out that the works of man are contrary to the mercy of God and never could acquire justification and salvation for man. Only the free grace of God can give justification and salvation to man *(Rom. 3:28, 6:23)*.

The New Testament talks not only about God's grace to man but also man's response to God's grace. Because man receives grace which he did not earn, the proper response of man must be mercy to other men *(Luke 6:36)* which can take the form of charity *(Acts 9:36; 2 Cor. 9:7)* and thanksgiving to God *(2 Cor. 9:11 f)*[(3)].

2. What is Faith?

Faith along with grace also has fundamental importance for Christian theology and religion. Here we look at the Biblical understanding of faith; an analysis of faith will be made in the following chapter.

In the Old Testament there are a good number of words for faith: *chasah* to seek refuge, *quawah* to wait for, to hope for, *yachal* to hope, *aman* and *he'emin* to put trust in, to rely on, to take God seriously as God. In the Old Testament, faith is closely related to the Covenant. It is expected and demanded by the members of the covenant people that they remain faithful to the covenant God. This faithfulness, *hesedh,* is absolutely required, so that faith in God is equivalent to being faithful to God. Thus "faith" in the Old Testament means primarily not a theoretical belief in God but a practice: to do God's will as it is expressed is in the Decalogue, the charter of the covenant.

The New Testament has an important word for faith: *pistis,* which we may translate as faith, belief or trust. In Christ's message, the demand for faith has a central importance besides the calling for repentance *(Mark 1:15)*. Jesus Christ grasped the opportunity to call His hearers to faith in God, in Himself and in the good news that He announced about the arrival of the Kingdom of God in His person. In Christ's teaching and preaching faith in God always meant not only accepting God as our heavenly Father but trusting in God's Almighty power and infinite love to men and utmost obedience to the will of God. Jesus Christ required faith in Him because He is the Son of God and he was sent by God to announce the arrival and the reality of the new age of the Kingdom of God[(4)].

111

In the Apostolic age the importance of faith grew considerably, as the means through which the vicarious suffering and death of Jesus Christ accomplished the redemption of mankind. Because they understood this so clearly, the Apostles logically stressed the importance of faith in Jesus Christ as redeemer, saviour and lord *(Acts 2:36)*. Since then Christian faith meant faith in Jesus Christ *(Gal. 3:22; Rev. 14:12)*. Consequently, faith meant the hearty acceptance and trust in the message - in preaching and witnessing - about salvation in Jesus Christ.

3. Grace and Faith as a Unity

Grace and faith belong together as the two sides of a coin. The grace of God is materialized in the salvation he offers to man. Faith is man's answer of acceptance for God's grace in salvation. Grace and faith therefore belong together because of the logic of the act of giving and receiving. There can be no successful giving without receiving what is given, and there is no act of receiving without the act of giving. For example, if one is invited for dinner, it is not enough to sit down to the table with plenty of food. The guest must stretch out his hands and take the food to his plate and eat. Otherwise, he remains hungry while sitting at a full table. Likewise the mercy of God offers salvation and invites us to receive it. Our faith in God's gift is the act of possessing and identifying salvation as our own. By faith objective salvation becomes subjective. Hence, faith may appear as an entirely human act, but many theologians insist that even the faith by which we grasp the divine grace is itself a product of God's grace because faith is the gift of God *(Eph. 2:8)*, a doctrine Augustine encapsulated in his saying "He who created the sun created eyes to see it".

Grace and faith are two important issues of Christian theology not only on a theoretical or academic level but also at the practical level too. Priests, ministers and pastors are called by God to become the stewards of God's mercy to men. Preachers offer the salvation of God to men; their sacred duty is to call people to faith in God, in Jesus Christ and in His good news of salvation.

NOTES

1.   See Part I, Section 2, Chapter 5, Point 7.
2.   A. Richardson: An Introduction to the Theology of the New Testament, p.281.f.
3.   ibid, p.282.
4.   See Part II, Section 2, Chapter 1, Points 2.3

Chapter 3

The Gifts of Spirit

The Fruits of Spirit, Biblical and Cardinal Virtues
Faith, Hope, Love, Other Virtues, Charismas

In the first chapter of this section we studied the work of the Holy Spirit in conversion, justification and sanctification. There we spoke about sanctification primarily from a formal point of view, that is, sanctification as the work both of the Holy Spirit and of man. However, we ought also to consider sanctification from the material point of view, that is, what is the content of sanctification? The answer is that a human life is in the process of sanctification when the gifts of the Holy Spirit progressively become apparent. So the sanctification of a human life occurs by and through the growing presence of the gifts of the Holy Spirit. The Holy Spirit which comes to dwell in man in a subjective and individual way after conversion and justification, has as His goal the sanctification of man's life. The Holy Spirit is in man's life influencing, inspiring, leading, comforting and presenting to him those gifts which are essential for the building up of a new being, pleasing to God. The material answer to the question: What are these gifts of the Holy Spirit in man? is twofold: The gifts of the Holy Spirit are the fruits of the Spirit; they are also those gifts called "Charismas". Let us expound each of these terms.

1. The Fruits of the Spirit

In the New Testament, there are several passages which enumerate the ethical characteristics of Christians. These are developed as the good fruits of the Holy Spirit, and they signify stages in the process of sanctification. *1 Cor. 13:13* mentions faith, hope and love as a "more excellent way" for believers. *Gal. 5:22-23* speaks of "Love, joy, peace, patience, kindness, goodness, faithfulness, gentleness and self-control". *Col. 3:12-13* enumerates such fruits as: "compassion, kindness, lowliness, meekness, patience, forbearing, forgiving". *2 Peter 1:5-7* lists such gifts as: "faith, virtue, knowledge, self-control, steadfastness, godliness, kindness and love". These fruits are brought forth by the Holy Spirit working secretly in believers, and they appear as "virtues" of the believers.

2. Biblical and Cardinal Virtues

Because of the variety of the fruits of the Holy Spirit, classical theology and ethics grouped them together as "virtues" and classified them in two main groups known as the Biblical and the Cardinal virtues. Biblical virtues are three: faith, hope and love. Cardinal virtues are four: prudence, justice, temperance, and fortitude. The principal difference between Biblical and Cardinal virtues is that Cardinal virtues can be acquired by human effort and they are not the exclusive prerogative of Christians. Cardinal virtues are the result of the Holy Spirit's general work in the world. Thus while the cardinal virtues cannot be absent from the life of Christians, even the fallen man who may deny the existence of God is still under the care and providence of God (Matt. 5:45) and may also exhibit these virtues. The Biblical virtues, however, are regarded by theologians as the special gifts of the Holy Spirit, and they can only be present in those who are converted, justified and in the process of sanctification. Thus the Biblical virtues of faith, hope and love in their purest, genuine and divine form can only be present in the Christian life.

3. Faith

In the previous chapter we studied the Biblical understanding of faith and its relationship to grace. Such faith is one of the most important gifts of the Spirit, and it requires further elucidation.

We may distinguish three kinds of faith: The first can be called everyday faith, because we use this faith in our everyday life and activity. This faith underlies all our trust in one another. For example, if I buy a tin of food I believe that its contents are exactly what the label indicates. I must trust the knowlege and experience of a particular medical doctor to place myself in his care; lacking such confidence I might well look for another doctor. Similarly, if I want to travel and decide to take a flight I must have confidence that the aircraft is airworthy, the pilot is a master of his profession and the plane will fly to the announced destination. Without such confidence I might well cancel my flight. It is obvious from what was noted above that without this kind of faith man cannot live a normal human life and human society cannot exist.

The second sort of faith that we may distinguish is scientific faith. Science could not develop without constructing and believing certain theories, hypotheses or models. These are basically presuppositions in which guessing and belief have a prominent role. When a working theory is constructed, accepted and believed at least temporarily, scientific research aims to verify it. If it cannot be verified it may well be rejected; on the other hand, if it can be verified then it becomes a scientific truth.

The third is religious faith. We may use P. Tillich's definition: "Faith is the state of being ultimately concerned." If man's ultimate concern is the truly ultimate, that is God, then man has genuine religious faith that cannot be fulfilled in this life alone. But if one's religious faith is concerned with a penultimate, that which is less than God, then man's religious faith is idolatrous faith. The objects of idolatrous faith can be not only religious idols, but profane gods like wealth, career, pleasure, sex, power or ideology. In these cases the penultimate passes as the ultimate but does not possess the power of the ultimate; this is the danger of idols. Idols promise the utmost fulfillment of man's life without having the power to give it. They can only fulfill penultimate concerns. When the goals of an idolatrous faith are attained disappointment takes place, because man understands that this fulfillment is not what he expected and hoped for. When faith is being fulfilled the faith itself disappears and this throws man into existential crisis. This is because one cannot live without faith; faith is that which holds man's personality together. Without this holding-together power, man's personhood disintegrates[1]. In the light of understanding of idolatrous faith, man's existential necessity for genuine religious faith becomes obvious and properly argued. Christian religion and theology offer a genuine religious faith for man and call upon him to have faith in the living God who is the Father of Jesus Christ. Thus God promises a new and full life beginning in the present moment and wholly fulfilled in the future. Only this faith in the living God can really hold man's person together, can heal and transform man.

Christian theologians of a bygone ago distinguished two types of faith. They spoke of: "Fides quae creditur" - faith which is believed, and "fides qua creditur" - faith by which one believes. This distinction seems somewhat artificial because faith cannot be separated from its content. Christian faith has three important characteristics. Classical theology discerns these elements in faith: notitia, assensus, and fiducia. Noticia means knowledge. Faith must have a content. Without the content of faith there can be no faith at all. The content of the Christian faith is what God revealed in Jesus Christ about Himself, concerning man's sin and salvation and the new life which is possible through the work of the Holy Spirit[2]. Assensus means to agree to or to assent to the content of faith. It is to accept the knowledge communicated by faith as really true, important and valid. But the complete Christian faith also has the element of fiducia, that is a wholehearted trust in the content of the faith. On this basis of trust, the believer relies entirely on faith and on God who gave the promises. Each of these three elements is important in itself but only the three elements together constitute a genuine Christian faith. Without *notitia* faith is blind; without *assensus* one cannot reach the stage of *fiducia*; without *fiducia* faith remains theoretical. The three elements must be present in equal proportion in the faith of Christians, otherwise faith suffers distortion. If the intellectual element is dominant in faith without trust in its content, there is imminent danger that the Christian faith is distorted into an empty expression of a religious philosophy. If the emotional element becomes dominant in Christian faith the danger is of degradation into a chiliastic or "enthusiastic" type of faith which, in its extreme manifestations, proves to be distractive to non-Christians instead of being attractive to faith. In the sectarian movements one can find several examples of this. If *notitia* and *assensus* are present in the Christian faith without the element of *fiducia* then the temptation is for the believer to be easily caught by the trap of legalism; he himself wants to construct a basis from good works upon which his trust can rest, leading to an unbearable uncertainty of his own salvation. It can be seen that these three elements of faith correspond to the three main faculties of man, the intellectual, volitional and emotional faculties, so that healthy Christian faith claims the whole human person.

At this point let it be stressed that Christian ministers, priests and pastors must keep a keen eye on whether these three elements of faith are present in a healthy proportion in the faith of their parishioners. If not, they must make the necessary corrections to their teaching to re-establish the balance. Various types of Christians' faith exist on the practical level which can be discerned as follows:

Traditional faith can be found among those who are born into Christianity and educated in the Christian religion. They usually have a great deal of knowledge of the content of the Christian faith but they do not have personal trust in it. They accept Christianity intellectually but they do not allow it to affect, shape and lead their lives. They are nominal Christians only and for them Christianity is only one religion among others. They know what Christianity is but they deny its power *(2 Tim. 3:5)*.

Temporal faith is the next to be mentioned. Jesus Christ talked about it in *Matthew 13:20-22*, and it is referred to in *Hebrews 6:4-6* and *Acts 8:13*. It is a temporary faith which appears initially to be genuine faith but, after a time, turns out to have no roots and dies out when difficulties arise.

Faith in miracles expresses itself in two ways. The passive type accepts that God is able to perform miracles. The active type itself performs miracles *(Matt. 17:20)*. This latter type of faith is rare because it is a special gift of God, it is one of the "Charismas".

Genuine or redemptive faith is the gift of God and this is living in those who are the elect of God *(1 Cor. 12:9; Eph. 2:8)*. By this faith the believer accepts as true all words of God and with it the promises of God, namely the forgiveness of sins, the resurrection and eternal life through Jesus Christ. Through the exercise of redemptive faith these will all become reality in his personal life[3].

As well as these positive characteristics, faith has two sicknesses: doubt and anxiety. Doubt is mainly intellectual in character and paralyses the element of notitia in faith, making it weak if not impossible. Doubt is not always destructive, however, and when it is overcome the result is a stronger faith *(Mark 9:24)*. Anxiety indicates a lack of faith. When faith dies its place is occupied by anxiety. Anxiety is a complex feeling and it is an unnatural state of the human soul. Among its ingredients are doubt, fear, restlessness, tension, meaninglessness, cynicism, alienation and a sense of isolation. Anxiety comes from lack of *fiducia*, the unconditional trust in God.

The Christian minister's duty is to kindle and to nurture faith in the parishioners. Faith is the *Sine qua non* of the Christian life. Without faith a Christian life is not possible at all *(Heb. 11:6)*. Man through faith experiences forgiveness and the New Life, and by faith may become the son of God again *(John 1:12)*. Faith is one of the most precious gifts of God. It is necessary for this life where everything is in transition. When this life fades and with it everything that was precious, only faith remains to lead one home to God *(2 Tim. 4:7-8)*.

4. Hope

Besides faith, hope - *elpis* in Greek - is also a Biblical virtue and is likewise the gift of the Holy Spirit. Paul mentions hope immediately after faith *(1 Cor. 13:13)* and by so doing he emphasises the indispensability and importance of hope in the Christian life.

Hope is necessary for all human life. The ancient Greco-Roman thinkers realized the importance of human hope and enshrined it in the sentence: *"Dum spiro spero"*, that is: "While I am breathing, I am hoping".

Greek mythology narrates that the gods, having been offended by man, punished men by taking away their gifts from them. Only hope was not taken, so that men should comfort themselves with it. Human hope is immanent hope, that is, it hopes for something that can be found in this world. If human hope does not materialize, disappointment, pessimism and sorrow overtake man. In contrast, Christian hope is transcendental and can be properly understood only in relation to faith. Hope presupposes faith and is, in fact, the content of faith for which one goes on hoping. J. Moltmann says that "Faith believes God to be true, Hope awaits the time when this truth shall be manifested"[(4)]. The characteristics of Christian hope include a trust that the promise of God will surely be fulfilled even though it be in the future. This trust comes from the acceptance of God's self-revelation, that He is almighty and faithful and that what He promised will be realized sooner or later. He is able to do it and His words and promises stand firm *(Pss. 33:4, 119:89; Isa. 40:8; 1 Peter 1:23, 25)*.

We may distinguish between the great hope which waits for the ultimate fulfillment of God's promises of resurrection, the Kingdom of God and the new creation, which will occur at the end of this world in the *eschaton*, and small hopes, which the believer expects from God in this world and in his everyday life. When hope disappears, anxiety and despair occupy its place in the human soul. So the presence of these in one's daily life indicates weakness or lack of hope. Jesus Christ warned His followers against being anxious *(Matt. 6:25-34)*. Paul warned the Thessalonians against over-strong enthusiasm and chiliasm *(2 Thess. 2:1-5)* which can be equally dangerous. The Christian minister's task is to nurture a truly Christian hope in his parishioners and to fight against anxiety, despair, pessimism, hopelessness and fear. Only those Christians can have a healthy faith in whom hope is alive and strong.

5. Love

The third Biblical virtue is love, the crown of Biblical virtues. Paul stresses that faith and hope will be fulfilled and thus become superfluous, but love remain forever *(1. Cor. 13:13)*. This is not the only reason love is the main Biblical virtue. There is a second reason, namely that love binds the believer both to God and to his fellow man, while faith and hope are directed to God only. This is why Jesus Christ stresses love as the great commandment for man *(Mark 12:30-31)*.

Because confusion and misunderstanding surround the word Love we have to clarify its Biblical and theological meaning. There are different ideas conveyed by the one word love. The ancient Greeks knew five kinds of love, four of which recur in the New Testament. *Philia* means love between friends which makes friendship possible. *Philadelphia* means the love of sisters and brothers. *Epithymia* means desire of the flesh, sinful desire or lust. *Eros,* which does not occur in the New Testament, is the name of the god of love in Greek mythology, hence its meaning in modern psychology, of sexual drive and passion, although its original meaning is "longing for values". Lastly, there is *Agape* which, in the New Testament usage, describes God's love for man and man's love toward God. *Agape* love is what the Bible and theology are concerned to discuss and hence is regarded as the third Biblical virtue.

Genuine love is a complex virtue. Firstly, in this love some of the elements of other types of love are present in greater or lesser proportion. So in this love, desire, longing and aspiration values are present latently; even the element of self-love is present. In some cases even *eros* love can colour it. Secondly, love is not only a matter of emotion as it is often supposed to be, but in this love the whole person participates including the intellectual and volitional faculties. This is because love is the most profound factor of human life. Theologically speaking it is because man is created by the love of God for the love of God[5]. Philosophically speaking, love is the basic desire and drive of man to re-unite with that from which he is separated but originally belonged. Love is therefore the existential desire of man to overcome this separateness and to reestablish the state of original unity. Love is born from the feeling of the lack of its object and love mobilizes the whole person to acquire that which is painfully lacking[6].

Thus, the central importance of love in man's life derives from the fact that God himself is love and the source of love *(1 John 4:16)*. Jesus Christ called upon His followers to realize the principles of the great commandment: "You shall love the Lord your God with all your heart, and with all your soul and with all your mind and with all your strength...You shall love your neighbour as yourself" *(Mark 12:30-31)*. This is why the Christian religion was traditionally called the religion of love. This is why outstanding theologians of all ages emphasized the importance of love for the Christian life[7]. This is why the Christian life in the process of sanctification must reach the stage where life is not only a life lived in faith and hope, but which lives in love too. Christian believers have to follow the principle of the divine love and realize it in every relation of their life.

119

The sanctified man's attitude to God is love. It originates from the love of God. The Christian understands that the infinite extension of God's love culminates in God's work for the redemption of Man *(Eph. 2:4-7, 3:18, 19)*. Only this divine love can kindle answering love in man's heart. Man's love to God must materialize in true worship of God. This ought to happen in man's heart because there the Holy Spirit is dwelling making man's body the temple of God *(2 Cor. 3:16)*. This includes in itself not only adoration, thanksgiving, confession of sin and supplication but listening to and accepting God's will. Those in whom God is dwelling cleanse themselves from all sin and withstand temptations and expell evil thoughts *(Eph. 6:11 f; Phil. 4:8)*. Moreover, they develop an inner community with God which is described by theology as the "mystical union with God". Only God in us, with whom we are in this union, can give to us the inner conviction and assurance about the reality of our salvation and the conviction that inseparably belong to God forever *(Rom. 8:38-39)*. This is the testimony of the Holy Spirit in our soul and therefore we can say: *Abba* - "Father" to God *(Rom. 8:15)*. Only those in whom God dwells through the Holy Spirit can be the true disciples of Christ and carry out their duty of witnessing by word and by deed *(Matt. 28:18-20, 7:21)*.

According to the great commandment of Jesus Christ the right attitude of man to other men is love; "Love your neighbour as yourself". The love Jesus Christ meant is revealed to us in His new commandment: "You love one another; even as I have loved you, that you also love one another" *(John 13:34)*.

Jesus Christ's love to men has three features: His love was a forgiving, benefitting and sacrificing love. We are dedicated as Christians to follow these three principles in our relationship with other men. We forgive those who have wronged us. We are to understand that the only real solution to sin is forgiveness, the divine solution. Without forgiveness, sin will grow and multiply and destroy both its subject and its object. Sin is born from hatred and kindles revenge. Both of them aim at man's destruction. Only forgiveness can neutralize the poison of sin, but Man has not yet learned this lesson. Divorces, the falling apart of families, violence and wars provide sufficient illustration of man's unwillingness to forgive. Where there is human life there is sin, and where there is sin there must be forgiveness for life's sake.

The process of sanctification also requires the desire to benefit one's fellow man, if one really is following the example of Jesus Christ. He lived not to seek His own well-being or benefit but that of others. He wished to enrich others and not Himself. His whole attitude was not of one who came to rule but of one who came to serve *(Matt. 20:28)*. He knew that one of the basic principles of life is serving. He said: "My Father is working still, and I am working" *(John 5:17)*. Jesus Christ rendered a service which aimed to heal the wounds caused by sin. He healed the sick, granted forgiveness to those who needed it. He gave comfort to the broken hearted, hope to the hopeless and an inner freedom to the poor and oppressed. So the disciples of Jesus Christ have to continue His work in seeking and doing such acts which are for the benefit of others. Therefore the Christian attitude to others never can be motivated by selfish interests, by the desire to obtain gain from others, but by seeking how can one help others. Christians offer themselves as those who sincerely want to help, mediate and serve. They have to be honest, sincere and true friends of others. In doing this they prove to be the "salt of the earth" *(Matt. 5:13)*.

Jesus Christ's love for us has a third feature. His love was so great that it made Him ready for self sacrifice to redeem mankind. The cross of Christ is the utmost proof of His self-sacrificing love to us. The validity of love can be measured by the sacrifice born from it. Jesus knew well the other great principle of life; the principle of sacrifice. He said "unless a grain of wheat falls into the earth and dies, it remains alone but if dies, it bears much fruit" *(John 12:24)*. Life can be promoted only by sacrifice. For example: If the student does not sacrifice time for study he will not make progress. If a mother does not sacrifice her time, energy and life for her children they will never learn how to fit into a complex society. The worker must devote himself to his work in the factory: Without this there would be no modern machines to run modern life. There is only life where there is sacrifice.

Christians must follow Jesus Christ's footsteps in this respect also. They must understand, follow and practise wholeheartedly this principle and show their love through sacrifice. The process of sanctification is not found in one who expects sacrifice from others, but in one who gives sacrificially to others. Only then can man be sure that God's Spirit is dwelling in him, that he is a true child of God and fellow worker for God *(I Cor. 3:9)*.

Christian life is life lived in love. This love is not the product of man, t is the gift of God the Holy Spirit. He who stands in the beaming rays of God's love which flows from the cross of Christ will be filled by love. He can mirror this divine love around this world to men. Humanity is hungry or this divine love. Man cannot live without love; he was created for love. _ove for man is the same as sunshine is for the flower: without sunshine, the flower will never bloom and just vegetates without its essential colour and fragrance. Man may possess many things, such as philosophies, economic and political systems, culture and civilization, but the world is short of love. Man needs love in personal relations, in family life, in the community, in offices and in factories, even in international life. Because of the lack of love the world is as it is. Christians are called by God to be the transmitters of the divine love in this world.

Love also has its sicknesses. When man is not loving the living God he will love idols which will eventually corrupt him. Love deteriorated becomes selfish love. When love disappears or dies indifference appears; in extreme cases, hatred arises, the antipode of love. Hate is a destructive force not only for others but for those who exercise it.

Christian ministers are called by God to be the advocates of this divine love. They should not preach a message of Mosaic law to establich righteousness, but the love of God unconditionally and unrestrictedly. If a minister is well aware of this task and performs it then the congregation will be awake and will show the signs of life.

6. Other Virtues

Besides the Biblical virtues there are cardinal virtues which also must be present in the life of believers in the process of sanctification. Cardinal virtues are also the gifts or fruits of the Holy Spirit. But because of the universal work of the Holy Spirit in the life of the whole of mankind the cardinal virtues can equally be present in the life of non-believers too.

It was noted that the New Testament contains a list of different qualities *(Gal. 5:22-23; Col. 3:12-13; 2 Pet. 1:5-7; Phil. 4:8)*, which the medieval theologians summarized in four cardinal virtues. These are:

Prudence, which includes in itself knowledge, wisdom and cleverness. Prudence is the virtue which suggests the possible solution or action in any given situation.
Justice, which enables one to treat individuals in different ways but according to the principle of love.
Temperance, which enables one to exercise necessary and sufficient self-control, and
Fortitude is the virtue which encourages one to withstand temptations and endure the burdens of life.

The cardinal virtues accompany the Biblical virtues and they flow from them. Where the Biblical virtues are present the cardinal virtues necessarily will be present. Both of them are the gifts of the Holy Spirit in the life of believers in the process of sanctification.

7. The Charismas

There are other gifts of the Holy Spirit beside the virtues which Classical theology calls "Charismas", those "Spiritual gifts" mentioned in *1 Corinthians 12:8-10*. Here Paul lists nine charismas: wisdom, knowledge, faith, healing, miracles, prophecy, distinguishing between spirits, tongues and interpretation of tongues. The charismas are the special gifts of the Spirit. Not all believers receive these gifts, although the fruits of the Holy Spirit are available to every believer. God gives charismas to those whom He wants according to His free will.

Some of these charismas are very attractive, such as healing and speaking in tongues. There are groups within contemporary Christendom who hold healing sessions for the sick while some even practice exorcism - the casting out of evil spirits. Speaking in tongues is practised mainly in the Pentecostal Church. Because of its spectacular character, it has attracted much attention in some places, but it is certainly unattractive to others. Moreover, the spiritual value of speaking in tongues may be questioned. Even Paul who mentions it warns: "In Church I would rather speak five words with my mind in order to instruct others than ten thousand words in tongues" *(1 Cor. 14:19)*.

To close this section let it be emphasized that the sum of the meaning of the Christian ministry is to help people to undergo conversion, to experience justification and to help in the process of sanctification with the goal that they become mature Christian persons so that they will find the meaning of their life in living for the service of mankind and for the glory of God. Without maintaining this aim constantly, Christian ministers, priests, and pastors easily become something else. They may become a celebrant of a religion or a religious philosopher or a social reformer or simply a clerical manager of a congregation. In such cases, they miss their calling to be fellow-workers of God in His grand work of the salvation of mankind and the world.

NOTES

1.   P. Tillich: Dynamics of Faith (Harper Colophon Books, 1957) p.1.f.
2.   See Part I, Section 1, Chapter 4, Point 5.
3.   W. Heyns: Dogmatics, p. 302.f (Budapest, 1925).
4.   J. Moltmann: Theology of Hope, p.20.
5.   E. Brunner: Dogmatics, Vol. II, p.73.
6.   P. Tillich: Systematic Theology, Vol III, p.134 f.
7.   Augustine said: *Ama et fac quod vis* - "love, and do what you wish". He understood love will guide man's activity to a good end. In modern Theology P. Tillich emphasised the importance of love. J. Fletcher in his Situation Ethics said "love is the only commandment".

SECTION THREE

The Doctrine of the Church

Chapter 1

Biblical Understanding of the Church

Introduction, The Church in the Bible
The Characteristics of the first Church
The Biblical Symbols of the Church

1. Introduction

It has been said before that the work of the Holy Spirit is twofold. He works in individuals creating new life in man by leading him through conversion, justification and sanctification. The Holy Spirit also creates a new community among the believers, which is the Church. (See Part III, Section 2, Ch. 1.). We have yet to examine this aspect of the Holy Spirit's work, an important part of our study because faith in the Church is an article of the Christian Faith. The Apostolic Creed says: "I believe in...the Holy Catholic Church; the communion of saints".

The area of doctrine which deals with the Church is called "Ecclesiology", from the Greek word *ecclesia*, which means those called out from the sinful world by God and organized into a special community. *Ecclesia* simply means "Church". The English word Church, however, comes from the Greek word *Kyriakon* which means "The house of the Lord". Other names of the Church like *Kirk, Kerk* and the German *Kirche* all come from the same root. Ecclesiology means the theological understanding the Church has of itself. Ecclesiology deals with such questions as: What is the Church? What is its task? What means has the Church for completing its task? What is the structure of the Church? What is the role of the clergy and laity? etc.

To answer these different questions, Ecclesiology has developed branches which deal with specific aspects of the Church's life. Ecclesiology in the narrow sense deals with the nature of the Church and

125

the criteria for the Church. Sacramentology studies the means by which the Church accomplishes its task. Missiology deals with the task and mission of the Church, including *diakonia* which studies Christian service both in the Church and in the world. Ecumenology seeks the ways of unity among the various denominations of the Church. Ecclesiology is actually the third main aspect of pneumatology besides soteriology, the study of salvation and pneumatology, the study of the Holy Spirit[1].

We will deal with these three main branches of Ecclesiology in subsequent chapters.

2. The Church in the Bible

The Church is not a result of realization of a human idea or plan, but is the work of the Holy Spirit. Its origin goes back to the Bible and it is found both in the Old and the New Testaments. The Old Testament Church is the predecessor of the New, and the Christian Church as we know it has its origin at the first Pentecost.

The name of the Old Testament Church is *Qahal Jahweh*. Its Hebrew root means "to call", hence the name means "those whom Jahweh called" or the "elect people" the "people of God". The origin of the Old Testament Church goes back to the calling of Abraham by God. God elected Abraham and his offspring and successors as the people of Israel and as God's covenant people they were given the law of Moses as a sign of God's lordship over the world *(Ex. 19:5-6)*.[2]

In the New Testament, *Acts of the Apostles* Ch.2 narrates the birth of the first Christian Church in Jerusalem on the first Pentecost. This was not an unexpected event since Jesus Christ promised His disciples the coming of the Holy Spirit which would give them power to accomplish the task of founding His Church. Ten days after the ascension of the resurrected Christ, the Holy Spirit arrived in the form of a mighty wind and tongues of fire distributed and resting on the disciples. This outpouring of the Holy Spirit transformed the disciples into Apostles, filling them with divine power. They spoke in tongues, which attracted interest among the different nationalities gathered in Jerusalem for the festivities. Peter delivered the first sermon of the Church. In it he preached about Jesus Christ as the crucified and risen Lord and urged the crowd: "Repent, and be baptized every one of you in the name of Jesus Christ, and you shall receive the gift of the Holy Spirit" *(Acts 2:38)*. Three thousand men were baptized on that day and they founded the first Church, the "Mother

Church" of all Churches around the world. The Church then and now is the work of the Holy Spirit.

3. The Characteristics of the First Church

The first Christian Church serves as the model in many respects for the Church of all ages. Let us survey the characteristics of this early Church.

First is that the *Kerygma* was preached, the good news of the Salvation of man in the name of the crucified and risen Lord Jesus Christ. Salvation is a free gift of God and available for everyone who repents and is baptized. Those who believe in it will receive the Holy Spirit as an assurance of salvation and as a guide in their new life.

The Church is born out of the preaching of the Gospel. Without preaching the Gospel there is no Church. This is one of the mysteries and wonders of the Church. Priests, ministers and pastors have to learn it well: when and where the Gospel is preached, the Church is born, because the Holy Spirit leads people to repentance.

The second characteristic of the first Church was *Koinonia*, the community and the fellowship of the believers *(Acts 2:42)*. Those who repented and were baptized could not live in isolation. They accepted each other as brothers and sisters in faith, partners in salvation and the members of the family of God and co-inheritors of the Kingdom of God. This fellowship of community of the believers is the visible side of the Church. It is expressed wherever the believers came together for worship, prayer and eucharist or for any other occasion. To be a Christian means belonging to a new type of community called the Church.

Without true *koinonia* there is no strong Church. The lack of *koinonia* in our age weakens Churches. Many church-members attend services to seek their own salvation, comfort and peace but are not interested in those who sit beside them in the pews. The leaders of the Church have to promote friendship, fellowship and community life in the Church.

The third characteristic of the first Church was *diakonia*, which is service *(Acts 2:45)*. The first Christians could not accept that some of them should live in need and poverty. The rich members of the Church found a way to help the needy among them, even to the extent of selling their property and placing their funds at the disposal of the Church. In doing so they created a communal community. This was also the work of the

Holy Spirit.

This *diakonia* is the ground of the social responsibility of the Church, and the basis of its charity. On a broader front, Christians bear responsibility not only for their own brethren but for the society and the world in which they are living. Without *diakonia* there is no true fellowship and its lack proves that either the *kerygma* which is proclaimed is not proclaimed validly or the Christians who hear it are not obeying it. Where any of these special marks of the Church are lacking the presence of the true Church is questionable.

4. The Biblical Symbols of the Church

There are other names in the Bible for the Church beside *Qahal Jahweh, Ecclesia,* and the "People of God." The Church is also called the "Flock of God" *(Acts 20:28)*, its shepherd is Christ and the guardians are the pastors. Another symbol of the Church is the "temple", "building" or "home" of God where God chooses to dwell *(1 Cor. 3:9, 16; Eph. 2:21-22)*. The Church is also called the "household of God" where God is the father and the members are the children *(Eph. 2:19)*. In the Pauline writings the Church is frequently called the "body of Christ", its head is Christ and the individual believers are the members of the mystical body of Christ *(1 Cor. 12:12-30; Eph. 1:22, 23, 5:23; Col. 1:18)*. The Church is also called the "bride of Christ" with whom Christ will unite in the Kingdom of God *(Eph. 5:25; Revel. 19:7)*[3].

NOTES

1.   See Part III, Introduction, Point 3.
2.   A. Richardson: An Introduction to the Theology of the New Testament, p.284.f.
3.   ibid. p. 254.f.

Chapter 2

The Marks of the Church

**The Classical Definition, Marks, Notes and the Protestant
Principle of the Church, the Paradox of the Church**

1. The Classical Definition of the Church

In the previous chapter we mentioned three characteristics of the
Church which can be regarded as a kind of definition: The Church is there
where the *kerygma* is preached, *koinonia* exists and *diakonia* is practised
(if we presuppose that *koinonia* includes the observation of the
sacraments). The classical definition of the Church in dogmatic theology
contains three statements. According to this the Church is *coetus
electorum* - the Company of the Elect, *corpus Christi* - the Body of Christ
and *communio sanctorum* - the Communion of Saints.

The idea of the Church as *coetus electorum* comes from *John 15:16*.
Here Jesus Christ says to the disciples: "You did not choose me, but I
chose you." According to E. Brunner this points out the "eternal election"
of God as the basis of the Church. Those who were elected by God, are
called by God into the Church. This is the transcendent ground of the
Church and the eternal election of God is being realized in the course of
the history of the Church[1].

The Church defined as the *corpus Christi* is based on Paul's
concept of the Church as the "Body of Christ." *(1 Cor. 11:12-30; Eph.
1:22)*. This idea is drawn from the conviction of the first Christians that
they belonged to the new covenant of Jesus Christ which is in His broken
body and shed blood. They participated in the covenant by faith and by
their continued life in the Church community, they are continuing the work
of Jesus Christ. Therefore they consider those who are assembled in the
Church as the members of the mystical body of Christ. The Church's head
is Christ and members execute the will of the Head of the Church *(Gal.
2:20; Eph. 4:15-16)*. The Church is one body with many members, which
body has one head *(Rom. 12:5; Eph. 5:23)*.

The Church can be described as *communio sanctorum* which is
based on *Acts 2:42*. There the Church is regarded as a community of
believers who were being called out of the world by God into the Church,

the spiritual community of the saved. They are called saints because they are redeemed from their sins by Christ and sanctified by the Holy Spirit for entering into the Kingdom of God *(1 Cor. 1:2; 2 Thess. 2:13; Rev. 21:27)*, where they serve both God and man.

We can say together with Brunner that each of these definitions represents a special aspect of the Church. The first points to its transcendent origin, the second to its historical reality and the third to its spiritual character. The unity of the three must be maintained in a balanced way because only this can secure the real Church[2].

2. Marks of the Church

Beside the definition of the Church classical theology speaks about the traditional marks of the Church, those features which are the distinctive characteristics of the Church only. These marks are described in the Nicene Creed (381 A.D.): "I believe...One Holy Catholic and Apostolic Church". Hence the four traditional marks of the Church are One, Holy, Catholic and Apostolic. Let us look at the meaning of them.

The Church is "One". It cannot be otherwise because there is only one Christ, there is only one salvation and the Apostles founded only one Church *(Eph. 4:4-5; Acts 2:41)*. The New Testament talks about "Churches" but this refers to the different local Churches which were, for example, in Ephesus, Corinth, Philippi, Rome, etc., and they all belong to the One Church and they can be regarded as the branches of the one Church. Because the Church is the body of Christ, there cannot be two bodies or more *(1 Cor. 12:12-30)*. Even the various denominations which like to call themselves the true Church are but the parts of the "One" Church.

The Church is "Holy" not because of itself but because of the sanctifying work of the Holy Spirit. This is achieved by the Word of God and by His Spirit. Consequently the Church belongs to Holy God and is obedient to his will. The sanctity of the Church is not derived from its moral quality or otherworldliness, but from its spiritual origin, a situation which includes in itself the other two qualities. The Church is neither infallible nor indefectible. Church history provides enough examples of the opposite. But the Church is able to overcome all weaknesses because of the work of the Holy Spirit in it[3].

The Church is "Catholic". One may misunderstand this as speaking of the Roman Catholic Church solely. But catholicity in its original meaning encompasses both universality and authenticity. The Church is "universal" in that it exists for all humans, it accepts everybody and therefore is an open community for all people. This universality also means that the Church is interested in man as the creation of God and not as a creature distinguished by class, race, sex or age *(Gal. 3:28)*. The Church even tries to remove the divisive borders among men *(Eph. 2:14)*. The catholicity of the Church also means its authenticity, that is what the Church preaches and practices. It is from God and is sufficient for salvation because God says so.

The Church is "Apostolic". This means that the Church is "built upon the foundation of the apostles and prophets, Christ Jesus himself being the cornerstone" *(Eph. 2:20)*. The apostolicity of the Church involves in itself at least three important concepts. First, the foundation of the Church is Jesus Christ who is called the cornerstone of the Church, the underlying strength by which it all holds together. This is the only right of the Church to exist and the purpose for which the Church exists. Second, apostolicity suggests continuity which involves mission. The work of salvation by Jesus Christ was prepared by the Prophets and carried on by the Apostles, so that as the Church stretches out in time the same thing occurs as happened in the first Church: The *kerygma* is preached, the sacraments are administered, *koinonia* and *diakonia* practised. Third, the Church remains apostolic so far as it remains faithful to Jesus Christ. Thus, the Church has to stand on the cornerstone of Jesus Christ and to withstand the destabilizing impact of heretical temptations. These features give a static interpretation of apostolicity. Its dynamic meaning is that when the Spirit of Jesus Christ is living and acting in the Church, it is led on its way in accordance with the will of God. This true apostolicity of the Church is the work of the Holy Spirit together with the other marks[4].

3. Notes of the Church

The words '"Mark" and "Note" actually have the same meaning but we use them separately in order to make a clearer distinction between the "Traditional Marks" of the Church and the "Notes of the Church" recognized by the Reformers. In the age of Reformation the question of the signs, marks or notes of the true Church were raised. This was because the "Old" Church accused the Protestant Churches of not being the "true" Church. The Reformers had to work out the criteria by which the presence of the "true" Church could be determined. They set out these criteria in the doctrine of the *Nota Ecclesiae* - the Notes of the Church, which is in the following form: "The true Church exists where the word of God is preached and the Sacraments are truly administered"[5]. Some Reformers add a further criterion of Church discipline.

This formula is based on the Scriptures and it is a precious heritage of the Protestant Churches not only to establish themselves as Churches, but to defend themselves against any accusation that calls in question their true nature.

4. The Protestant Principle of the Church

There is one more lesson which the Reformers offer to us in connection with the Church. this was formulated in the principle of *semper reformanda*, that is the Church must be continuously reformed. This is an important principle and Protestant ecclesiology must take it seriously. There is a constant danger as generations follow each other that the Church clings to the traditions of the forefathers, to old theological concepts and obsolete language and liturgy which have lost their relevance for contemporary members of the Church. As a result the Church easily becomes petrified and lifeless and a museum of the past, unable to fulfill its vocation in the present. It is therefore necessary for the Church to be reformed, renewed and rejuvenated from age to age, from generation to generation, on the local, national, and world level. Only this principle of continuous reformation can give the Church the necessary flexibility and adaptability to cope with new problems and situations as they arise in contemporary society [6].

The principle of *semper reformanda* must not be misused and should not lead to the opposite extreme, which would renew the Church by discarding all tradition, precious values of the past and the treasures of the preceeding generations. In the process of continuous reformation the question is not which *new* things could replace the *old* one, but rather how the *old* concepts, doctrine and ceremonies can be made relevant in a new situation.

5. The Paradox of the Church

There are at least three more characterisitics of the Church which should be regarded as essential attributes or marks of the Church. Their common feature is that they contain contradictions, so that we use the word "paradox" to describe them. These are as follows:

The Church is both "visible" and "invisible" at the same time. The visible Church is the institutionalized, organized Church as it appears in this world. Membership of the invisible Church is known only to God. The invisible Church also unites believers of the past and of the future with those who belong to the present visible Church. These are "all the saints" who from the beginning of the world were called, justified and sanctified by God. It should also be stressed that there are not two churches but only one, and that the invisible Church is somehow present in the visible Church.

The Church is both" militant" and "triumphant". The first term describes the Church as it is living in this world: witnessing worshipping and serving amidst temptations, abuse and persecution and this is the reason why the Church has often had a militant attitude and life-style in this world fighting the good fight so that the will of God may be implemented. The second expression denotes the future, eschatological position of the Church, when temptations, trial and persecution will be overcome and it will be victorious, triumphant and glorious. *(Rev. 21)*.

The Church has both "horizontal" and "vertical" dimensions. This is because the Church is "living on the earth but belonging to heaven"; the Church is not from this world but for this world. The calling of the Church is from "above" but it is sent to serve here "below". From this unique situation comes the meaning of its service: to be the communicator of a transcendent wisdom, a plan of salvation and of power to this world. In this dialectical situation, the Church must face two temptations. First, the Church is tempted to be transcendent, that is to deal with only heavenly things, forgetting that she also has to provide answers and solutions to earthly problems. The second occurs when the Church is tempted with immanence becoming so involved in worldly, everyday things, problems and ideas that she forgets her transcendent vocation. The horizontal and vertical dimensions of the Church must be kept in balance.

Theologians have to know these main characteristics of the Church which result in a better and deeper understanding of the nature of the Church as a living organism in this world. Without this understanding it is likely that the Church will yield to these constant temptations, becoming deformed, other than she ought to be.

NOTES

1. E. Brunner: Dogmatics, Vol. III, p.23.f.
2. ibid. p.27.
3. J. Macquarrie: Principles of Christian Theology, p.401.f.
4. E. Brunner: Dogmatics, Vol III, p.1119.f.
5. J. Calvin: Institutes IV.I.10.
6. E. Brunner: Dogmatics, Vol, III,p.91.

Chapter 3

The Mission of the Church

The Missionary Commandment, Various Concepts of Mission
Medieval, Liberal, Modern

1. The Missionary Commandment

In the previous chapters we have studied the doctrine of the Church to see precisely what should be its character. Now it is time to answer the questions of what the Church is for, what is its vocation, what its task and mission might be in this world. Christian theology is in a favourable position to answer this question because Jesus Christ did not leave the Church in doubt about its task. In what has become known as the "missionary commandment". He plainly told the disciples their task: "Go therefore and make disciples of all nations, baptizing them in the name of the Father and of the Son and of the Holy Spirit, teaching them to observe all that I commanded you" *(Matt. 28:19-20)*. Mark and Luke report this commandment of Jesus Christ in their own style *(Mark 16:15; Luke 24:47)* The commandment was not unexpected because first the twelve and then seventy disciples were sent by Jesus for mission during the years of His messianic activity *(Matt. 10:1-15; Mark 6:7-13; Luke 9:1-9, 10:1-12)*. The book of the *Acts of the Apostles* shows how they executed this missionary commandment.

The content of mission can be found in Christ's commandment and is threefold: preaching, teaching and baptizing. Preaching means the proclamation of the good news, that is, the forgiveness of sins and eternal life in the name of Jesus Christ. Teaching means to educate people in the secrets of the Kingdom of God and its implications for this life. Finally, the commandment was to baptize those who repent and introduce them into the Church which is the communion of the saints and the body of Christ, which Church keeps and leads them to the coming Kingdom of God. In the Church they can worship God and serve men.

The mission of the Church can be regarded as one of the marks of the Church[1]. Where the Church is there must be a mission.

If there is no sense of mission the presence of the true Church may be questioned. The mission of the Church demonstrates the life of the

Church. Where there is a Church but mission is lacking there is something basically wrong with that Church. The sign of life is growth, so the sign of a living Church is its growth - although this growth is not always numerical but it certainly should be spiritual.

To preach the Gospel to all nations is only one side of the mission of the Church. Its other side is to gather into the Church those who listen to the witnessing of the Church and organise them into congregations and to raise them in faith, hope and love, to help them in their way of sanctification and preserve them for the Kingdom of God. One ancient symbol of the Church is the ark which Noah was ordered by God to build in order to save men and animals from the flood *(Gen. 6-9)*. Likewise the Church is built by God to save those who are elect from the sinful and perishing world for the new life, preserving them for the Kingdom of God. Because of this understanding of the Church many an old Church was built in the shape of an ark.

2. Various Concepts of Mission

During its two thousand year history the Church has always been more or less aware of its missionary commitment. But the Church has understood and practised its missionary task in different ways at different times. Let us review briefly the most distinctive concepts of this understanding of the mission.

3. The Older Concepts of Mission

The concept of mission which prevailed for many years was based on Augustine's teaching. He regarded the Church as the sole and exclusive institution where salvation was available. This was conceptualized in the statement: *Extra Ecclesiam non est salus*. "Outside the Church there is no salvation". Therefore the main aim of mission was to help people to enter the Church, even by force summarized in the *expelle intrare* principle. The practical aim was to baptise as many people as possible. This attitude of the Church coincided with the great migration from the Asian steppe to Europe that occurred in successive waves throughout the early medieval period. The Church baptized them, sometimes whole tribes at a time, and grew enormously. In the middle of the medieval period the concept of mission was radically altered. Now its aim was to win the world, which practically meant the extension of the political authority of the Popes over all nations. This aim necessarily involved political means and the use of force. This can be seen in the Crusades and later in the political ambitions and practices of the Popes. The reaction against the interference of the Church in political matters helped the spread of the Reformation and it later resulted in the separation of Church from state in many countries. Meanwhile monastic orders made enormous efforts to bring Christianity to the peoples of Africa, Asia and America by converting, baptizing and teaching. They established mission-stations on the coast of these continents where missionaries faced many troubles and many of them suffered martyrdom.

Since the 16th century Rome has relied on its counter-reformation effort to conquer Protestantism. In the 19th century Ultramontanism strengthened the pope's political influence[2]. "Proselytism" also was considered as a proper form of mission. The goal was to gain people from other Churches and convert them. The high tide of this process is now over, but sporadically it is still practiced by some Churches.

4. The Liberal Concept of Mission

In the 19th century the missionary activity of the Churches reached its peak. The western "Christian" countries wanted to "Christianize" the whole world, mainly what we now think of as the "third world." It is not our task to analyse the work of these modern missionaries. However, one positive and two negative facts should be mentioned. The positive fact is that beside promoting Christianity in the Third World, these countries laid down systems of education and health services. The negative results, however, are that in many regions they were the supporters of the colonial systems and Christianizing meant also to "civilize". Usually this involved urging people to abandon not only their tribal religious customs but also their socio-cultural heritage. In doing so missionaries caused great damage to the cultural life of the third world people and upset their traditional social system, which caused serious problems. After the Second World War when the former colonies gradually gained independence and with the emergence of new peoples, the so-called Young Churches also emerged, many of whom have insisted on working out an indiginous Christian theology of their own.

In the period of Protestant Liberal Theology German theologians worked out two concepts of mission in the Church. They distinguished between foreign mission and home mission. The first meant the missionary activity of the Church abroad, which aimed at the Christianization of non-Christian people the world over. The second meant the missionary work of the Church at home, to make real Christians of the growing number of the nominal members of the Church. This kind of home mission was necessary because of the secularizing effect of the burgeoise positivist and sceptical philosophies on the one hand and the growing leftist and revolutionary ideologies on the other hand.

In this period the Churches put huge energy into missions. Missionary stations were established in practically every part of the world. The enthusiasm and optimism for the success of the mission can be seen from the programme of J.R. Mott, a renowned evangelist of that age whose aim was: "evangelizing the world in this generation".

5. Some Modern Concepts of Mission

During and after the Second World War the Christian Churches gradually re-evaluated the concept of mission.

D. Bonhoeffer (1906-1945), the German theologian who suffered martyrdom in the last days of the war, was pre-occupied with the problem of "What does it mean to be a Christian today?" He observed that modern man is not religious. He reached the conclusion that the non-religious man must not be asked to become religious first in order to believe in Christ. Man must be liberated for fuller participation in the tasks and problems of the world. This attitude of the Church also involves entering into dialogue with non-Christian religions and ideologies[3]. This concept, however, has to be received with caution because the Church cannot in any circumstances depart from Christ's commandment to make people Christian and remain the true Church. In that case, the Church will melt away and there will be none to advise people to "fuller participation in the affairs of the world".

J. MacQuarrie proposes a similar theory to that of Bonhoeffer when he asks: "Is it necessary to all men to be gathered into the Church before the Kingdom can come? Or is the Church a representative community - both representing the world toward God in its serving, witnessing and praying among and for all men[4]. In this case the Church is leaven, salt and light in this world, - the "pioneers" of the coming Kingdom. And in this case the motive of mission is love which means self-giving, not to win the world but to identify itself with the world, even lose itself in the world as Christ did. He suggests that the Church instead of gaining converts, or winning the world, or expanding itself, should share with other great world religions to lead a mission to the loveless masses of humanity[5].

In recent decades, the East-European Protestant Churches developed a theology of Mission, the so-called Theology of Service or Theology of Diaconia. These Churches were living in a secularized and atheist-socialist society and have tried to find their way by developing this theology. They understood the Church as the continuation of Christ's work. Because Christ served the needs of man, hence the work of the Church must also serve the people among whom the Church is living. In practice, it means that the Church associates itself with and supports the humanistic, good aims of the state and took up the case of the destitute, the handicapped, children and lonely aged people. It tries to save those who are in the bondage of alcohol and other drugs. The Church was also an active supporter of peace movements, considering its work as true witnessing about the Lord of the Church not by words but by deeds[6]. A closer scrutiny of this theology shows that it is politically motivated. These Churches became the collaborants of the atheist-communist political systems of those countries and that the Theology of Service was in fact a Theology of Servitude[7].

The Western Churches' concept of mission has gone through a radical change in the last decades. This is due to the fact that the former missionary Churches became independent, the so called Young Churches in the third world. The mother Churches have become less anxious to send out missionaries to work under the authority of the sending Churches or missionary societies. Instead of sending missionaries they now send "fraternal workers" who as expatriates are working under the authority of the young Churches. The fraternal workers are not only priests or ministers or theological educators but doctors, nurses, teachers, and engineers who help build and run hospitals, health centres and various development projects of the young churches. The sending Churches also provide material and financial aid when and where necessary.

The various concepts of mission have often led to extremes such as worldliness or other-worldliness, aggressiveness or self-negation. The best standpoint may be a dialectical one. On the one hand the Church must keep what is good from the traditional concepts of mission: to preach the Gospel, convert people and expand Christianity. On the other hand, the Church must enter into dialogue with other world religions and ideologies by recognizing the values that are inherent in them because in them too, the Holy Spirit is also working. But the Church should reject what is sinful in them. Moreover, the Church must realize that mere preaching is not enough in an age where the value of words is so degraded. The Church must reinforce its words by deeds as a particular form of witnessing about its Lord. The missionary Church must become the serving Church. The warning words of James are relevant for the Church of today: "I by my works will show you my faith" *(James 2:18).* The healthy missionary Church has two dimensions: one is vertical and the other is horizontal. The vertical dimension is that the Church receives vocation, inspiration and power from "above" into the horizontal level of the everyday life of the world. The Church infuses these gifts into the human community "down" here. Without the vertical dimension, the horizontal work of the Church is ineffective or non-existent. Without the horizontal dimension the Church is guilty of selfishly retaining God's gifts, and by doing so proves itself useless and superfluous in the world.

The two thousand year history of the Church shows that the Church intended to take seriously the missionary commandment of Jesus Christ. By honouring it the Church grew from its modest beginnings to a world Church. The mission of the Church is not yet ended because the Kingdom of God is not yet here in its totality. Every generation of mankind is a new challenge for the Church to help them towards Christ. Christian ministers and the members of the Church must take seriously Jesus Christ's missionary commandment.

NOTES

1. J. MacQuarrie: Principles of Christian Theology, p. 441.
2. The Latin word "Ultramontanism" denotes the ambitions of the Popes to extend their political authority "Beyond the Hills" of Rome.
3. D. Bonhoeffer: Letters and Papers from Prison, (Collins Tartan Books) p. 90.f.
4. J. MacQuarrie: Principles of Christian Theology, pp. 441.f.
5. ibid.
6. K. Toth: The Voice of Christians for Peace, pp. 17.f, Budapest
7. Afer the collapse of the communist regime in Hungary the Theology of Service lost its relevance, and the Churches have distanced themselves from it. Bishop E. Kocsis of the Reformed Church in Hungary stated that: "This theology was employed mainly in dialogue with the Marxists...Since this reason is over, this theology has no role and function any more." Presbyterian Record, p. 45, June, 1991, Toronto.

Chapter 4

The Word and Sacraments

**The Word of God, The Sacraments, Baptism, Lord's Supper
The Church as the means of Grace**

In the former chapter we studied the task of the Church mission. That is witnessing about Jesus Christ as the crucified and risen Lord and the salvation in his name. God not only gave this task to the Church, He also provided the necessary means for the Church to perform its task. These are the Word of God and the Sacraments, also called the means of grace, by which God's saving grace is communicated to man.

1. The Word of God

God has entrusted His Word to the Church to preach and to teach to keep it and observe it. The Word of God is given to the Church in the special revelation of God which can be found in the Scriptures, that is in the Bible. The Bible contains God's plan for the salvation of humanity and tells how this plan was prepared in history and realized in the person, life and history of Jesus Christ the Son of God. It tells how man can have access to this salvation and sets out its consequences for the life of man. The Word of God was entrusted to the Church in order that the Church should proclaim it.

Why has the Word of God such enormous importance? This is because the Word of God is not only the "speech" of God but at the same time it is also the "power" of God. As we saw before the Hebrew word *dabar* means both word and deed. In human experience word and deed are usually separated from each other. But with God the two are the same. When God speaks it means that He acts at the same time. God's talk is not only His "opinion", His "wish", His "imagination"; but it is His will which is being realized at the same time as it is uttered by God. God's word is the creative activity of God; when God speaks it means that God acts. This is why the Bible is right in saying that the world was created by the Word of God. God said: "Let it be" and the world came into existence. The New Testament took over the Old Testament concept of the Word of God, which appears as *Logos tou theou* in Greek. The New Testament understands that the *Logos* of God, the expression of His will which brings about his purpose in the world, is Jesus Christ the Son of God *(John.*

1:14). The creation occurred through and by the Word of God. The New Creation - salvation from sin and the gift of eternal life - also occurs through and by the Word of God. But because the Word of God is the Son the New Creation also takes place in, through and by the Son of God Jesus Christ *(2 Cor. 5:17; Eph. 3:9; Col. 1:16, 3:10)*. This is why the Word of God is so important for the Church [1].

At this stage it will help us, before we go further, to note the three forms of the Word of God distinguished by K. Barth. These are: the revealed word of God, whose peak is Jesus Christ because He himself is the revelation of God; the written Word of God as it is recorded for posterity in the Scriptures; and the proclaimed Word of God as it is uttered in the preaching service of the Church [2].

Hence we can understand that when and where the Church proclaims the Word of God in its evangelizing, preaching and teaching service, which is the human testimony about the revelation of God in Jesus Christ, the creative activity of God is present. By the proclamation of the Word of God the New Creation takes place in man who by listening, believing and obeying it experiences the forgiveness of sins, entering into a new relationship with God and participating in the redemption. Man experiences in himself the birth of the New Being which will inherit the Kingdom of God.

This is why the Reformers, having understood this secret of the Word of God, said: *Predicatio Verbi Dei est Verbum*, that is "The preaching of the Word of God is the Word of God". When the Word of God is proclaimed a miracle happens. In reading and proclaiming the Word of God from the Bible, in meditating on it and explaining it and applying it to one's life, the Holy Spirit is at work. He makes the old words, the sentences of the Bible as it is appears through the human words of the preachers, to be the living word of God to man, and by it man is drawn into the presence of the living God. God speaks to me, judging, forgiving and promising me blessings, and His word becomes a "burning ember" in my life and a creative force in my heart, mind and soul which wants to bring forth the New Being in me. In the proclamation of the Word of God a transubstantiation takes place: the human testimony about God becomes God's testimony about Himself and a creative force in man's life.

How does the New Creation commence in man's soul by the impact of the Word of God? This is because God wants to start with the new Creation at the very point where sin entered into man and the world, and with it the fall and corruption of man, and this is the soul of man. The fall occurred in the soul of man by listening to the voice of temptation, and here man decided to rebel against God. God wants to save man by giving man His Word so that man should listen to it by his mind and accept it in his soul and in his heart. Where the corruption has occurred, there must start the healing process too[3].

To sum up all this: the Word of God is the power of God which created the world and creates New Life in man. The Word was entrusted to the Church to proclaim, that by it man should be saved and by it the Church be created and maintained. The Church can proclaim the Word of God effectively because of the presence and the work of the Holy Spirit in the Church.

Because of the importance of the proclamation of the Word of God; ministers, priests and pastors have to take very seriously their preaching service. This is because the salvation of man and the existence of the Church depend on it. The Church was born by preaching the Word of God. The growth of the Church depends on the preaching of the Word of God. So the secret, the meaning and the task of the Church is in the honest, relevant and valid proclamation of the Word of God.

2. The Sacraments

The word "Sacrament" comes from the Latin *Sacramentum* which originally meant the soldier's oath of allegiance. In Christian theology it means the believer's oath to Christ and also the secret, mysterious and sacred ceremonies. This is because the Early Christians regarded both Baptism and the Eucharist or Lord's Supper as secret, sacred and mysterious ceremonies. The Christian tradition kept the word Sacrament and meant by it the ceremonies of baptism and eucharist. The part of dogmatic theology which deals with the theology of Sacraments is called Sacramentology.

Roman Catholic theology acknowledges seven sacraments - baptism, confirmation, eucharist, penance, unction, ordination and matrimony. The Protestant Churches accept only two sacraments: baptism and eucharist. This is because only these two were instituted and ordered by Jesus Christ. Jesus Christ's commandment for Baptism is recorded in *Matthew 28: 18-20*: "Go therefore and make disciples of all nations, baptizing them in the name of the Father and of the Son and of the Holy Spirit." The Lord's Supper also was ordained by Jesus Christ, according to Paul in *1 Corinthians 11:24-25*: "Do this in remembrance of

143

me". Regarding the acceptance of only two sacraments, Protestant theology adds a second argument to the first, in saying that only these two, baptism and eucharist, are necessary for salvation. Accepting only two sacraments does not mean that the Protestant Churches do not take seriously the acts which are involved in most of the other Roman Catholic sacraments, but that Protestant theology does not regard them as sacraments because of the lack of evidence that they were instituted as direct commands of Christ. Only two Protestant groups, the Salvation Army and the Society of Friends (or Quakers), do not administer the sacraments as a formal part of corporate worship.

Why are sacraments necessary? Classical theology calls sacraments the *Verbum Visible* - the visible form of the word of God. In the sacraments, God presents us His Word in a materialized and visible form. This is necessary because of our weakness, in that we can more readily believe what we experience than what we hear. So in the sacraments the Word of God is still vitally important. The material parts of the sacraments are the bearers of the Word of God and at the same time they are the seals of the promises of God which point to the mercy and merit of Jesus Christ. The sacraments as the materialized Word of God are tangible; they can be touched and experienced. The sacraments include in themselves an outward, visible sign and an inward spiritual grace. Hence the sacraments are frequently called the means of Grace because they are the vehicle of the Divine grace to men.[4]

The sacraments are important because they are the signs of the forgiveness of sin and assurance of salvation. This is because Christ - who is the Word of God - is the substance and therefore the essence of the sacraments as the source of Grace. Christ is the source of Grace and not the outer materials of the Sacraments. The sacraments only guide us to Christ and, by guiding us to Christ, present to us Christ and Christ's gifts, forgiveness and salvation. No one can have the gifts of Christ without having Christ Himself. So the sacraments have a serving function like the Word. But the sacraments communicate Christ in a fuller way. The Spirit and the Body of Christ are communicated by the sacraments while the Word communicates only the spiritual Christ. Sacraments can effectively communicate Christ only if faith is present, the blessing conveyed by the sacraments can be received only in faith. As with the Word of God, taking the sacraments will be unproductive unless received by faith. At the same time the sacraments strengthen the faith of believers. In the act of participation in the sacraments the Holy Spirit has a dominant function.

For the sacraments to achieve their guiding, serving and communicating function the Holy Spirit must be present and makes possible the participant receiving the full Christ together with His gifts of forgiveness and salvation.

Because of the importance of the sacraments as the means of grace they must be present in the Church. The Reformers considered the proper administration of the sacraments as one of the notes of the Church. Without offering and serving sacraments there cannot be a healthy, efficient and true Church. Only those Christians who participate in the sacraments can be regarded as mature and full members of the Church.

3. Baptism

The word "Baptism" is the English form of the Greek word *Baptisma*. Its verbal form means "To submerge into water, to wash". Baptism has always been practiced in the Church and was regarded as a sacrament because it was instituted by Christ *(Matt. 28:18-20)*, and its practice was ordered by Christ to the Disciples. In baptism the visible sign is the water. Its spiritual meaning is the forgiveness of sins and as the consequence of it is the rising up to a New Life.

As a religious ceremony baptism was well known in the ancient Middle East. In Old Testament religion a form of baptism was also practiced, the washing of the body and clothes which was necessary as a symbolic act of cleansing from sins *(Lev. 14:8; Ezek. 36:25; Zach. 13:1; 2 Kings 5)*. In New Testament times John the Baptist baptized those who repented at the River Jordan for the forgiveness of sins *(Mark 1:4)*. Jesus Christ himself was baptized by John *(Matt. 3:13-17)*. Jesus Christ did not baptize but his disciples did *(John 4:2)*. The ceremony of Baptism was taken over by Jesus from Old Testament religion and He gave to it a new meaning. It became the outer sign of repentance and the forgiveness of sins and salvation in His name and the sign of belonging to Him.

Baptism as a symbol has many meanings: the sign of the vocation of God, the sign of repentance and justification. Baptism is also the sign of the birth of the New Life in the place of the "dead" one, the submersion in water symbolizing the death of the old life, the emerging from the water symbolizing the birth of a new person *(Rom. 6:3; Col. 2:12)*. The new person in baptism received a new, Christian name. Hence Baptism serves as the solemn occasion of name giving and receiving. Baptism is also the sign of fellowship with Christ *(Gal. 3:27)* indicating that sanctification has already begun in the life of the baptized person. Baptism is thus the

145

initiation ceremony of entering the Church and as such it is the sign of belonging to the Church[5].

Baptism by water, however, points beyond itself to baptism by the Spirit. This has to follow water baptism *(Acts 8:16; Tit.3:5)*. To ensure the possibility of the baptism of the Holy Spirit, the Church later introduced the practice of confirmation. Confirmation involves a preparation for mature Christian life. This is practiced in those Churches which baptize infants because the initial vow that the infants will be raised as Christians is usually made by the parents, godparents and the congregation on behalf of the infants. Before the solemn moment of confirmation the candidates compulsorily take part in the confirmation course where they receive the essential teachings of Christian faith and life. The child reaching the threshold of being an adult and mature person takes over the vow in confirmation and confesses that he or she acknowledges Jesus Christ as Saviour and Lord over his or her life and wants to live in obedience to Him. This declaration in confirmation is the moment of the baptism of the Holy Spirit, because no one can confess Jesus Christ as Lord unless by the help of the Holy Spirit *(1 Cor. 12:3)*. This is essential for entering into the Kingdom of God *(John 3:5)*. Only those who are confirmed in their faith are allowed to participate in the Lord's Supper which is the other sacrament. However, recently some churches occupy a more liberal stand in this matter. Confirmation signifies one's full membership of the Church. Those Churches who practice adult baptism organize preparatory courses of instruction in the Christian faith and life for their baptismal candidates.

In connection with baptism three problems have to be clarified. First is the "Baptism for the Dead" that was practiced in the early Corinthian Church *(1 Cor. 15:29)*. This was an extreme act of the early Christians, who were anxious about the salvation of their passed-away relatives and friends who had died without knowing about salvation in Jesus Christ. By baptizing themselves on behalf of their beloved dead ones they expressed faith in their salvation. Today this practice is not used because salvation is preached and available to every man.

The second problem is whether infant or adult baptism should be practiced. The various Baptist Churches insist on adult or believer's baptism, while the majority of the Churches practise mostly infant baptism and occasionally adult baptism only as occasion demands. It is true that at the very beginning in the early Church adult baptism was practised but it could not be otherwise. The first Church in Jerusalem was constituted of adults who having heard Peter's preaching repented and were baptized. But the early Church practised infant baptism as well. When Cornelius' family was baptized it included the children too *(Acts 10)*. Jesus Christ called even the children to Him *(Mark. 10:14)*. Since that time the Church has practised infant baptism. Not only the Church practice upholds the right of infants to baptism; there are also at least two theological arguments to support it too. First, the theology of the Covenant also supports infant baptism. The children of the Covenant people of the Old Testament also belonged to the Covenant. The children of Christian parents cannot be excluded from the new Covenant either since they closely belong to this Covenant. In the Old Testament, the circumscision of the male infant was the sign of belonging to the Covenant people. In the Church, baptism of infants is the sign of belonging to the people of the New Covenant. Second, infant baptism also can be justified by the theology of the mercy of God. One of the features of the mercy of God is that it is always *Gratia Antecedens*, Antecendent Grace, which means that the Grace of God preceeds all human activity, merit or response and always is the initiating factor in the God-man relation. Thus, infant baptism can be justified in the context of this antecedent grace. God offers His mercy to the infant in advance and God expects the child's assent answer when he or she becomes old enough to understand the commitment required.

The third question is connected with the mode of baptism. Churches use different methods in the cermony of baptism, either sprinkling or pouring the water or touching the head of the peson with water on the one hand, or immersing the person in water on the other. The mode of baptism is insignificant from the theological point of view. Every Church has the right to practice baptism in accordance with its own tradition. Churches usually acknowledge each others' baptism.

4. The Lord's Supper

The Lord's Supper as a Sacrament has always been accepted and observed in the Church. The New Testament mentions it under different names: The Lord's Supper *(1 Cor. 11:20)*, "Breaking of bread" *(Acts 23:42, 46)*, *Eucharist* which really means thanksgiving *(1 Cor. 14:16)* or "Holy Communion" *(1 Cor. 10:16 f)*. The Early Christians frequently linked the Lord's Supper with their common meal or "love feast" the so called *Agape (1 Cor. 11:17; Acts 2:46; Jude 12)*. The Lord's Supper name in the Roman Catholic Church is called "Mass". This name is derived from the Latin word *missus* which means sending, dispatching or throwing, which refers to the central act of the Mass, the forgiveness of sins, either at the moment when the sins of the communicants are absolved (thrown away) or to the end of the celebration of the Mass when the priest dismisses the people. In the mass the Roman Catholic Church offers only the bread or the "host" to the communicants while the Protestant Churches serve both elements, the wine and the bread as signifying the blood and body of Christ.

The Lord's Supper is regarded as a sacrament in the Church because it was instituted by Christ, at the eve of the Jewish feast of Passover before Christ's betrayal, when Jesus Christ took his last supper together with the disciples. Jesus Christ ordained the repetition of this supper, saying: "Do it ... in remembrance of me" *(Mark 14:22-25; Matt. 26:26-28; Luke 22:19-20; 1 Cor. 11:23-26)*. As a sacrament, it has the visible signs of the bread and the wine; it also has a spiritual meaning, the redemptive death of Jesus Christ on the cross.

The meaning of the Lord's Supper is as follows. Jesus Christ took over this ceremony from an Old Testamant observance *(Ex. 12)*. Originally this was the *Pessah*, the Passover feast of the Jews which was one of their three main festivals. The *Pessah* was a memorial of the deliverance of the Jews from Egypt. On this occasion unleaven breads were eaten, a lamb was killed, prepared and eaten and wine was drunk amidst an elaborate cermony. Jesus Christ instituted the Lord's Supper on the eve of the Passover. He took the elements of the Passover feast and filled them with new content, giving them new meaning. He himself is the "Lamb of God" *(John 1:36)* who sacrifices Himself for the expiation of the sins of mankind *(1 Cor. 5:7)*. The shared bread signifies His broken body. Christ said: "This is my body which is given for you" *(1 Cor. 11:24)*. The shared wine signifies His blood shed for us: "This cup is the New Covenant in my blood" *(1 Cor. 22:25)*. Thus, Christ interpreted his own death as the real and unique sacrifice of His body and blood, by which a New Covenant was established between God and man *(Heb 9:11-15)*. All the promises of God about redemption, salvation and the new creation began to materialize. The elements of the Lord's Supper, the bread and the wine, are the material seal and assurance from God that the forgiveness of sins and salvation are complete. As the bread and wine feed us for this life, so Jesus Christ's broken body and shed blood feed us for eternal life. The elements of the Lord's Supper communicate to us the mercy of God. But this does not happen *ex opera operato*, that is, not by the act of eating and drinking them automatically but only if the elements are received by faith. This faith is indispensible in connection with the elements, which are the *Verbum Visible*, just as faith is indispensible in connection with the Word of God which is the *Verbum Audible*.

148

Three aspects of the Lord's Supper require our special attention. The Lord's Supper points to the past, because Christ ordered it as a remembrance of Him. At the Lord's Supper the community of the believers recalls that evening when Jesus Christ ate bread and drank wine together with His disciples. In this recollection the Church evokes the passion and the death of Jesus Christ and understands anew that all that happened to Jesus Christ in His passion and death happened for the benefit and blessing of His followers: for the forgiveness of their sins and for their redemption and salvation. The Lord's Supper has also an eschatological character. The Lord's Supper points to the future, to the "Messianic Banquet" which will take place in the Kingdom of God *(Luke 13:29; Mark 10:37, 40)*. Jesus Christ promised it when He said at the Last Supper: "I shall not drink again of the fruit of the vine until I drink it new in the Kingdom of God" *(Mark 14:25)*. The Lord's Supper is only a token of this promised banquet, but in it this banquet is already present as a sign. So the Lord's Supper ties us not only to the past but to the future as well. This is how the Lord's Supper nurtures hope in believers.

But there is more than past and future in the Lord's Supper. When in the Lord's Supper the past is being evoked and the future is there in advance, in the present moment a miracle happens: the living Lord is present spiritually but realistically to us. The communicant is convinced the Jesus Christ Himself gives him forgiveness, redemption and salvation. This miracle is similar to what the disciples at Emmaus experienced at the moment when He broke the bread for them *(Luke 24:30-31)*. The presence of Christ in the Lord's Supper is the work of the Holy Spirit who brings to us Christ's salvation. In this way we can talk about the real presence of Christ in the Lord's Supper[6].

We ought also to review the different interpretations of the Lord's Supper, recognized by different branches of Christianity. Roman Catholic theology of the eucharist is based upon the doctrine of transubstantiation. This means that at the moment when the priest repeats Christ's words: "This is my body" and "This is my blood", the elements of the Mass, the bread and the wine, change into the body and the blood of Christ. Outwardly the elements remain the same but their substance is trans-substantiated into the physical body and blood of Christ. Moreover, in Roman Catholic understanding, the elements are effective *ex opera operato* that is, the act itself - the receiving and eating - communicates the divine grace irrespective of whether the communicant is wicked or pious or whether the priest is a worthy or unworthy person. This doctrine comes from a literal interpretation of Christ's words: "This is my body" when Christ gave the bread of the Supper to each of His disciples. It is obvious to us that Christ did give them bread, a piece of a loaf, and not a piece of His body. Therefore, Christ's words should be understood symbolically and spiritually. As the Passover meal was a symbolic act, so is the Lord's Supper - but with a new and deeper meaning. It is no wonder therefore that the Reformers criticized and rejected the Roman Catholic doctrine of the mass and set out to reinterpret the meaning of the Lord's Supper.

According to the interpretation of Zwingli, the Lord's Supper is essentially the occasion for remembering Christ's redemptive death. He stressed Christ's advice to the disciples: "Do this in remembrance of me". This interpretation links the Lord's Supper entirely to the past and disregards its other dimensions. Zwingli did not work out fully the doctrine of the Lord's Supper because of his premature death.

Luther could not accept the doctrine of transubstantiation and replaced it with the doctrine of consubstantiation, according to which Christ is mystically but really present not in the elements but with them, beside, above or around them. Because Luther insisted upon the real presence of the physical body of Christ at the Lord's Supper, he had to interpret how Christ could be present simultaneously on every altar where the Lord's Supper was observed. He did so with the help of the ancient doctrine of *communicatio idiomatum*, that the glorified human body of Christ shares in the omnipresence of God, and therefore Christ can be really present everywhere at the Lord's Supper[7].

Calvin rejected both the Roman Catholic and the Lutheran doctrines of the Lord's Supper, that is the idea of Christ's physical presence in one or another form in the elements. Calvin interpreted the presence of Christ in the Lord's Supper spritually. When the communicant receives the elements he receives the whole Christ by faith and with that all that Christ means: forgiveness and eternal life. This spiritual, mystical communion of the communicant with Christ is the work of the Holy Spirit. This interpretation is more realistic than the former two[8]. In Calvinist understanding, the problem of the presence of Christ in the Lord's Supper, is not a Christological but a Pneumatological issue.

The doctrine of eucharist is quite diverse among Christian Churches. With the growth of the ecumenical movement, theologians have made a serious effort to reach a consensus. One result is the "Leuenberg Concordat" between the Lutheran and Reformed Churches in Europe in which they reached an agreement on the Lord's Supper. The World Council of Churches published the result of a fifty year study on eucharist, baptism and the ministry, the "Lima Text," for the collective study and official response of the member Churches[9].

5. The Church as a Means of Grace.

Because it pleased God to entrust His word and the sacraments to the Church, the Church should use them as the means of Grace by which salvaltion is communicated to men and by which the Church can achieve its missionary task. Moreover, since the Church serves as the trustee of the means of Grace it can also be regarded as a means of Grace itself.

The Church itself is a means of Grace insofar as the activity of the Church is centered on the Word of God and the sacraments. This creates the conditions for the true worship of God *(latreia)* which in turn creates both fellowship *(koinonia)* and service of man *(diakonia)*. These three essential elements under the work of the Holy Spirit qualify the Church to be a means of Grace, that is, enabling the Church to become the communicator of God's saving Grace for the salvation of mankind. These three duties of the Church are dependent upon each other.

The Church is the place where the true worship of God takes place in preaching the Word of God and celebrating the sacraments, and by answering and reponding to them in prayers, hymns and by a life of obedience. The Church provides occasions for services and worship where the people of God come together. Singing hymns and saying prayers prepares God's people for the hearing of the Word of God and for participating in and responding to the sacraments with new dedication. The preaching of the Word of God may take different forms according to the needs of the congregation and according to the Church calendar. It can be in the form of evangelizing, teaching or thematic sermons, homilies or Biblical exposition. Or it can be made specially suitable for various occasions such as Christmas, Easter or Pentecost, or baptism, wedding or funeral services. The Church as an institution organizes and provides various special opportunities for listening to the Word of God in Bible-study groups, in Sunday school, youth groups or women's guilds.

Because of the work of the Holy Spirit in the Church, the Word and the sacraments create new life in the believers and organize them into the Church by calling and keeping them there. The concrete form of the organized community is *koinonia* - fellowship. The Church becomes this spiritual community because of the presence of God in the Word, in the sacraments and in the Holy Spirit. In the fellowship, there are at least three important elements: friendship, brotherhood and responsibility. By the inspiration of the Holy Spirit the members of the Church understand that

151

they closely belong together because each of them has the same God, Redeemer and Holy Spirit, the same faith and the same salvation, and each of them is a member of the spiritual body of Christ which is the Church. Therefore, they accept each other as brothers and sisters in faith, and each of them bears responsibility for the others. The Church as an institution promotes fellowship among its members by providing special occasions such as meetings, gatherings, and conferences.

Out of true worship and true fellowship flows the *diakonia*, the helping service of the Church. This is because both the true worship and true fellowship evoke responsibility. This in turn commands care, assistance and help, not only spiritual but material. *Diakonia* has two directions, inward and outward. The members of the Church have to look inward at those who are in need, poverty, sickness or in other trouble in its midst and find a way to help them, as occurred in the first Chruch in Jerusalem *(Acts 2:44-45)*. *Diakonia* also has an outward direction towards the world, because the Church feels responsibility not only for its members but for the world as well. The Church is well aware that Christ died not only for believers but for the whole world too. *(John 3:16)*. God wants to save the whole world, because the world is the object of His love *(1 John 4:14)*. The Church as an institution organizes both the inner and the outer *diakonia*, be it charity or social work or assistance for solving social issues in society. Only in these ways can the Church truly be the means of Grace.

To close this chapter let us remind Christian priests, ministers and pastors of their most important and sacred duties of faithful preaching of the Word of God, the correct administraction of the sacraments and organization of the Church as an institution for the effective conveyance of the Grace of God. This is because they are the main means of spreading abroad the grace of God by which God wants to save men and preserve them for the coming Kingdom of God.

NOTES

1. See Part I, Section 1, Chapter 3, Point 2 and Section 3, Chapter 3, Point 1
2. K. Barth: Church Dogmatics Vol 1.1, p. 98.f.
3. See Part I, Section 1, Chapter 3, Point 2.3.
4. J. Calvin: Institutes, IV, XIV, 6.17.
5. J. MacQuaqrrie: Principles of Christian Theology, p.481.
6. ibid, p.474.f.
7. See Part II, Section 3, Chapter 3, Point 1.4.
8. J. Calvin: Institutes IV, XVII.26.
9. Baptism, Eucharist and Ministry, Faith and Order Paper No.111/WCC, 1982

Chapter 5

Ministry in the Church

Ministry in the New Testament, Ministerial Structure of the Churches, The Apostolic Succession and Papacy

In the previous two chapters we have seen the mission of the Church and its task and its means - the Word and the Sacraments - by which the Church accomplishes its mission. The question arises: who is the subject both of the Mission and of the administration of the Word and the Sacraments who carries out and executes all this? The answer of theology is: in the broader sense the subject is the people of God, in the narrower sense it is the ministers of the Church. Let us deal with the doctrine of the Christian ministry in this chapter.

1. Ministry in the New Testament

The New Testament stresses the importance of the "universal priesthood" of all believers. This idea was taken from the Old Testament where Israel the covenant people of God were called to be "a kingdom of priests and a holy nation" *(Ex. 19:6)*. The physical Israel became unworthy of this calling and Isaiah prophesied that with the coming of the Messiah, His people would be called the "Priests of the Lord" *(Isa. 61:6)*. This is why the New Testament says of those who accept Christ as Saviour: "You are a chosen race, a royal priesthood, a holy nation, God's own people" *(1 Peter 2:9)*. On this basis Christian theology talks about the universal priesthood of the people of God.

What does the universal priesthood of believers mean? Simply stated, it is the continuation of Christ's ministry in the world. Christ calls men and women to Himself so that they may be ministered to by Him and that they should benefit from His ministry. This means that Christ serves them by offering them the forgiveness of sins and the new life in Him and with Him. This happens through the work of the Holy Spirit in the Church. But Christ not only calls men and women to himself; after he has minstered to them, he sends them into the world that they should continue His work through witnessing, showing their new life as an example to others and serving the needs of other people. Christ wants to work in the world through the service of His followers, the Christians. Christ is in this world so far as the Christians are able to show Him to the world. Christians can achieve this ministry because the Holy Spirit equips them with wisdom, power and zeal *(1 Cor. 3:9; Acts 4:33; 1 John 1:2-3; Eph. 3:7).*

In addition to, and based upon the universal priesthood of all believers, the New Testament deals with special ministries. Out of the ranks of the ordinary believers were chosen those who seemed to be suitable for special ministries. They were endowed with special gifts and charismas by the Holy Spirit; the community of the believers recognized the gifts and set them apart for special ministry. This was what happened in the election of seven deacons in the first Church in Jerusalem *(Acts 6:1-6)*. Because of the rapid growth of the Church it was necessary to elect or to appoint special ministers for specific tasks. The New Testament knows various special ministries. *Ephesians 4:11* mentions: apostles, prophets, evangelists, pastors and teachers. *Philippians* 1:1 talks about bishops and deacons. *Romans 16:12* talks of deaconesses and *1 Timothy 5:17* of presbyters. The office of the Apostles was unique because they were the disciples of Christ and the founders of the Church. This office died out with them. The Bishops were the successors of the Apostles. The Prophet - a special ministry - soon disappeared, but his function lived on partly in the work of the preacher. The evangelists spread the Gospel from towns to villages. The pastors, priests or presbyters were ministers of the local congregations. The deacons originally helped at the celebration of the Lord's Supper and at the *agape,* and beyond that they helped the Apostles in various ways *(1 Tim. 3:8f)*. Deaconesses mainly helped in caring for the poor and the sick *(1 Tim. 5:9-10)*. The New Testament Church provided a variety of ministries for the proper conduct of Church life.

The main ministries however were the bishops, presbyters and evangelists. Two important conditions prevailed in the new Testament [1]. The first condition was the "inner calling", the secret work of the Holy Spirit in some members of the Church by which they became willing to dedicate their life to the special service of God. The second condition was the "outer calling" by the Church for the ministry, as can be seen in the election of the seven deacons by the Church of Jerusalem *(Acts 6:1-6)*[2].

2. Ministerial Structure of the Churches

Special ministries in the Church developed in a complicated way from the time of the early Church. This development followed its own line in the Roman Catholic Church, in the Orthodox Churches and in the Churches of the Reformation. It is not our task to give an elaborate and comprehensive study of all this; we confine ourselves to two basic doctrines and structures of ministry.

First, there is the Roman Catholic type of ministry and those closely related to it. In the Roman Catholic Church there is a characteristic doctrine and structure of ministry. Here, because of the doctrine of the Papacy - the Pope is considered as the successor of the chief Apostle, Peter, and therefore the representative of Christ - ministerial authority and structure come from "above" to "below". The Pope appoints bishops who lead each diocese on behalf of the Pope. Because the bishop cannot be present in each parish of the diocese, he in turn appoints "vicars" who represent the bishop in the parishes and work vicariously on behalf of the bishop. The Roman Catholic minister is a priest because he is considered *Sacerdos* - the sacrificer when he administers the Mass in which Christ is sacrificed anew. The Roman Catholic priesthood has retained much of the concept of Old Testament priesthood. In the Roman Catholic Church the priesthood is a sacrament, and consequently the priests have an indelible character. The priests constitute the "clergy" in distinction to the "laity", all the rest of the believers. The word clergy comes from the Greek *kleros* which means inheritance, so the clergy means those who inherited Christ's service. From the Greek word *laos*, "people", comes the concept of the laity. The clergy are considered to be independent of the Church because they precede the Church. the Roman Catholic ministry is organized in a hierarchy, meaning that according to a sacred rule they are organized into different levels of authority and duties, including major and minor orders.

The ministry in the Orthodox Church developed along similar lines to the Roman Catholic ministry. However, in so many ways it has characteristic orders of hierarchy like patriarch and metropolitan, without acknowledging the supermacy of the Pope. Here the clergy are not regarded as an independent body apart from the Church but as an integral part of it. The ministry in the Anglican and Lutheran Churches retained many characteristics of the Roman Catholic concept of ministry, but they do not accept the Pope as the head of the Church and regard the ministry as a constituent part of the Church.

Second, there is the Reformed or Presbyterian type of ministry. The Reformers, principally Calvin, reconsidered and constituted ministry in the light of the Scriptures and put forward an alternative doctrine of ministry to that of the Roman Catholics. Calvin reintroduced the word "minister" as the replacement for the "priest". Rather than one who repeats the sacrifice of

Christ, minister means servant of the Word of God and the Sacraments, servant of the Lord and of the Church.

Here the structure of the ministry is "from below to above". Following the pattern of the ministry of the universal priesthood of all believers. The minister is not appointed from "above" by a higher authority but he is chosen or elected and called by the members of the Church. This is a recognition that the Holy Spirit lives and works in the congregations of the Church which is the body of Christ. The will of the Holy Spirit is manifested through the decision of the congregations. The congregations elect elders and other officials of the Church, including ministers. The governing body of the congregation is the Session, the council of elders. Higher governing bodies like Presbyteries, Synods and the General Assembly are made up of representatives of the sessions and are lead by a Moderator. The General Assembly, which is the highest legislative and govening body of the Church, usually meet yearly and elects its moderator. The clear structure of the Presbyterian-Reformed type of ministry has been coloured over the centuries by the traditions of the various national churches; however, it has retained the basic and fundamental elements of Calvin's pattern.

These two basic types of ministry are sometimes present in a mixed form and produce a great variety of ministerial titles and ranks in the Churches. The traditions of the respective Churches and their particular needs also play an important role. There are, for instance, Churches which reject both systems and the organizational structure that goes with them, and call their local leaders "pastor" or simply "brother".

3. The Apostolic Succession and the Papacy

There is a controversy between the historic Churches on the Roman Catholic doctrines of the Papacy and apostolic succession. In this respect the Roman Catholic Church attaches great importance to three passages of the New Testament. The first is *Matthew 16:18* where Jesus said: "I tell you, you are Peter and on this rook I will build my Church". The next is in *John 21:15-17* where the risen Lord gave a special commandment to Peter, saying to him: "Feed my Lambs" and "Tend my sheep". The third is in *1 Peter 5:2* where Peter gave a commission to his fellow elders to "Tend the flock of God that is in your charge." From these three texts the Roman Catholic Church not only derives and justifies the institution and authority of the Papacy, but with it the apostolic succession too by arguing that

Jesus Christ appointed Peter as the foundation of the Church and gave him a special commandment to be the chief pastor of the Church. The Roman tradition contends that Peter did exercise this authority and, as the first bishop of Rome, handed over this commandment and authority to his successor towards the end of his life. Since then this succession has been prevalent in the Roman Catholic Church so that there is a continuous line of apostolic succession in the Church from Christ through Peter to the latest Pope. The apostolicity of the Church in the Roman Catholic understanding involves an unbreakable line of apostolic succession[3].

The majority of the Churches do not accept this interpretation and more or less reject the office of the pope and this view of apostolic succession. They argue that *Matthew 16:18* is a later insertion and Peter was only a fellow Apostle among other Apostles. Peter left Jerusalem after the death of Jesus Christ and His resurrection and tried to resume his old fishing job, so Christ's commission "tend my sheep" was actually a reminder to Peter of his vocation because he was about to desert from Christ's cause. They also argue that by the introduction of the apostolic succession, the Church was trying to guarantee the fidelity of the traditions and teaching of the Church. But this stratagem failed to work, because some of the successors of Peter as bishop of Rome clearly distorted Church doctrine instead of protecting its traditions.

Apostolic succession with a different meaning is still recognized in the majority of the non-Roman Catholic Churches in the act of the ordination of ministers and at the induction ceremony of higher ministerial officers. During the ceremonies there is an act of "Laying on of hands" on the head of the person to be ordained or inducted. "Laying on of hands", was common in the Old Testament *(Lev. 24:14; Ex. 29:10; Deut. 34:9)*. It also was practiced by the Apostles *(Acts 6:6)* and the tradition has remained in the Church to this day, because it is considered an important act symbolizing receiving the special gift of the Holy Spirit which is needed for the adequate exercise of the particular office. This is also considered as the sign of the Church community identifying with the one entering into the rightly understood succession of the Apostles.

Theological students have to take seriously their preparation for ordination and entering into the ministry. They have to dedicate themselves not only to their studies, but should follow the direction of the old Christian tradition of the triple process of purification, illumination and perfection. By doing so they might be prepared adequately for the weighty duties of the Christian theologian and minister.

157

NOTES

1. J. MacQuarrie: Principles of Christian Theology, p.420.f.
2. L. Berkhof: Systematic Theology, p.587.
3. A. Richardson: An Introduction to the Theology of the New Testament p.294.

Chapter 6

Church Relations

Relations between Churches, Church and the World, Church and State, Church and the Kingdom of God

The Church is living on earth but belongs to heaven. This statement refers to the divine origin of the Church which, however, has to accomplish its task on earth: to gather people of the earth and to lead them towards the Kingdom of God. Thus the Church's work has two dimensions. One is horizontal, the worldly dimension. The Church has to live and work in this world, resulting in rich relations. First, the Church gathers people into itself from the world and leads them towards the Kingdom of God. We examined this in an earlier chapter, and we might call it the Church's relation to itself. Second, the Church is divided into Churches and denominations, thus giving rise to many questions of the relations between the various elements. Third, the Church by living in the world inevitably enters into some kind of relation with the world, state and society. This poses a further question: What relationship should exist between the Church and the world? The other is a vertical dimension, which links the Church to the Kingdom of God. The result of the kingdom of God's relation to the Church is that the powers of the Kingdom of God are present and act through the Church in this world. This has already been studied[1]. The other issue which has yet to be studied concerns the Church's relationship to the Kingdom of God.

In this chapter we intend to answer these three questions: What relationship should exist between the Churches? What kind of relationship should exist between the Church and the World, including the State? and what is the Church's relation to the Kingdom of God?

1. Relations Between Churches

The fragmentation of the one Church into many Churches and denominations is a sad and painful fact which shows the weakness of the people of God. The first major division occurred in 1054 AD when the Orthodox Churches separated from the Roman Catholic Church. The second main division took place in 1517 with the Reformation; the followers of the Reformation were excommunicated by the Roman Catholic Church. The division of the Church went on when various of the Reformation

Churches split into different denominations: Lutheran, Calvinist, Anglican and Baptist, and so on.   Later on the Methodist Church came into existence as the result of the great revivalist movement in the Anglican Church let by the Wesley brothers, John and Charles. More recently, many other groups have formed, such as Adventists and Pentecostalists. A number of smaller religious communities have since developed.

Sporadic attempts have been made in the past centuries to restore the unity of the Church but without any important result or success. Instead of the spirit of brotherhood, we see competition, proselytism and animosity between the denominations. This has resulted in an adverse effect especially in the mission field. There, the Churches have to face the problems regarding the effectivenes of their missions overseas which grew out of their divisions.   Many missionary societies came together in Edinburgh in 1910 to sort out their difficulties, a historic meeting regarded as the beginning of modern ecumenism - the Church's search for unity. Two movements played an important role in its development: the "Faith and Order" movement led by the Anglican Bishop Brent, aimed at overcoming the differences of faith and order within the Churches, and the "Life and Work" movement led by the Swedish Lutheran Bishop Soderblom, aimed at the practising of Christian love.   The present Ecumenical Movement was born in 1948 following the destructions of the Second World War, with the aim of promoting ecumenism and cooperation between the Churches and to lead them towards unity. The Roman Catholic Church did not join the World Council of Churches, but it acknowledged the work of the Holy Spirit in this movement, and did send observers. After the Second Vatican Council the Roman Catholic Church entered into dialogue with the World Council of Churches and with other Protestant and Orthodox Churches, and now a growing ecumenical cooperation and joint action can be seen between the various Churches of Christendom.

This ecumenical dialogue is taking place between different Churches on a range of subjects such as the nature of the Church, the meaning of ministry, the problems of tradition and of Scripture, the eucharist, the relationship between Church and society, and so on. The spirit of co-operation is growing among the denominations. This takes concrete form in ecumenical meetings and conferences on various levels, in joint worship and action. These ecumenical relations between the Churches exist and grow on local, national and world levels. At the same time co-operative efforts are being made for mutual approaches and for actual corporate unity between Churches. For example, in the "Leuenberger Concordat" the European Lutheran and Reformed Churches have reached an agreement on the Eucharist. In some cases Churches have united or are on the way to unification; the Presbyterian Church in England and the Congregationalist Church in England have united with each other. There is a "Uniting Church in Australia" in which Presbyterian and Methodist Churches are working towards organizational unification.

The modern ecumenical movement is the response of the Churches to their painful disunity. Christians are expected to realize that despite forces of separation there is much more linking them together. They all have the same God, Christ and Holy Spirit, the same Bible, faith and services, and they share in the same forgiveness of sins, new life and salvation[2]. Christians ought to promote Christian unity in the framework of their respective Churches.

2. Church and the World

The Church is in a dialectical situation in respect to the world. This is because the Church is not "of the world" but "for the world". The Church is "*ecclesia*", the community of those who have been called out from the world by the Holy Spirit. This means that they have a heavenly calling and destination, since they have been created anew for the World to Come and are sanctified by the Holy Spirit. All this occurred in order that they should live in this world and for this world, serving the witnessing to God in this world. So the world belongs to the Church's horizontal dimension as its field of service.

The Church must be well aware of its dialectical situation because only this can prevent it from falling into two temptations. The first temptation is an isolationism deriving from the Church overemphasizing on her "other-worldliness", her separatedness from the sinful world. She forgets that she is sent on a mission to this sinful world, and easily becomes a ghetto Church by separating and isolating herself from the world and selfishly pursuing what is for her benefit only. In this case the Church becomes useless, superfluous and a burden in the world. The second temptation is for the Church to overemphasize the importance of its role in worldly affairs, so that it gradually forgets its "other-worldly" character and vocation and regards itself as merely a religious group of people who are willing to help in solving the various problems of the world. In this case the Church assumes a voluntary role in the varied plans of society and gradually abandons its unique witnessing service to the salvation of mankind in Jesus Christ's name. A balance must always be maintained between the two kinds of witnessing, in words and in deeds.

161

Good deeds and relevant actions must always be accompanied by witnessing in words. And out of the proclamation of the Word of God must follow good deeds, action with responsibility and charity towards the world.

Witnessing by words about God must be made real and backed up by deeds in the world which point out the love of God for mankind. The deeds must bear testimony to the same love of God. Only by maintaining the unity between the proclamation of the Word of God in speech and proclamation of the Word of God through action can the Church perform its mission authentically and effectively in this world.

The responsibility of the Church to the world takes several forms. The Church feels responsibility for both man's spiritual and material needs. In its concern to satisfy mankind's material needs, the Church never should abandon its spritual duty, the preaching of the Gospel. In order to help in satisfying man's material needs, the Church has to be involved in a wide range of activities which varies from region to region and is conditioned by the actual needs of people. For example, the responsibility of the Church living in an affluent society may differ from the responsibility of the Church living in a poor one. Naturally, too, the service of the Church living in a Muslim country is different from the service of the Church living in a secularized non-Christian society. The Church which lives in a developed country has a different task in comparison to the Church which lives in a developing country. These differences in service reflect the differences in problems which the Church encounters in different regions. Consequently, we understand why the Church is involved in so wide a range of activities: fighting against unemployment, exploitation, social injustice, racism, discrimination, illiteracy, underdevelopment, drugs, wars, also poverty, caring for marginal peoples, refugees, the victims of violence, the victims of natural disaster, the destitute, crippled and handicapped, dumb and blind people, orphans, the aged and abandoned.

3. Church and State

Because the Church includes within itself a certain group of people it constitutes a particular entity in society, and because society is organized and lives in a particular state the right attitude of the Church to the State has to be examined. The Church's relation to the state is a dialectical one, for two reasons. First, because the State is a part of the world to which the Church must relate. Secondly, because the members of the Church have two citizenships, as the citizens of a given State and at the same time they are "citizens of the Kingdom of God" *(John 18:36; Eph. 2:19; Phil. 3:20).*

The Church exists in this world, but her calling is from heaven and for heaven - the Kingdom of God. From this two temptations derive for the Church in its relation to the State. The first is called "Ultramontanism". (See Part III, Section 3, Chapter 3, Note 2). Such a view asserts that the Church as the agent of God considers herself as the supreme authority who by divine authorization is above the state authority. The state has to obey the will of the Church authorities who for other reasons depend upon it. This is when the Church tries to acquire political power. The symbol of this ruling Church is the cross and the sword. The second temptation of the Church in relation to the State is "Segregationism". This occurs when the Church considers that she has nothing to do with the state and shows indifference and passivity to the politico-social and cultural affairs of the state. The result is that she isolates and segregates herself completely from the state and dedicates herself like a hermit exclusively to her inner spiritual life.

There are three main forms of Church-State relations. The first is characterized as antagonism, when the State and the Church fight each other. The Second is separation, when the State and the Church each live in a completely divorced manner, living alongside each other according to the rules of mutual agreement. The third can be called alliance, when the State claims the ethical, ideological or socio-political support of the Church and in return provides protection for the Church, offers financial or material help and grants privileges to the Church. The history of Church-State relations provides many examples of these patterns of relationship and even of their combination.

God did not leave the Church without guidance in this matter. The Scriptures contain ample references: *(Rom. 13:1-7; Matt. 22:21; Heb. 13:17; 1 Pet. 2:13-17, Tit. 3:1; 1 Tim. 2:1-2)*. To sum up the Church's attitude to the State, it may be said that the Church, wherever and in whatever conditions she lives, has to show a threefold attitude to the State: "priestly", "prophetic" and "royal" attitude. The priestly attitude means that the Church offers prayers and supplications for the State, for its authorities and for its people, for the peace, prosperity and unity of the State. The prophetic attitude of the Church is threefold. First, the Church by its proclamation of the Word of God calls upon the citizens of the State to be converted and live their lives according to the will of God. Second, the Church where necessary raises its voice against every deformation of State life. Third, the Church tries to point to guiding principles which should be followed by the State. The "Royal" attitude of the Church is not a ruling but a serving attitude, in accordance with Christ's example. This means that the Church offers a helping hand to promote all the good plans and initiatives of the State for the benefit of its citizens. Of these three attitudes or functions of the Church within the state, undoubtedly the prophetic function is the most critical. The Church often tends to forget this function, resulting in damage in credibility. The Church which becomes merely a part of the establishment usually pays dearly for the privilege.

The servants and the leaders of the Church have to take seriously all the three offices of the Church in relation to the State.

4. The Church and the Kingdom of God

At the beginning of this chapter it was said that the Church has two dimensions to its work: the horizontal and the vertical. So far, we have dealt with the task of the Church on the horizontal dimension, its relation to other Churches, to the World and to the State. In this paragraph we turn our attention to the vertical dimension and we look at the Church's relation to the Kingdom of God.

It has also been said before that the Church has its calling from "above" a calling from God directed toward the Kingdom of God. From this calling originates the vertical dimension of the Church's task. Hence, the Church is not a static but a dynamic entity; the Church is founded not for itself but for the Kingdom of God. Consequently, the Church has its meaning not in itself but in the Kingdom of God. This also means that the Church is not a "sitting" one but is "on the way" from here to somewhere else, from this world to the coming world of the Kingdom of God. Hence, the task of the Church is to "carry" people from the old age to the new one.

The Church is in a dialectical situation in relation to the Kingdom of God. On the one hand the Church was created among men because the Kingdom is a possibility for men. In the Church, the Kingdom is already here because the Church is the point where the kingship of God breaks into this world and through it His Kingdom is present in this world. On the other hand, the Kingdom of God in its fullness has not yet arrived; the Church here and now is only a sign and a token of the Kingdom of God. Members of Christ's Church belong to the Kingdom in faith and through faith they receive the gifts, wealth and blessings of the Kingdom of God. The Church of Christ carries its people towards the Kingdom but the Kingdom of God still has yet to come in its fullness.

The Church in itself is not the full Kingdom of God but in it the powers of the Kingdom of God are present; with it and in it the Kingdom of God is really present in its essence. This is because in the Church established and nurtured in and through the Word, the Sacraments and the Holy Spirit, God the Trinity is present and creates the new people of God for the Kingdom of God. The Church is the "Embassy" of the Kingdom of God where the traveller receives his "visa", "information", and "means" for the journey to the Kingdom of God. The Church belongs to the Kingdom and represents it as an embassy belongs to and represents its State. He who enters into an embassy enters into the State which the embassy represents even if he has not yet actually arrived at that state. Likewise, whoever enters into the Church enters into the Kingdom and feels the atmosphere, power, majesty and magnificence of the Kingdom, although he is but only symbolically in the Kingdom of God. He is not yet in the Kingdom but he already benefits from it and actually is on the way to it, because he wants to go there and the Kingdom has granted him all assurances for entering into it and living in it.

Christians and Christian ministers have to understand well the importance of the Church in relation to the Kingdom of God. The Church is not a club or a society of religious people, nor yet a mere gymnasium for spiritual exercises, but a place where the coming Kingdom of God is already present with its newness, power and majesty. The living God is present in the Church through the Holy Spirit who forgives sins, creates faith and obedience and with it the new Life which inherits the Kingdom of God.

NOTES

1.   See Part III, Section 3, Chapter 4.
2.   J. MacQuarrie: Principles of Christian Theology, p.402.f.

165

SECTION FOUR

The Doctrine of the Last Things

Chapter 1

Eschatology in the Early Church

General Remarks, Eschatology in the Old Testament, Eschatology in the New Testament, the Reinterpretation of Eschatology

1. General Remarks

Eschatology is the last and final aspect of classical Christian theology. The word "Eschatology" comes from the Greek *eschatos* which means the last, ultimate or utmost. Eschatology as a theological discipline deals with the last things which await the individual, the Church and the world. Christian theology is in a position to give a summary of the main features of the End because the revelation of God does not leave man in darkness about what the End will bring. The dominant factor in eschatology is the Holy Spirit. By Him we receive the revelation of the last things, by Him we have hope in the promises and the arrival of the *eschaton* is the work of the Holy Spirit - yet in this work, as in all things, the Father and the Son also participate. Christian Faith is future-oriented, in that it accepts the promises of God about resurrection, the last judgement and the new creation with salvation and eternal life. But this is not yet here. It is still in the future, theologically speaking in the *eschaton*. Yet, by faith these things are already a reality in a token form to the Christian whose hope looks forward to the time when God's promises will be fulfilled. Therefore, the Christian life means living in hope and in expectation, waiting for the fulfilment of God's promises.

Because the Christian's faith is future-oriented, so is Christian theology. This cannot be otherwise because both faith and theology derive their true meaning from the *Eschaton*. If there is no resurrection, new creation and eternal life then theology and faith have lost their meaning, their relevance and importance, and consequently there is no reason to pursue them. However, God in His revelation gave firm promise of a new beginning, a new and perfect life in the framework of the new creation. There will be no sin, no pain or death, and man will live in the presence of God (Rev. 21:4). Consequently, both faith and theology become very important, indeed the most important things of all.

Christian theology has always taken eschatology seriously, but there have been periods in its history when eschatology was given more stress and importance. These periods can be found in the early Church, in the later part of early Medieval theology and in our contemporary theology. In these periods the growth of the importance of eschatology was not without reason. The early Church expected the immediate *parousia*, the second coming of Christ. Medieval theologians expected the second coming of Christ at the end of the first millenium. Hence the stress on eschatology in these periods. In our present time eschatology has become one of the main issues of theological thinking, because the sudden end of mankind and of the world in a possible nuclear catastrophe was a growing danger.

In the following sections we will study the eschatology of the Bible and then the doctrine of the last things: the future of individuals as well as of the Church and the world. Lastly we give a brief review of eschatology in modern theology.

2. Eschatology in the Old Testament.

The concept of eschatology in the Old Testament is centered around the concept of *Jom Jahweh* - the "Day of God'. This idea appears in the prophetic writings and has two features. On the one hand it is the day of "wrath and judgement" (Isa. 7:18, 13:9; Jer. 46:10). On the other hand it is the day of "mercy and salvation" (Isa. 49:8, 54:3, 61:2; Jer. 33:15-16). Later the concept of *Jom Jahweh* was linked with the concept of the Messiah who was to come to restore the mighty kingdom of David and to gather all nations around Israel.

The idea of *Jom Jahweh* was linked not only with the idea of the promised Messiah but also with the idea of the Kingdom of God, *Malkuthammaim*, in the belief that the appearance of the Messiah heralds the arrival of the Kingdom (Zeph. 3:9; Micah 4:2). However, two different types of the Kingdom can be found in the Old Testament. There is a secular and political type which inspired many rebellions and upheavals in Israel, and there is the concept of a spiritual type of Kingdom. The belief

167

in and expectation of this type of Kingdom was maintained by pious persons like Enoch and communities like the Essenes, and the Qumran sect. They were not expecting a political Messiah who creates an earthly kingdom but a Messiah who would bring forth the direct kingship of God. They expected the end of this world in the near future. They hoped for nothing from weapons, upheavals and wars, but they were busy in preparing their souls for the coming of the Messiah by repentance and a pious life. The new, divine rule would be preceeded by the messianic work which materializes in painful judgement on ungodly and pagan peoples, on Satan and his allies. The divine person of the Messiah will rule over the whole world and will be triumphant over all demonic power, subjecting the world to God. But only the last generation of mankind has the fortune to participate in the Kingdom and not the generations of the past[1].

In connection with the *eschaton*, hope has to be seen as the link between the present and the future. The concept of hope in the Old Testament is not a neutral one; it is either good or bad. Hope always stands over against fear and it hopes something good (Pss. 22:5, 40:4-5, 62:5-6, 115:9). Hope is connected with trust. To hope means to possess the future and this belongs to the welfare of man. The importance of hope becomes obvious in the life of those who are in distress, because the God-fearing man in this situation does hope and trust in the liberation of God. Hope and trust are demanded from man (Pss. 37:5, 42:6, 125:1). The hope is not always hope for a definite something but may be a generalized trust in God's defence and help (Jer. 17:13; Ps. 61:1-4). When the hope is placed in something other than God, God crushes it and changes it into fear (Amos 6:1; Isa 32:9-11). No one can trust in his wealth (Ps. 52:7) or in his righteousness (Job 25:4), or in his religious achievement or in the Temple (Jer. 7:4) or in idols (Hab. 2:18) Israel cannot trust in its power or its alliance (Hos. 10:13; Isa 31:10); the godly depend on the will of God. In earlier ages the elect people asked and expected God's help in concrete problems. This was gradually transformed into eschatological hope, and every temporal, earthly problem was expected to be solved in the eschaton[2].

3. Eschatology in the New Testament.

The New Testament concept of the *Eschaton* was taken over by the early Christians from its beginning in the Synagogue and it received a new content: the *Parousia*, the second coming of Christ, and with it the end of the world and the beginning of a new one characterized by resurrection, judgement and eternal life in the Kingdom of God.

According to the Synoptic Gospels the centre of Jesus Christ's teaching was the proclamation of the arrival of the Kingdom of God in His person (Matt. 4:17)[3]. Around this was the teaching about Chirst's second coming, the Resurrection, the Last Judgement and the Kingdom of God in its fullness.

The Apostolic letters show the growth of the concept of eschatology. In the epistles of Paul the idea of the *parousia* comes into the foreground and with it the resurrection, the transformation of the living and the Last Judgement (1 Cor. 15). The Kingdom is already here in essence but still has to come in its fullness, perfection and glory (Matt. 6:10; 2 Thess. 2:1-12). The letters of John mention the appearance of the Antichrist before the second coming of Christ (1 John 2:18-22, 4:3). Christ will judge the living and the dead (2 Tim. 4:1). The righteous will enter into the Kingdom and receive eternal life (Heb. 6:19; James 2:5, 1:12; 1 Peter 5:4; Jude 21) while the ungodly people will be devoured by the fire of the Judgement as will earth and heaven (Heb. 10:27; 2 Pet. 3:7; 10-12). There will be a new earth and a new heaven (2 Peter 3:13). The Book of Revelation is particularly eschatological and apocalyptical. This book colours the above-mentioned elements of the End with the idea of double resurrection and double judgement. The first resurrection occurs at the *parousia* when the saints who suffered martyrdom are raised from the dead and rule with Christ for a thousand years. The first judgement is on the "Beast" and the "false prophet", when Satan will be bound for a thousand years. After the millenium Satan will be released to make an onslaught on Christ and the Church, but it will be the last fight. The army of Satan and that of Gog and Magog will perish in flames. Satan will be thrown into the "lake of fire". Then the general resurrection takes place and it in turn is followed by the Judgement and the elimination of death and Hell. Those whose names were not recorded in the "Book of Life" will be thrown into the "Lake of Fire". The reward of the redeemed is salvation and eternal life, service before the throne of God and life in the "heavenly Jerusalem"-the Kingdom of God. Here there will be no night or darkness because the eternal light of God shines (Rev. 19, 20, 21).

169

4. The Reinterpretation of Eschatology

It is evident from the Apostolic letters that the early Church was expecting the immediate second coming of Christ (2 Thess. 2:1; Col. 3:4; James 5:7-8; 2 Peter 1:16, 3:4,12). But the *parousia* did not take place when they thought it would and the Church had to find its way in the world. Eschatology was slowly removed from the centre of theology to its periphery. The importance of doctrine grew as the result of the de-eschatologization of theology.[4] Origen gave a spiritual-allegorical interpretation to the second coming of Christ by saying that Christ comes back in the soul of the believers.[5] Augustine assumed the *parousia* would occur at the end of the first millenium, the "thousand years" period of the Church. He also equated the Kingdom of God and the Church by saying that the Church is the Kingdom of God in the first thousand years. The first resurrection happens spiritually inside the Church because the Church resurrects the souls of those who were under judgement and damnation. This resurrection takes place in those who believe in the message of the Church and by faith these persons already have new life. The second resurrection is the bodily one which occurs at the end of time when Christ returns for the Last Judgement. Augustine reached these conclusions by reinterpreting the doctrine of the Millenium of the Book of Revelation. In the late period of the early Church eschatology gradually faded away and the importance of the Church as the institution of salvation was gradually strengthened.[6]

NOTES

1.   E. Benz: Evolution and Christian Hope, p.3 f. (V. Gollanz, London 1967)
2.   Bultmann and Rengstorf: Hope, p.9 f, Adam and Black.
3.   See Part II, Section 2, Chapter 1, Point 2.
4.   M. Werner: Formation of Christian Dogma, p.669, Beacon, Boston, 1963.
5.   Origen: Matthaus Kommentar, p.312, C.C.S Leipzig, 1933.
6.   E. Benz: Op. cit. p.26 f.

Chapter 2

The last Things

**The Parousia, The Mystery of Death, The Wonder of Resurrection
The Last Judgement, Hell and the Question of Purgatory
Heaven, the Kingdom of God and The Consummation of the World
The Question of Universal Salvation**

1. The Parousia

Christian theology has always taken seriously Jesus Christ's promise of His second coming in glory at the end of time. Jesus foretold His *parousia* and the Apostles proclaimed it *(Matt 24:3, 25:13; Luke 18:8; Acts 1:11; 1 Thess. 1:10; Col. 3:4; Phil. 3:20; James 5:8; 2 Pet. 1:16, 3:12).* There will be apocalyptic events as the sign of Christ's coming; both man-made wars and natural disasters *(Matt. 24:6, 29; Luke 21:20-28; 2 Peter 3:10; Rev. 8-9).* But before this the Gospel will be proclaimed all over the world *(Matt. 24:14; Rev. 14:6).* Lastly, Christ will appear in His glory.

In connection with Christ's *parousia* the question of its place in time emerges: When will He come back? The first Christians hoped for Christ's immediate second coming. As we have seen, Augustine put its date at the end of the first millenium. Since then extremist theologians have tried to predict the exact date of Christ's coming by the help of mystical calculations. The Seventh Day Adventist theologians have in the past tied themselves to specific dates with regard to Christ's *Parousia.* Each of the promised dates came and went and today they tend to interpret Christ's second coming spiritually.

Nowadays the belief is gathering strength in certain Christian circles that the time of the second coming of Christ is near. It is probably that the end of the second millenium is around the corner. Sober Christians have to avoid the temptation to try to calculate that date. Instead they accept Christ's answer to the question about His returning: "But of that day and hour no one knows, not even the angels of heaven, nor the Son, but the Father only" *(Matt. 24:36).* The fact of Christ's resurrection created the possibility of His *parousia.* Christians who accept in faith the resurrection of Christ also have to accept Christ's promise of His returning, and are living in the expectation of the second coming of their Lord. *(Matt. 25:1-30).*

2. The Mystery of Death

What will happen at the second coming of Christ? First of all there will be general resurrection of the dead *(1 Cor. 15:22 f; Rom. 8:11; 2 Cor. 1:9; 1 Thess. 4:13 f)*, but before we come to grip with that, let us try to give an understanding of Death itself.

Classical theology connects death to sin; death is the consequence of sin. Man was originally created for life without death, but because of the Fall that type of life was taken away from man and what is left is only a temporary life *(Gen. 3:19)*. Death thus occurs as a direct result of sin because sinful flesh can not inherit the Kingdom of God *(1 Cor. 15:50)*.

The heralds of death, sickness, pain and fear appear in man's life and they are at work in man's being from the day of his birth and in due course yield man up to the inevitable end of life. The tragic human situation is that he who is born to this life is born to die. Man is the only creature on the earth who is aware of his unavoidable death.[1]

Man tries to do everything to avoid or at least postpone his death. Man tries to find practices and medicines to prolong life. Through religions and philosophies man tries to find consolation and hope in a better after-life. The cults of the dead in all religions provide sufficient proof that man always believed in a life after death. The excavated tombs of past ages show how man equipped the graves of the deceased with food, utensils, clothes and valuables which were considered necessary for the after-life. Man also invented philosophies and theologies to acquaint himself with death and the after-life. In some of these death was sometimes considered as a natural part of life which had to be accepted, while in others man simply tried to forget death and kept himself busy in order to have no time for thinking about the end.

In modern theology the problem of death is dealt with seriously as never before. Reinhold Niebuhr considers that the fear of the anticipation of death is unbearable. Man is the only creature which knows this fear. Only Christian faith can overcome the fear of death, knowing that neither life nor death is able to separate us from the love of God *(Rom. 8:39)*, and those who do not have this faith approach death with fear and trembling. E. Brunner points out that the result of sin is not only that man dies but that he dies with anxiety, fear and agony because of his uncertainty about what awaits him on the other side of death. K. Barth views death in relation to Christ's death on the cross, and says that death is not natural because it is not from God's creation. Death is the most dreadful enemy of man, which frightens man with the possibility of Hell, the utmost and final separation from God. In death man inevitably faces God. Because man is sinful he can only expect rejection and condemnation. So death derives its fearfulness not from death itself but from God whom man meets in his death (Eccl. 12:7). But the Christian belief is that Christ accepted His own death voluntarily, a death in which the full consequences of sin can be seen. Because of Christ's vicarious death, believers are exempted from the second death, that is the ultimate separation from God. Christians know that they died with Christ and they will rise as Christ rose from the dead to eternal life.[2]

In connection with death the question arises whether man's being perishes absolutely in death or something imperishable survives. The ancient belief that only the body perishes but the soul survives death was adopted by Christian theology. This theory is not a Christian one, but its elements can be found in the Bible. This thought infiltrated into Christian theology from ancient religions on the one hand and from Platonic philosophy on the other. Both of them considered the human soul as the "Divine spark" in man which survives death because it cannot perish in it. If that is so the question arises: Where are the souls of those who have died? Either they can be in Hades or Sheol, which is the realm of the dead, or they can be with God. If they are with God, are they already in the Kingdom of God without the Last Judgement and Resurrection? Or if they are separated from God, are they all rejected without judgement? These are weighty questions, and indeed the theory of the survivial of the soul itself also comes under attack from many directions. Many thinkers and scientists insist that in death man's complete being perishes; body, soul and spirit perish. What then of the Christian belief that in death man's "imperishable" soul returns to God"?

The answer is that man's body and soul (Hebrew *nephesh*, Greek *psyche*), that which makes man a living being *(Gen. 1:7)*, are completely eliminated in death and become dust *(Gen. 3:19)*. But man's spirit (Hebrew *ruach*, Greek *pneuma*) which is the bearer of the "Image of God" in man *(Gen. 1:27)* by which we mean man's personality, character and memory, the unique pattern of each individual, returns to God *(Eccles. 12:7)*. (See: Part I, Section 4, Chapter 1:3 and 6). This should not be confused with the non-Christian "immortality of the soul",which proposes that human soul lives consciously forever apart from the body. Man's being definitely perishes in death, however, the dead "live to God". Christ said: "that God is not God of the dead but of the living, for all live to him" *(Luke 20:38)*. Those dead are living in God's memory, they are remembered by God and none of them is forgotten. The dead are living

173

in God and known by God as a "pattern" According to this "pattern" the dead will be created anew. Consequently, it is not necessary for Christians to rely on such a theory as the eternity of the soul. The believers' assurance is in God himself. This faith alone can give comfort against the dread of death. He who once created man out of nothing by doing so proved Himself to be able to create man again out of nothing, for a new and perfect life according to the pattern hidden in God in the likeness of the resurrected Christ.

From this understanding of death it follows that the dead cease to exist completely for this world and the world ceases to exist for the dead, just as the sleeping man ceases to exist for the world and the world for him. As the sleeping man does not know what is happening around him and does not feel the passing of the time, remembering only the moment before having fallen asleep and the next conscious moment when he awakes, so something like this happens in death too. Paul plainly refers to death as sleep *(1 Thess. 4:13)*. In death the passage of time between the last moment of life and the resurrection is completely lacking. Objectively this time may be measured by millions of years but subjectively for the dead person it is only a moment. During this million year "moment" the history of the world will happen and reaches its end. The next conscious moment of the dead will be at the Resurrection, and in it the re-created person faces God for judgement. This is the mystery of death; its purpose is to deliver man by the help of the resurrection to God his creator from whom he originates and to whom man must return. By this understanding of death it gets meaning and loses its fearful character. It now appears not as the enemy of man but an important element in the plan of salvation. Consequently, the believer can accept it patiently from the hand of God, knowing that even this enemy serves the purpose of God *(Ps. 23:4)*.

3. The Wonder of Resurrection

Faith in the Resurrection is one of the main cornerstones of the Christian faith and as such it is included in the Apostolic Creed. Only faith in resurrection gives the real meaning to being a Christian from the human point of view. Paul clearly and rightly says. "If there is no resurrection ... then our preaching is in vain and your faith is vain ... your faith is futile and you are still in your sins. If for this life only we have hope in Christ, we are of all men most to be pitied: *(1 Cor. 15:16-19)*.

Faith in the Resurrection is also widely disputed. This is because the idea of resurrection is in sharp contradiction to the basic natural laws, to human experience and logic and to science. Everything in this world seems to prove the oppposite: the unavoidable end of every living being is death, from where there is no returning. The human mind cannot imagine resurrection because human thinking is trained by experience to accept the unavoidability of death and opposed to acceping the thought of returning from it. At this point it is important to note that although the human mind proves the inevitability of death, history shows that mankind never can accept this, because death is so absolutely alien to man. This is because man is created for something other than death - for eternal life. Because of the inability of the corrupted human mind, the natural man cannot accept the idea of resurrection; only by faith can man accept it - a leap of faith to which the believer happily agrees.

Christian faith in the Resurrection is not a myth or utopian vision. Resurrection is definitely and firmly promised by God: *(John 11:25; 1 Cor. 6:14, 15:54-56; Acts 24:14; Eph. 2:6).* The reality of the Resurrection was demonstrated by God in the resurrection of Jesus Christ *(Rom. 1:4, 4:24; Gal. 1:1).* By raising Christ from the dead God proved three things: that Christ is God as He claimed and His death is a vicarious death for sinners; that God is able to raise the dead; that as Christ was raised so all men will be resurrected. Christian faith in the Resurrection is deeply rooted in Christ's resurrection and springs triumphantly from it *(1 Cor. 15:12; Col. 2:12; 1 Thess. 4:14).*

Resurrection does not mean a simple return to this life, as happened to those who were raised from the dead by Christ during His earthly ministry *(Luke 7:11 f; Mark 5:22 f; John 11:1f).* Resurrection means God's second *creatio ex nihilo* to a perfect life, in which there will be no sin, sickness, pain and death *(Rev. 21:4).* This resurrection will be the wonder of wonders. Even this life which we are living is a wonder. The Resurrection, which is God's second creation, is a greater wonder yet. In the picturesque description of the Bible, the introduction of resurrection will be a "trumpet" blown by an angel and resurrection will come about in a moment of time *(1 Cor. 15:52; Matt. 24:31; Thess. 4:16).* We may assume that in this "moment" time will be speeded up as in the creation.[3]

In the Resurrection, the "old" body will not be recreated as it was before; a new body will be created which is a spiritual body *(pneumatikos).* This is like the one which Christ had after his resurrection. The person in this new body will be the same, with the same identity and features, according to the pattern of the person hidden in God. The characteristics of this spiritual body will be not under the slavery of matter but the spirit will be complete master over the new matter and this new body will receive a renovated spirit and soul. This new being will be different from that of the old and it will be like that of the angels *(Matt. 22:30).*

One has to keep in his mind that God did not reveal everything about resurrection and man cannot push his imagination beyond what is revealed without the danger of going astray. The believer receives the promise of God about resurrection with gratitude and lives with it, accepting that it contradicts human reason. Still, the believer knows that resurrection is what he needs, and trusts to God that what He promised He will be able to perform in due time.

4. The Last Judgement

God in His revelation plainly says that after resurrection will come the Last Judgement *(Matt. 16:27, 25:31 f; John 5:22, 27-28; 2 Cor. 5:10; 2 Tim. 4:1; 1 Pet. 4:5),* when God and Christ judge the dead and the living, that is, those who are being resurrected from the dead and those who are still living at the *parousia* of Christ *(1 Thess. 4:16, 17; 1 Cor. 15:52).*

There are theological and moral reasons which point to the necessity of judgement and punishment of evil. First, from the theological standpoint, the holiness of God does not tolerate the uncleanness of sin forever; he who commits sin must bear its consequences. Second, the sovereign God does not tolerate a will which contradicts His will. Because the core of sin is rebellion against God's will, the sinner must bear the consequences of his sin. Third, sin spoils God's glory; in the act of sin, God is mocked by sinners, but God is not prepared to tolerate this and judges and punishes sinners. Fourth, there is a moral reason for the Last Judgement and punishment. This reason is two-sided. On one hand, man's moral awareness could not accept the fact that a man with grave sins remains unpunished. On the other hand, the moral law claims that even those sinners who escaped unpunished should be met with judgement after death. Christians believe that God and Christ will together execute the Last Judgement, at which the angels and even the saints will be present. *(John 5:22, 27; Matt. 25:31-46; 1 Thess. 5:13; 1 Cor. 6:3).*

We have to see clearly what is happening in the last Judgement. First, there will be no doubt that the whole of mankind, every individual, believer and unbeliever, has to stand before God for judgement *(Rom. 14:10; 2 Cor. 5:10; Rev. 21:11-15)* Second, God will judge men

176

according to their deeds *(Matt. 16:27)*. Third, there will be no one who, on the basis of his deeds, will not be condemned. Fourth, condemned mankind will be divided into two groups. The first group, that of the believers, will be spared from the punishment because the righteousness of Christ covers them from the punishment. The righteousness of Christ is what He gave to those who believed Him, loved Him and followed Him. And this is possible because Christ on the Cross and in death has voluntarily suffered the punishment of our sins on behalf of us. The "exchange" between us and Christ on the cross, accepted by faith, now becomes reality; the miracle of salvation now takes place and the result is that the sinner is justified and qualified to enter into the Kingdom of God. The second group, that of the unbelievers, are to suffer the consequence of their sins and their unbelief, which is eternal separation from the God they have spurned *(Matt. 10:15, 25:30; Mark 9:46; Rev. 20:15)* [4]

The seriousness of the Last Judgement has to motivate Christians to become responsible persons who are willing to demonstrate their faith to others in actions of love *(Matt. 7:21, 1 John 3:14)*.

5. Hell and the Question of Purgatory

The concept of Hell, both in the Bible and in theology, went through a process of development from its Old Testament beginnings through the New Testament writings and into the recent period. In its development this concept was undoubtedly influenced by other religions, mainly from Mesopotamia, Egypt and the Orient. Later, different philosophies influenced it. The concept of Hell is closely related to the idea of "Hades" which in ancient religions is considered as the world of the dead. Its Old Testament equivalent is *"Sheol"* which is under the earth. This is the destination of all the dead, where they continue their life but in a shadowy and colourless way. It is a place of silence, forgetting and of sleeping *(Job 17:1, 11-16; Pss. 115:7, 6:5)*. At one time it was considered that *Sheol* fell outside the rule of *Jahweh* and there was no return from it *(Job 7:9-10, 10:21-22)*, but later, it was believed that *Jahweh* is Lord not only over the living but even over the dead *(Amos 9:2; Pss. 86:113, 139:8)*.

This belief led to a radical change in the concept of *Sheol*, a change that gradually strengthened the belief that the world of *Sheol* will come to an end in the future and there will be the resurrection of the dead from *Sheol. (Isa. 26:19; Job 14:14, 19:25; Ezek. 37:1-14)*. With the belief in resurrection the idea of judgement was accepted gradually, and that beyond death and resurrection God will judge all men, punish the wicked

177

and reward the righteous *(Isa. 40:10; Pss 11:6, 58:11, 28:4; Job 20:29; Matt. 16:26; 2 Cor. 5:10; 1 Peter 4:5; Rev. 22:12)*. Because of the belief in the Last Judgement, the concept of *Sheol* was transformed into the place of punishment and recieved a new name: *Gyehenna* or "Hell" *(Num. 16:30; Job 24:19; Isa. 66:24; Matt. 5:29, 25:41)*. The pious and the righteous will be qualified in the Judgement for entering into "Paradise" or "Heaven" or the "Kingdom of God" *(Luke 23:43; 2 Cor. 12:3; Revel. 2:7, 22:2)*. Jesus Christ and the first Christians adopted this concept of Hell *(Luke 16:19.f; John 14:2; Mark 9:45-48; Matt. 6:20; Luke 10:20)*.[5]

The notion of Hell as a physical place is closely connected with the ancient "three-storey" world-model. In this model the underworld, the location of Hell, was imagined as really existing under the surface of the earth and ruled by Satan and devils who torment the inmates. Heaven, the world "above" the earth, was believed to be the physical place of God and the angels and that of "Paradise" which is the place of the good, pious and righteous. This model of Hell and Heaven is now outdated. Today the majority of theologians consider Hell and Heaven as symbols which adequately describe two basic states of man in relation with God. Hell means man's state eternally apart from God, that is man's rejection and separation from God which means "despair". Heaven describes man's state of "blessedness" in the nearness and presence of God, which means fullness of life.[6]

In connection with Hell we have to mention the idea of Purgatory which was developed in the Medieval Church. Its origin goes back to the later period of the early Church. Augustine mentions this idea in the "City of God", saying that between death and judgement souls are being purified by fire. Hence the name of "Purgatory" which means the place of purging or purifying. The doctrine was officially formulized only in late Medieval times (1439). The Reformers, however, rejected this doctrine. Neither Protestant nor Orthodox theology accepts it, because the doctrine lacks adequate Biblical foundation.

6. Heaven, the Kingdom of God and the Consummation of the World

Like the idea of Hell, the concept of Heaven also went through a process of development both in the Bible and in theology. The Hebrew *Samaim* and the Greek *Uranos* mean both the visible sky and the invisible heaven above it, which were created by God *(Gen. 1:1; Neh. 9:6; Pss. 33:6, 96:5, 121:2)*. The visible sky was considered as a massive tent which stands on the mountains as pillars, its ends resting on the edges of the earth *(Gen. 1:6f; Job 26:11; Pss. 75:3, 104:5; Amos 9:6)*. On this tent-like surface the stars were fixed, and each moves along on it on its way *(Gen. 1:14 f; Ps. 19:6; Isa. 40:26; Jer. 33:25)*. The heavens have gates and through them God gives gifts and blessing like rain and dew onto the earth. Moreover, if it is necessary, punishment descends through these gates upon the earth as flood, fire, lighting and drought *(Gen. 7:4, 19:24; Deut. 11:17, 28:24; Luke 4:25; James 5:27)*. The throne of God is in heaven, where He lives with the angels *(Ps. 103:19; Isa. 66:1)*. From heaven God looks down at the earth and men *(Pss. 11:4, 14:2)*.

Heaven is also called the Kingdom of Heaven or the Kingdom of God, where God's sovereign will reigns. God wants to re-establish His Kingdom on the Earth *(Jer. 33:13; Ezek. 36:24 f; Dan. 2:44; Matt. 6:10)*. Heaven is out of the reach of man, but God can lift man up to it *(Gen. 5:24; 2 Kings 2:11; Heb. 11:5)*. The Son of God came down from Heaven. In Him the Kingdom of God is here among men and when He comes again He brings those who are His own into the Kingdom of God *(Matt. 24:31, 25:34; 2 Cor. 5:1; 1 Thess. 4:17)*. Heaven must not be considered as spatial and imagined to be somewhere "out there" in space. As God cannot be located because He is Spirit, so the Kingdom of God cannot be located because it is spiritual. This does not mean unreality but rather a higher reality. Heaven and the Kingdom of God can be considered as being in the state of the presence of God, where and when His eternal presence can be felt.[7]

Beside the doctrine of the Kingdom of God where God's elect and saved people will dwell, there is the doctrine of the consummation of the World. God cares not only for those saved out of the world but for the world as well. God creates a new heaven and earth upon which the Kingdom of God will be fully established. *(Isa. 65:17, 66:22; Rev. 21:1)*. The characteristic of this new creation is that there will be no death, sickness, pain, distress, nor tears *(Rev. 21:1)*. There will be no separation between man and man, between man and God, between God and the whole universe; "God will be everything to everyone" *(1 Cor. 15:28)*. Man can look at God face to face without fear and trembling. This life will be one of eternal love and perfection. Man, like the angels, will render voluntary, free service to God, will live in peace, harmony and joy. In this new creation Satan, sin and death have no place at all and God's original plan for the world will be realized. The salvation, the Kingdom of God and the consummation of the world are alike objects of Christian hope *(John 10:28; Rom. 8:30; 2 Cor. 5:17; 2 Pet. 3:13; Rev. 21:1-4, 22:4)*.

By faith believers already enjoy the Kingdom of God and experience its blessings, looking forward in hope and expectation to the full coming of the Kingdom of God. They know that the Kingdom of God is not an empty utopia, a fond imagination or an unreal dream, because the Kingdom of God has already appeared in the life. The resurrection and ascension of Christ are the divine seals and assurances of the reality of the promised Kingdom. Out of the dialectical character of the Kingdom - that the Kingdom of God is already here in the believers and in the Church but still has to come in its fullness - comes the right attitude of believers to the Kingdom of God. They cannot wait passively for its full coming, but have to work for its spreading and coming by infusing into this world the power, love and gifts they received from the Kingdom of God. In doing this the believers are aware that the coming of the Kingdom is not the result of their work, but will arrive because of the sovereign will of God. Therefore, believers are living in expectation of the Kingdom of God *(Matt. 25:1-13)*.

7. The Question of Universal Salvation

There have been theologians since Clement of Alexandria (c 150-215), Origen (c 185-254) and Gregory of Nyssa (c 330-395), and such modern theologians as E. Brunner, K. Barth and P. Tillich, who implicitly could not accept the end of the world according to the interpretation of the doctrine of the "Double Decree" in its classical meaning. This decree teaches that the drama of the World will end with the eternal salvation of the elect and the eternal damnation of the rejected. This theory was maintained by Augustine and Calvin, and is maintained by many present day fundamentalist or conservative theologians.[8].

The doctrine of Universal Salvation or *Apocatastasis* from a Greek word meaning "complete restoration, reestablishment" says that the punishment of condemned sinners could not be eternal, but at the very end the whole of mankind will be taken up into salvation. In its most radical version this doctrine insists that even Satan will be converted. The doctrine was condemned by the Synod of Constantinople in 543 AD and it is not the official teaching of the majority of the Christian Churches. However, this doctrine was accepted by some Christian groups such as the Arminians, the Anabaptists and Moravians, and it is taught by many liberal theologians. As was mentioned above, some leading contemporary theologians show an inclination towards this notion, which suggests that the doctrine deserves more of our attention and consideration.

Undoubtedly there are passages in the Bible which indicate the rejection and punishment of unrepentant sinners in the last Judgement will be eternal *(Matt. 3:12, 25:41; Mark 3:29; Revel. 14:11, 20:10).* But there are also texts in the Bible which show God's universal saving will. For example, *1 Timothy 2:4* speaks of God: "Who desires all men to be saved". The Greek text uses *Thelo* which means "will"; God wills that all men be saved. *1 Corinthians 15:27-28* says that "all things are put in subjection under Him ... that God may be everything to everyone". In the light of this the eternal rejection of part of mankind would prove the opposite; God's saving will only be partially fulfilled in the saved few, God cannot be "everything to everyone", only in those who have been saved but not in the rejected. If the rejection of a significant part of mankind is eternal, then how can Christ's redemptive work be regarded as perfect in its consequences for the whole of mankind? God's plan for the restoration of sinful mankind also cannot succeed perfectly, and God's glory will not be restored fully if the condemnation of a significant part of mankind is eternal. How then can it be said that God's love is unconditional and unfathomable? Can the punishment of a finite being be infinite? Can a temporal sin be punished eternally? Brunner says with reason that the doctrine of the Double Decree shows God as one who has two wills and transforms the unconditional love of God into a particular love which cares only for a part of humanity.[9]

No doubt there is a tension between God's saving will and God's judging will, between God's mercy and God's punishment, between God's divine love and God's holy wrath. The solution of this tension is in Christ's vicarious punishment and in His rejection in His death. In Christ's redemptive work God's judgement and punishment were satisfied, His wrath and anger died out and God's love, mercy and saving will prevailed. The question is, to what degree? Unconditionally or conditionally, perfectly or provisionally? When the Early Church decided to condemn the doctrine of *Apocatastasis* we must presume a practical consideration was decisive in their decision. That is, a fear that if the Church preached universal salvation it would make itself superfluous and dispensable. If at the end both good and wicked, godly and ungodly, reach salvation, why then are repentance, faith and the Church necessary? This doctrine could lead people to irresponsibility and would encourage them fo commit and live in sin. But the outcome of this doctrine may not necessarily be so understood. The meaning of being a Christian is that he is spared from fear, uncertainty, despair and hopelessness in regard to the end, and from the feeling of the meaninglessness of existence. Christians know that they are saved and they live as the children of God, seeking and doing His will in the hope that at the last they will receive the award of eternal life *(2 Tim. 4:8).* The ungodly, on the other hand, live in fear, trembling, waiting for nothing but utter destruction in the end. They are living in sin and by doing so they waste their life. Only at the very end, after judgement and rejection, will they understand the unfathomable and unconditional love of God and they will regret and be ashamed of their wasted life. However, if Christians are not prepared to accept the unorthodox doctrine of universal salvation, at least they have to live in hope of not only their own salvation but even for the redeemed life of the whole of humanity. This is because they know that God's love is unconditional and unfathomable and beyond all human understanding.

Christian theologians have to deal with eschatology cautiously because two temptations surround it which must be avoided. First is to downplay or neglect the eschatological element which leads to the impoverishment of Christian faith and life. Second is to overemphasize the eschatological element, which leads to an extreme position which can be characterized as chiliasm. This results in a utopian situation which concentrates only on the future and disregards the importance and responsibility of the present. The eschatological aspect of Christian faith and teaching must be maintained in a balanced way so that Christians become people of God who understand "Here we have no lasting city, but we seek the city which is to come" *(Heb. 13:14).*

NOTES

1. See: Part I, Section 4, Chapter 5, Point 1
2. A. Richardson (ed): A Dictionary of Christian Theology, p.88, SCM 1969.
3. See: Part I. Section 3, Chapter 1, Point 2.3.
4. E. Brunner: Dogmatics, Vol III, p.420 f.
5. See Part II, Section 2, Chapter 3, Point 1.2.
6. P. Tillich: Systematic Theology, Vol III, p.418.
7. ibid, p.406.
8. J. Calvin: Institutes III, 2:5.
9. E. Brunner: Dogmatics, Vol. III, p.418 f.

Chapter 3

Eschatology in Contemporary Theology

The Theology of Hope
J. Moltmann, W. Pannenberg, E. Schillebeeckx, J. B. Metz

1. The Theology of Hope

Eschatology has always been an essential part of Christian theology. We have already seen in the first chapter of this section how the early Church took eschatology seriously in which the *Parousia* was given central importance. It is true that in subsequent ages eschatology gradually lost its central position in theological thinking and took a place on the periphery of Christian theology, as theologians of different ages were kept busy solving problems which emerged from the current life of the Church. However, eschatology has never been denied or discarded, and has always constituted an important (albiet peripheral) part in Christian theology. We also noted that there were periods when eschatology grew in importance, as at the end of the first millenium or in some modern sectarian movements.

Towards the end of the last century, eschatology became a major issue in theology as the result of the Bible criticism that was then fashionable. This was the achievement of the work of A. Schweitzer who suggests that the key to understanding Jesus' life and ministry is in the eschatology. His ideas of eschatology were taken up and taken to extremes by the two Swiss theologians, M. Werner and F. Buri around the middle of this century in their so called "Consequent Eschatology" They reached the conclusion that the Christological dogma of the Church is the result of the failure of Christ's immediate second coming. Therefore, they concluded, Christianity is based on an illusion. However, they tried to provide an existentialist interpretation of Christianity to save it one way or another. Little wonder they did not leave a lasting impression on theology[1].

The English scholar C. H. Dodd introduced a new concept of "realized eschatology" in the 1930's. His starting point was that mainly the epistles of Paul and the Acts regarded the kingdom of God as a state which is already present. Dodd, therefore, emphasized that Jesus Christ brought in the Kingdom with his messianic work[2].

183

R. H. Fuller, around the middle of the century, occupied a mediating stance with regard to the opposing views in eschatology. He insisted that Jesus Christ was well aware that the Kingdom of God was to come with His ministry. But in its fulness it will come only after His messianic death. So Jesus Christ in His life only inaugurated the *parousia*[3].

In the mid sixties of this century and onward, eschatology once more became one of the main focal points of theology through the work of the school of the "Theology of Hope" in Europe. A group of theologians, both Protestant and Roman Catholic, belong to this school and it has exercised a considerable impact upon contemporary theological thinking. It has rendered essential assistance to the birth of Liberation theologies. In the following paragraphs we review briefly some of the main ideas of some of the outstanding representatives of this school.

2. J. Moltmann

The founder of the school of Theology of Hope is the German Protestant theologian Jurgen Moltmann (b. 1926). His book Theology of Hope (1964) represents a milestone in the post-Barthian era of theology. The philosophy of Ernst Bloch (1888 - 1977), a Jewish born renegade Marxist, influenced Moltmann, particularly Bloch's principle of hope *(Prinzip Hoffnung)*. Moltmann attempted to reinterpret Christian theology in terms of hope, stressing that eschatology is not only one element of Christian theology but it is the centre and the key of Christian faith and of theology. Consequently, the problem of the future is the only real problem of theology. God speaks about Himself as One whose essential nature is the future. He is the God of hope. This is obvious from the Exodus and from the prophetic writings of the Old Testament. The New Testament writings not only talk about a Jesus Christ of the past, or who He was, but they speak about who the Christ will be in the future and what man can expect from Him. God is not only behind us or above us but He is before us. Consequently, eschatology is not the end of theology but is its beginning. This theology results in positive ethical implications. Christian hope must be materialized by the participation of Christians in the activity of society. Christians must be "creative disciples" who show "creative hope"[2].

3. W. Pannenberg

The theology of the German Protestant theologian Wolfhard Pannenberg (b. 1928) shows many common features with that of Moltmann, but he distinguishes himself from this school. According to

184

Pannenberg, the God of the Bible is the God of the Future. Every reality is related to the future and is eschatologically oriented. God is the God of promises, and in God's promises the future is proclaimed. God reveals Himself in history, particularly in Israel's history. By fulfilled promises God leads His people towards more bold hopes: His own coming, the resurrection of the dead and the Kingdom of God. The teaching and resurrection of Jesus Christ have great importance in Pannenberg's theology. In Christ's teaching the world to come already exists because of its relation with the Kingdom of God. God's love can be understood as the present expression of the coming Kingdom. Pannenberg regards Christ's resurrection as a historical fact, a fact of great importance because in it there is the promise of a universal resurrection. Without resurrection, life is meaningless; only in it can human existence reach its utmost fulfilment. Christ's resurrection is not an isolated miracle, it is the beginning of the universal resurrection. Because this theology insists upon the historicity of Christ's resurrection and because this Christ will appear at the end of human history, it follows that this theology takes history seriously. Pannenberg looks at history and the world with hope. Consequently the Christian faith could not lead to escapism from the world but to responsibility for this world and for its future. At this point in its ethical consequences Pannenberg's theology shows its positive and progressive character[5].

4. E. Schillebeeckx

Eduard Schillebeeckx (b. 1914), a Dutch Roman Catholic theologian of Belgian origin, is also a prominent representative of the school of the Theology of Hope. He looks at contemporary man as one who turns towards the future. This turn is the impact of our age's social, scientific and technological changes. This "turning towards the future" attitude of modern man exercises an influence upon his religion and it also turns towards the same direction. In the future-oriented religion the concept of God undergoes changes. In past cultures, which were past-oriented, the concept of God was also heavily tied to the past. The reconstruction of the concept of God in a future-oriented world is possible because God has revealed Himself as the God who is "coming". God shows Himself to man as the future of man and gives to us in Jesus Christ the possibility of creating the future. The content of Christian faith is the eschatological fulfillment of the promises of God. God who comes in history realizes His promises in history and thereby renews history. Christian faith means commitment to the future; Christians have to improve life by caring for humanity and defend life against every danger. Only then will the Christians' faith in the future be proven true[6].

5. J. B. Metz

Johannes B. Metz (b. 1928), a German Roman Catholic theologian, also can be counted in this school. He starts with the fact of the gradual secularization of the world and tries to seek the response of faith to it. He suggests that instead of a negative and militant attitude, theology should show a positive and conciliatory attitude to the process of world-secularization. In other words, theology should not understand secularization as the proof of the rejection of the word of God. This cannot be true, because God accepted the world in Jesus Christ and by it eschatologically determined the world. The Church in the world is the sign that God accepted this world. But the world is both accepted by God and resists this acceptance; hence its secularization. God is the God of history, who not only stands above and behind history but who is coming in history, and at the same time God stands over against history as its free and sovereign future. This gives an eschatological character to the world. He suggests that theology must be transformed into eschatological theology which is basically "World-Theology" in so far as it deals with the future of God's world. Christians are responsible that their faith be expressed as creative and militant hope. Christians must become the builders of the heavenly Jerusalem by constructive participation in the social and political problems of this world[7].

The birth of the Theology of Hope was helped by several factors. Among these we can trace the growing interest of humanity in the future of the world and in it that of the individual - in a world where the atomic catastrophy was a growing danger and which could mean the sudden and apocalyptic end of the world. Another factor is that historic dialectical and hermeneutic theologies stressed the importance of the "Here and Now" and distracted attention from the future. Another factor relates to the exestentialist theologies which narrowed the *kerygma* to the individual, with the result that theology had no answer to the problems of the future or to the burning issues of society, humanity and the world. The theologies of the school of the Theology of Hope try to provide the answers to all these problems, and to show God as the One who holds the future for Mankind and for the world[8].

NOTES

1. E. Brunner: Dogmatics, Vol III, p. 260.f.
2. C. H. Dodd: The Apostolic Preaching and its Development, 1936.
3. R. H. Fuller: The Mission and Achievement of Jesus, 1954.
4. J. Moltmann: Theology of Hope, p. 10, 17-18, 335.
5. W. Pannenberg: Basic Questions in Theology, Vol. II, p.237.f (SCM, 1971) and: Basic Questions in Theology, Vol III, p. 99.f and: Jesus-God and Man, p. 85.f.
6. E. Schillebeeckx: God and the Future of Man, p. 172.f (Sheed and Ward, 1969)
7. J. B. Metz: Theology of the World, p. 13.f, Burns and Oates (Herder, 1969)
8. J. MacQuarrie: Twentieth Century Religious Thought (SCM 1978) p.382..

SUGGESTED READING

PART TWO
Introduction

Chapter 1

1. E. Brunner, Dogmatics, Vol II (London: The Lutterworth Press, 1964), p.289 f.
2. K. Barth, Church Dogmatics, Vol IV, Part 1, §57, 58 (Edinburgh: T&T Clark, 1956), p.3 f.
3. P. Tillich, Systematic Theology, Vol II, Part 2, The Reality of Christ (The University of Chicago Press, 1957), p.97 f.
4. I.H. Marshall, The Origins of New Testament Christology (Inter Varsity Press, 1976).
5. C.F.D Moule, The Origin of Christology (Cambridge University Press, 1977).
6. W.R. Matthews, The Problem of Christ in the 20th Century (The Oxford University Press, 1951).
7. N. Hook, Christ in the Twentieth Century (The Lutterworth Press, 1968).
8. A.M. Fairbairn, The Place of Christ in Modern Theology (Hodder and Stoughton Ltd).
9. H. Berkhof, Christ the Meaning of History.
10. N.F.S Ferre, Christ and the Christians (Harper and Brothers, 1958).
11. J.K.S. Reid, Our Life in Christ (SCM, 1963).

Chapter 2

1. A. Schweitzer, The Quest of the Historical Jesus (Adam and Charles Black, 1956).
2. A. Schweitzer, The Mystery of the Kingdom of God (Adam and Charles Black, 1956).
3. J.M. Robinson, A New Quest of the Historical Jesus (SCM, 1958).
4. D.F. Strauss, The Life of Jesus Critically Examined (SCM, 1973).
5. J. E. Renan, The Life of Jesus (The World Publishing Co, 1941).
6. G. Bornkamm, Jesus of Nazareth (London: Hodder and Stoughton Ltd, 1960).
7. I.H. Marshall, I Believe in the Historical Jesus, (W.B. Eerdmans Publ. Co, 1977).

8.   W. Pannenberg, <u>Basic Questions in Theology</u>, Vol I, Ch 2, 3, 4, 5 (SCM), p.15 f.
9.   A. Richardson, <u>History Sacred and Profane</u> (SCM, 1964).
10. O. Brachert, <u>The Original Jesus</u> (The Lutterworth Press, 1933).
11. E. Fuchs, <u>Studies of the Historical Jesus</u> (SCM, 1964).

Chapter 3

1.   W. Pannenberg, <u>Jesus - God and Man</u> (SCM, 1968).
2.   J. Moltmann, <u>The Crucified God</u> (SCM, 1974).
3.   K. Barth, <u>Church Dogmatics</u>, Vol IV, Part 1 §59; Vol IV, Part 2, §64; Vol II, Part 2 (Edinburgh: T&T Clark, 1958), p.161 f, p.315 f.
4.   E. Brunner, <u>Dogmatics</u>, Vol II, Appendix A, B (London: The 'Lutterworth Press, 1964), p.260 f.
5.   P. Tillich, <u>Systematic Theology</u>, Vol II (The University of Chicago Press, 1957), p.260 f.

SECTION 1

Chapter 1

1.   O. Cullman, <u>Christ and Time</u> (SCM, 1971).
2.   E. Brunner, <u>Dogmatics</u>, Vol II, Ch 9, The Fullness of Time (London: The Lutterworth Press, 1964), p.231 f.
3.   P. Tillich, <u>Systematic Theology</u>, Vol III, Kairos and Kairoi (The University of Chicago Press, 1957), p.369 f.

Chapter 2

1.   J. Macquarrie, <u>Principles of Christian Theology</u>, p.280 f.
2.   R. Pannikar, <u>Virgin Birth and Bodily Resurrection</u> (Orbis).
3.   D.M. Baillie, <u>God was in Christ</u> (Faber, 1948).
4.   G.S. Hendry, <u>The Gospel of the Incarnation</u> (SCM, 1959).
5.   R.L. Ottley, <u>The Doctrine of the Incarnation</u>, 2 Vols (Methuen and Co, 1896).
6.   C. Gore, <u>The Incarnation of the Son of God</u> (John Murray, 1891).
7.   J. Hick, <u>The Myth of God Incarnate</u> (SCM, 1977).
8.   M. Green, (ed) <u>The Truth of God Incarnate</u> (Hodder and Stoughton Ltd. 1977).

9. R.E. Brown, The Virginal Conception and Bodily Resurrection of Jesus (Chapman and Paulist, Newman Press, 1973).
10. E. Brunner, The Mediator, Book II, Section 2, The Incarnation of the Son of God (London: The Lutterworth Press, 1934), p.285 f.
11. T. Bosloper, The Virgin Birth (SCM, 1961).

Chapter 3

1. O. Betz, What Do We Know About Jesus? (SCM, 1968).
2. G. Bornkamm, Jesus of Nazareth (Hodder and Stoughton Ltd, 1960).
3. P.C. Simpson, The Fact of Christ (Hodder and Stoughton Ltd).
4. A. Schweitzer, The Psychological Study of Jesus (The Beacon Press, 1958).
5. H. Johnson, The Humanity of the Saviour (Epworth Press, 1962).
6. J.M. Bowman, The Intention of Jesus (The Westminster Press, 1943).
7. P.DeRosa, Jesus Who Became Christ (Collins-Fontain, 1977).
8. E. Brunner, The Mediator, Book II, Section 3, The Humanity of the Son of God (The Lutterworth Press, 1934), p.328.
9. K. Barth, Church Dogmatics, Vol IV, Part 2, §64, 2.
    The Homecoming of the Son of Man (Edinburgh: T&T Clark, 1958), p.20 f.

Chapter 4

1. E. Brunner Dogmatics, Vol II, The Divinity of Christ (The Lutterworth Press, 1964), p.330 f.
2. H. Conzelmann, Jesus (Fortress Press, 1973).
3. O. Cullmann, The Christology of New Testament (SCM, 1959).
4. M. Hengel, The Son of God (Fortress Press, 1976).
5. R.C. Johnson, The Meaning of Christ (The Westminster Press, 1958).
6. W.R. Kramer, Christ, Lord, Son of God (SCM, 1966).
7. N. Pittenger, Christ For Us Today (SCM, 1968).
8. E. Brunner, The Mediator, Book II, Section 1, The Deity of the Mediator (The Lutterworth Press, 1934), p.201 f.
9. K. Barth, Church Dogmatics, Vol IV, Part 2, § 64, 3, The Royal Man (Edinburgh: T&T Clark, 1958), p.154 f.

Chapter 5

1. D. Baillie, God was in Christ (Faber, 1948).
2. D. Bonhoeffer, Christology (Collins Fount Paperbacks 1978).
3. C.F.D. Moule, The Origin of Christology (Cambridge UP, 1977).
4. F. Weston, The One Christ (Longmans, Green and Co, 1914).
5. S. Cave, The Doctrine of the Person of Christ (Duckworth, 1925).
6. A. Harnack, History of Dogma, 1894-9.
7. W.R. Matthews, The Problem of Christ in the 20th Century (Oxford UP, 1951).
8. W. Temple, Christ and the Younger Churches (SPCK, 1972).
9. G.K.A Bell, D.A. Deissmann (eds), Mysterium Christi (Longmans, Green & Co, 1930).
10. L. Berkhof, Systematic Theology, Part 3, The Unipersonality of Christ (The Banner of Truth Trust, 1959), p.321 f.

Chapter 6

1. N. Hook, Christ in the Twentieth Century (The Lutterworth Press, 1968).
2. W. Lillie, Jesus - Then and Now (SPCK, 1964).
3. W. E. Matthews, The Problem of Christ in the 20th Century (Oxford UP, 1951).
4. A. M. Fairbairn The Place of Christ in Modern Theology (Hodder and Stoughton Ltd, 1894).
5. N. Pittenger, Christ for Us Today (SCM, 1968).
6. A. Richardson, The Political Christ (SCM, 1973).
7. A.O. Dyson, Who is Jesus Christ? (SCM, 1969).
8. D.L. Carmody, J.T. Carmody, Jesus (Wadsworth Publishing Co, 1987).

SECTION 2

Chapter 1

1. E. Brunner, Dogmatics, Ch 2A, The Prophetic Office (London: The Lutterworth Press, 1964), p.271 f.
2. G. Bornkamm, Jesus of Nazareth (Hodder and Stoughton Ltd, 1960).
3. J.W. Bowman, The Intention of Jesus (The Westminster Press, 1943).

4. O. Betz, <u>What Do We Know About Jesus?</u> (SCM, 1968).
5. A. Richardson, <u>The Miracle - Stories of the Gospel</u> (SCM, 1959).
6. C.S. Lewis, <u>Miracles</u> (London: The Century Press, 1947).
7. A.M. Ramsey, R. Terwilliger, A.M. Allchin, <u>The Charismatic Christ</u>
   (Darton, Longman and Todd, 1974).
8. E. Keller, M. Keller, <u>Miracles in Dispute</u> (SCM)
9. M. Wilson, <u>The Church is Healing</u> (SCM, 1966).
10. L. Berkhof, <u>Systematic Theology</u>, Part 3, The Offices of Christ;
    Part 1, Introduction: The Prophetic Office (The Banner of Truth
    Trust, 1959) p.356 f.
11. W. Barclay, <u>The Mind of Jesus</u> (SCM, 1960).
12. J.A. Findlay, <u>What did Jesus Teach?</u> (London: 1953).
13. E.G. Ladd, <u>Jesus and the Kingdom</u> (SPCK 1964).
14. J. Weiss, <u>Jesus' Proclamation of the Kingdom of God</u> (Scholar
    Press, 1985).

Chapter 2

1. E. Brunner, <u>Dogmatics</u>, Vol II, Ch 2B, The Priestly Work
   (London: The Lutterworth Press, 1964), p.281 f.
2. L. Berkhof, <u>Systematic Theology</u>, Part 3, The Offices of Christ
   (The Banner of Truth Trust, 1959), p. 361.f.
3. J. Calvin, <u>Institutes</u>, II, XV.
4. M.D. Hooker, <u>Jesus and the Servant</u> (SPCK, 1959).
5. W.R. Kramer, <u>Christ, Lord, Son of God</u> (SCM, 1966).
6. W. Hanson, <u>Jesus The Messiah</u> (Hodder and Stoughton Ltd, 1944).
7. C.F.H. Henry (ed), <u>Christ, Lord, Son of God</u> (SCM, 1966).
8. E. Routley, <u>The Man for Others</u> (Peter Smith Ltd, 1964).
9. F.J. Powell, <u>The Trial of Jesus Christ</u> (London: 1949).

Chapter 3

1. A. Richardson, <u>An Introduction to the Theology of the New</u>
   <u>Testament</u>, Ch 9, The Resurrection, Ascension and Victory of
   Christ (Harper & Row), p.19O f.
2. E. Brunner, <u>Dogmatics</u>, Vol II, Ch 2C, The Royal Work of Christ,
   p.298 f and Ch 12E; The Risen and Exalted Lord
   (London: The Lutterworth Press, 1964), p.363 f.
3. E. Brunner, <u>The Mediator</u>, Book 3, The Work of the Mediator,
   p.399 f.
4. L. Berkhof, <u>Systematic Theology</u>, Part 3, Ch 2, The State of

Exaltation, p.344 f and Ch 8, The Kingly Office (The Banner of Truth Trust, 1959), p.406 f.

5. J.A.T. Robinson, The Body (SCM, 1952).
6. W. Pannikar, Virgin Birth and Bodily Resurrection (Orbis)
7. W. Pannenberg, Jesus God and Man, Part 1, Ch 3, Jesus' Resurrection as the Ground of His Unity with God, p.53 f.
8. R.E. Brown, The Virginal Conception and Bodily Resurrection of Jesus (Chapman and Paulist - Newman Press, 1973).
9. N. Clark, Interpreting Resurrection (SCM, 1967).
10. E.G. Ladd, I Believe in the Resurrection of Jesus (London: 1975).
11. S.H. Hooke, The Resurrection of Christ as History and Experience (London: 1967).
12. D.P. Fuller, Easter Faith and History (London: 1968).
13. J.G. Davies, He Ascended into Heaven (London: 1958).
14. E. Schweitzer, Jesus (John Knox Press, 1971).

Section 3

Chapter 1

1. E. Brunner, Dogmatics, Vol II (London: The Lutterworth Press, 1964), p.283 f.
2. J. Macquarrie, Principles of Christian Theology, Ch 3, The Work of Christ, p.311 f.
3. D. Bonhoeffer, Christology, Introduction, Ch 2, The Person and Work of Christ (Collins Fount Paperbacks, 1978), p.37 f.
4. O. Cullmann, The Christology of the New Testament (SCM, 1959).
5. I.H. Marshall, The Origin of New Testament Christology (Inter Varsity Press).
6. W. Manson, Jesus the Messiah (Hodder and Stoughton, 1944).
7. R.C. Johnson, The Meaning of Christ (The Westminster Press, 1958).
8. A. Richardson, An Introduction to the Theology of the New Testament, Ch 10, The Atonement Bought by Christ, (Harper & Row, 1958), p.215 f.
9. F.R. Barry, The Atonement (London: 1968).
10. M. Hengel, The Atonement (SCM, 1981).

Chapter 2

1. J. Macquarrie, Principles of Christian Theology, Ch.13, The Work of Christ, §15, The Classical View of Atonement, p.318 f.

2.   E. Brunner, Dogmatics, Vol II, (London: The Lutterworth Press, 1964), p.288 f.
3.   L. Berkhof, Systematic Theology, Part Three, Divergent Theories of the Atonement (The Banner of Truth Trust, 1959), p.384 f.
4.   J. Baillie, God was in Christ (Faber, 1948).
5.   C.F. Henry (ed), Jesus of Nazareth Saviour and Lord (The Tyndale Press, 1966).
6.   R.C. Johnson, The Meaning of Christ (The Westminster Press, 1958).
7.   L.J. Sherill, Guilt and Redemption (John Knox Press, 1960).
8.   St. Anselm, Cur Deus Homo? Why Did God Become Man? (T.E., 1863)
9.   W. Pannenberg, Jesus God and Man, Ch 7, The Meaning of Jesus' Vicarious Death on the Cross (SCM, 1968), p.45 f.
10.   E. Brunner, The Mediator, Book 3, Section 2, Reconcilliation (The Lutterworth Press, 1934), p.435 f.
11.   K. Barth, Church Dogmatics, Vol IV, Part 1 & 6l, The Justification b Man (Edinburgh: T&T Clark, 1956), p.514 f.
12.   F.W. Dillistone, Christian Understanding of Atonement (London, 1968).
13.   H.A. Hodges, The Pattern of Atonement (London: SCM, 1955).
14.   G. Aulen, Christus Victor (SPCK, 1978).
15.   T. Stott, The Cross of Christ (Inter Varsity Press).

Chapter 3

1.   E. Brunner, Mediator (London: The Lutterworth Press, 1934).
2.   K. Barth Church Dogmatics, Vol IV, Part 1, 2, 3 §1, 3 §2, (Edinburgh, T&T Clark, 1956-1962).
3.   D. Bonhoeffer, Christology (Collins Fount Paperbacks, 1978),
4.   G. Aulen, Christus Victor (SPCK, 1978).
5.   L. Berkhof, Systematic Theology, Part 3 and 4 (The Banner of Truth Trust, 1959), p.305 f.
6.   P. Tillich, Systematic Theology, Vol II (The University of Chicago Press, 1957).
7.   J. Moltmann, The Crucified God (SCM, 1977).
8.   R. Bultmann, Kerygma and Myth, New Testament and Mythology (New York: Harper Torchbook, 1961).
9.   W. Pannenberg, Jesus - God and Man (SCM, 1968).
10.   N. Pittenger, Christology Reconsidered, 1970
11.   E.H. Cousins (ed), Process Theology, Part 3, Christ and Redemption (New York, Toronto: Newmann Press), p.191 f.

12. A. Richardson, The Political Christ (SCM, 1973).
13. L. Boff, Jesus Christ Liberator (SPCK, 1980).

PART THREE

Introduction

1. A. Richardson, An Introduction to the Theology of the New Testament, Ch 5, The Holy Spirit (Harper and Row), p.318.
2. J. Macquarrie, Principles of Christian Theology, Ch 14, The Holy Spirit and Salvation, p.328 f.
3. E. Brunner, Dogmatics, Vol III, Ch 1, Church and Holy Spirit (London: The Lutterworth Press, 1964), p.4 f.
4. L. Berkhof, Systematic Theology, Part Four, Ch II, The Operation of the Holy Spirit in General (The Banner of Truth Trust, 1959), p.423 f.
5. P. Tillich, Systematic Theology, Vol 3, Part 4, Life and the Spirit (The University of Chicago Press, 1957), p.11 f.
6. J. Moltmann, The Church in the Power of the Spirit, Ch 4, The Church in the Trinitarian history of God, p.50 f.
7. G.S. Hendry, The Holy Spirit in Christian Theology, 1956.
8. H. Berkhof, The Doctrine of the Holy Spirit, 1964.

SECTION 1

Chapter 1

1. A. Richardson, An Introduction to the Theology of the New Testament, Ch 5, The Holy Spirit (SCM, 1958) p.103 f.
2. C.K. Barrett, The Holy Spirit and the Gospel Tradition (London: 1947).
3. H.B. Swete, Holy Spirit in the New Testament, 1909.
4. Wheeler Robinson, The Christian Experience of the Holy Spirit, 1928, 1947.
5. G. Smeaton, The Doctrine of the Holy Spirit (London: 1958).
6. M. Green, I Believe in the Holy Spirit (London: 1975).

195

Chapter 2

1. J. Macquarrie, Principles of Christian Theology, Ch 58-60, p.328 f.
2. A. Richardson, An Introduction to the Theology of the New Testament, Ch 5, The Holy Spirit (SCM, 1958), p.103 f.
3. H.P. van Dusen, Spirit, Son and Father, 1958.
4. C.C. Richardson, The Doctrine of the Trinity, 1958.
5. H. Berkhof, The Doctrine of the Holy Spirit, 1964.
6. T. Rees, The Holy Spirit in Thought and Experience, 1915.

Chapter 3

1. A.B. Come, Human Spirit and Holy Spirit (USA: 1959).
2. G. S. Hendry, The Holy Spirit in Christian Theology, 1956.
3. L. Dewar, The Holy Spirit and Modern Thought, 1959.
4. P. Tillich, Systematic Theology, Vol III, (The University of Chicago Press, 1957), p.111 f.

SECTION 2

Chapter 1

1. E. Brunner, Dogmatics, Vol III, Ch 20, 21 (London: The Lutterworth Press, 1964), p.276 f.
2. K. Barth, Church Dogmatics, Vol IV, Ch 2, § 66 (Edinburgh: T&T Clark, 1956), p.499 f.
3. L. Berkhof, Systematic Theology, Part 4, IV-XI (The Banner of Truth Trust, 1959), p.454 f.
4. P. Tillich, Systematic Theology, Vol 2, Part 3, Ch 2E (The University of Chicago Press, 1957), p.165 f.
5. J. Calvin, Institutes III, XIII, XIV.
6. J. J. Macquarrie, Principles of Christian Theology, p.337 f.
7. V. Taylor, Forgiveness and Reconciliation, 1952.
8. G.W.H. Lampe (ed), The Doctrine of Justification by Faith, 1954.
9. G. Aulen, The Faith of the Christian Church, 2nd ed, 1961.
10. H. Küng, Justification, 1964.
11. W.E. Hulme, The Dynamics of Sanctification, 1966.
12. S. Neill, Christian Holiness, 1960.
13. D.G. Bloesch, The Christian Life and Salvation, 1967.
14. R.N. Flew, The idea of Perfection in Christian Theology, 1934.
15. E.S. Jones, Conversion (London, 1960).
16. B. Citron, New Birth (Edinburgh, 1951).

Chapter 2

1. E. Brunner, Dogmatics, Vol II, Ch 10, p.239 f, and Vol III, Ch 16, (London: The Lutterworth Press, 1964), p 152 f.
2. P.S. Watson, The Concept of Grace, 1960.
3. P. Tournier, Guilt & Grace, 1974.
4. D.M. Baillie, God was in Christ, 1948.
5. D.M. Baillie, Faith in God and its Christian Consummation, 1964.
6. G.F. Forell, The Protestant Faith, 1960.
7. P. Tillich, The Dynamics of Faith, 1957.

Chapter 3

1. J. Macquarrie, Principles of Christian Theology, Ch 14, 61-62, p.337.f.
2. E. Brunner, Dogmatics, Vol II, Ch 12-118, p.152 f and Ch 21 (London: The Lutterworth Press, 1964), p.290 f.
3. G. Ebeling, The Nature of Faith, 1961.
4. J. Moltmann, Theology of Hope, Meditation of Hope, p.15 f.
5. P. Tillich, The Dynamics of Faith, 1957.
6. P. Tillich, Love, Power and Justice, 1960.
7. P. Tillich, Systematic Theology, Vol III (The University of Chicago Press, 1957), p.129 f.
8. P. Tillich, The Courage to Be, 1952.
9. P. Hessert, The Christian Life, 1967.
10. W.E. Hulme, The Dynamics of Sanctification, 1966.
11. J.O. Sanders, The Holy Spirit and His Gifts (London: 1970).
12. A.E. Dyson, Freedom and Love (SPCK, 1975).
13. C.S. Lewis, Christian Behaviour (London: 1943).
14. W. Pannenberg, Faith and Reality (London: 1977).

SECTION 3

Chapter 1

1. J. Macquarrie, Principles of Christian Theology, Ch 69, p.386 f.
2. E. Brunner, Dogmatics, Vol III, Ch 1-8 (London: The Lutterworth Press, 1964), p.4 f.
3. L. Berkhof, Systematic Theology, Part 5, The Church (The Banner of Truth Trust, 1959), p.555 f.
4. P. Tillich, Systematic Theology, Vol III, Part 4, Ch 3A, §1-3 (The

University of Chicago Press, 1957), p.162 f.
5.   K. Barth, Church Dogmatics, Vol IV, Ch 2, §67, (Edinburgh: T&T Clark, 1956), p.614 f.
6.   J. Moltmann, The Church in the Power of the Holy Spirit, Ch 3, p.66 f.
7.   J.L. Houlden, Exploration in Theology 3, Ch 4, The Idea of the Church, p.53 f (SCM, 1978).
8.   J.G. Davies, The Spirit, The Church and the Sacraments, 1954.
9.   G. Johnson, The Doctrine of the Church in the New Testament, 1943.
10.   W. Pannenberg, Spirit, Faith and Church (USA: 1970).

Chapter 2

1.   A. Richardson, An Introduction to the Theology of the New Testament (SCM, 1958), p.286 f.
2.   E. Brunner, Dogmatics, Vol 3, (London: The Lutterworth Press, 1964), p.117 f, p.23 f.
3.   J. Macquarrie, Principles of Christian Theology, p.401 f.
4.   P. Tillich, Systematic Theology, Vol III (The University of Chicago Press, 1957), p.165 f.
5.   L. Berkhof, Systematic Theology, Part 5, Ch II (The Banner of Truth Trust, 1959), p.562 f.
6.   D. Bonhoeffer, The Cost of Discipleship, Ch 29-31, (SCM, 1959), p.212.
7.   J. Calvin, Institutes IV, 1, 2.
8.   E. Schweitzer, The Church as the Body of Christ (London: 1965).
9.   H.B. Swete, The Holy Catholic Church, The Communion of Saints, 1915.
10.   V. De Vaal, What is Church? (SCM, 1965).

Chapter 3

1.   J. Macquarrie, Principles of Christian Theology, Ch 78, p.441 f.
2.   E. Brunner: Dogmatics, Vol III, Ch 23 (London: The Lutterworth Press, 1964), p.314 f.
3.   K. Barth, Church Dogmatics, Vol IV, Part 3, §72 (Edinburgh: T&T Clark, 1956), p.681 f.
4.   J. Moltmann, The Church in the Power of the Holy Spirit, Preface Volume I, Part 2, p.7 f.
5.   A. Harnack, The Expansion of Christianity, 1904.

6.   J. Blauw, The Missionary Nature of the Church, 1952.
7.   R. Allen, Missionary Principles, 1964.
8.   J.V. Taylor, The Go-Between God (SCM, 1972).
9.   C.W. Forman, A Faith for the Nations (USA, 1957).
10. G.E. Anderson, T.F. Stransky, Mission Trends, 1,2,3
     (New York: 1974-76).
11. C.A. Robinson, History of Christian Missions (Edinburgh: 1915).
12. S. Neill, Christian Missions (Penguin, 1964).
13. J.V. Taylor, For All the World (London: 1966).
14. W.C.C. Report, Your Kingdom Come - Mission Perspective
     (Geneva: 1980).

Chapter 4

1.   J. Macquarrie, Principles of Christian Theology Ch 19, p.447 f.
2.   E. Brunner, Dogmatics, Vol III, Appendix, p.53 and Ch 4/I (London:
     The Lutterworth Press, 1964), p.60 f.
3.   K. Barth Church Dogmatics, Vol IV, Part 4 (T&T Clark, Edinburgh:
     1956), p.3 f.
4.   L. Berkhof, Systematic Theology, Part 5 (The Banner of Truth
     Trust, 1959), p.604 f.
5.   J. Moltmann, The Church in the Power of the Holy Spirit,
     Ch.5, p.197.f.
6.   J.L. Houden, Exploration in Theology 3, Ch 6, p.65 f (SCM, 1978).
7.   J.G. Davies, The Spirit, the Church and the Sacraments, 1954.
8.   F.D. Dillistone, The Structure of the Divine Society, 1951.
9.   G.E. Harris, A Ministry Renewed, 1968.
10. W.K. Lowther Clarke, ed, Liturgy and Worship, 1932.
11. J.D.G. Dunn, Baptism in the Holy Spirit (SCM, 1970).
12. J. Calvin, Institutes, IV, XV-XVII.
13. N. Clark, An Approach to the Theology of the Sacraments
     (SCM, 1956).
14. O. Cullmann, Baptism in the New Testament (SCM, 1950).
15. R.S. Paul, The Atonement and the Sacraments (USA, 1960).
16. Baptism, Eucharist and Ministry (Geneva: World Council of
     Churches, 1982).
17. W. H. Lazareth, Growing Together in Baptism, Eucharist and
     Ministry (Geneva: World Council of Churches, 1982).

Chapter 5

1. J. Macquarrie, Principles of Christian Theology, Ch 18, p.420 f.
2. L. Berkhof, Systematic Theology, Part 5, Ch 3 (The Banner of Truth Trust), p.579 f.
3. M. Green, Called to Serve, Christian Foundation Series.
4. S. Neil, On the Ministry, 1965.
5. J. Kennedy, The Minister's Vocation, 1963.
6. H. Thielicke, The Trouble with the Church, 1966.
7. B. Sundkler, The Christian Minister in Africa, 1960.
8. Baptism, Eucharist and Ministry (Geneva: World Council of Churches, 1982).
9. W.P. Lazareth, Growing together in Baptism, Eucharist and Ministry (Geneva: World Council of Churches, 1982).

Chapter 6

1. J. Macquarrie, Principles of Christian Theology, Ch 72, p.401 f and Ch. 80, p.512 f.
2. E. Brunner, Dogmatics, Vol. III, Ch. 23 (London: The Lutterworth Press, 1964), p.314 f.
3. D. Bonhoeffer, Ethics, Part 2, Ch. 3, p.297; Ch 4, p.289 f.
5. W. Pannenberg, Ethics.
6. N. Goodall, The Ecumenical Movement, 1964.
7. B. Lambert, Ecumenism, 1967.
8. B. Leeming, The Vatican Council and Christian Unity, 1966.
9. O. Cullmann, The State in the New Testament, 1956.
10. K. Barth, Church and State, 1939.
11. J.C. Bennett, Christians and the State, 1958.
12. E. Troeltsch, The Social Teaching of the Christian Churches, 1931.
13. J. Bright, The Kingdom of God, 1953.
14. W.G. Kümmel, Promise and Fulfilment, 1957.
15. N. Goodall, The Ecumenical Movement, (London: 1961).
16. J. Macquarrie, Christian Unity and Christian Diversity (SCM, 1975).
17. P. R. Clifford, The Mission of the Local Church (SCM, 1953).
18. G. R. Cragg, The Church and the World (Toronto: 1976).
19. J. Rossel Mission in a Dynamic Society (SCM, 1968).
20. K. Barth, Ethics; 1973 (Edinburgh, T&T Clark)

Section 4

Chapter 1

1.   A. Schweitzer, The Mystery of the Kingdom of God
    (London: (1901) 1956).
2.   E. Brunner, Dogmatics, Vol III, Part 4, Ch 1, (London: The
    Lutterworth Press, 1964), p.339 f.
3.   L. Berkhof, Systematic Theology, Part Six, Ch 1,
    Introductory Ch, (The Banner of Truth Trust, 1959), p.661 f.
4.   E. Benz, Evolution and Christian Hope, 1967.
5.   J. Macquarrie, Principles of Christian Theology, Ch 15, p.351 f.
6.   J. Moltmann, Theology of Hope, 1967.
7.   J.A.T. Robinson, In the End God, 1950.
8.   T.F. Glasson, The Second Advent, 1945.

Chapter 2

1.   J.A.T. Robinson Honest to God, 1963.
2.   R. Williams, Resurrection (Darton, Longman & Todd, 1982).
3.   J. Baillie, And the Life Everlasting, 1934.
4.   E. Brunner, Eternal Hope (The Westminster Press, 1954).
5.   E. Brunner, Dogmatics, Vol III, Part 4, p.339 f.
6.   M. Green, Satan's Downfall (Hodder and Stoughton Ltd, 1981).
7.   L. Berkhof, Systematic Theology, Part Six (The Banner of Truth
    Trust, 1959), p.661 f.
8.   J. Macquarrie, Principles of Christian Theology, Ch.4, p.351 f.
9.   J. Moltmann, Theology of Hope, 1967.
10.   J. Moltmann, The Future of Creation (SCM, 1979).
12.   L. Morris, The Biblical Doctrine of Judgement (London:, 1960).
13.   T.F. Francis, His Appearing and His Kingdom (London:, 1953).
14.   O. Cullman, Immortality of the Soul or
    Resurrection of the Dead?, 1958.
15.   R.P. Lightner, The Last Days Handbook (Nelson, USA).

Chapter 3

1.   J. Moltmann, Theology of Hope, 1967.
2.   W. Pannenberg, Basic Questions in Theology, Vol I,II,III.
3.   E. Schillebeeckx, God the Future of Man, 1969.
4.   J.B. Metz, Theology of the World, 1969.
5.   J. Macquarrie, Twentieth Century Religious Thought, 1978.
6.   Ruben A. Alves, Tomorrow's Child, 1972.

INDEX